What Reviewers Said About
Winning the War on Terror

Dr. James Forest, Terrorism Center, U.S. Military Academy at West Point:

"The authors have assembled a useful synthesis of the history behind the threat posed by al Qaeda. Their analysis of the religious ideology that fuels radical Islamists, rooted in the socio-political history of Saudi Arabia, adds a useful dimension to our understanding of the current global security environment. This is also one of the first pieces of scholarship to draw solid connections between the struggle in Iraq and global Islamic jihad led by al Qaeda. The authors provide a balanced view of our successes, failures and challenges in Iraq, and how these impact our ability to successfully prosecute the global war on terrorism. In doing so, they add some new insights to the national debate about the Iraq campaign, and offer some hope that our struggle for global peace and security does have an end in sight.....I would recommend that West Point's library purchase this book."

Peter Huessy, Member of the Committee on the Present Danger and President, GeoStrategic Analysis, Washington, DC:

"A key insight of this book reveals the network of killers motivated by a fanatical and twisted Wahhabist faith, sponsored by vast oil wealth and given s⟨ rogue states. Another is that free institutions and due process will d terrorists, an effort begun in Afghanistan and Iraq."

Peter J. Bergerson, Ph.D., Professor of Public Affairs, Florida Gulf Coast University:

"Readers will find this book a valuable resource to understand the origins of radical militant Islamic philosophy and how it became a jihad to threaten western society. Quist and Drake have provided a sober picture of an international deadly disease yet an optimistic picture of the future of U. S. national security interest as we enter the 21st century."

Reverend Ralph A. Baumgartner, Bishop's Associate, Saint Paul Area Synod, Evangelical Lutheran Church in America:

"The novel argument…that [the authors] make is that the invasion of Iraq does serve the war against terrorism because it puts pressure on Saudi Arabia to change its behavior and to make reforms that lead to democracy."

Winning the War on Terror

Winning the War on Terror

✦

A Triumph of American Values

Colonel B. Wayne Quist and Dr. David F. Drake

iUniverse, Inc.
New York Lincoln Shanghai

Winning the War on Terror
A Triumph of American Values

iUniverse books may be ordered through booksellers or by contacting:

iUniverse
2021 Pine Lake Road, Suite 100
Lincoln, NE 68512
www.iuniverse.com
1-800-Authors (1-800-288-4677)

ISBN-13: 978-0-595-35776-5 (pbk)
ISBN-13: 978-0-595-67272-1 (cloth)
ISBN-13: 978-0-595-80247-0 (ebk)
ISBN-10: 0-595-35776-8 (pbk)
ISBN-10: 0-595-67272-8 (cloth)
ISBN-10: 0-595-80247-8 (ebk)

Printed in the United States of America

To Charlie Nelson—"Rawhide"
for bringing us together and for his significant contributions,

and to Christian Quist and Ethan and Abby Drake
because your generation has been elected to take up the challenge.

Contents

Authors' Preface xiii

CHAPTER 1   The Saudi Kingdom and Its People 1

- *THE DESERT KINGDOM* *2*
- *THE FOUNDING OF SAUDI ARABIA* 4
  The Founder of the Kingdom 4
  The Role of Wahhabism 7
- *THE KINGDOM OF OIL AND ALLAH* *10*
  Discovery of Oil 11
  Impact of Oil on the Kingdom and the World 13
- *MODERN SAUDI ARABIA* *20*
  American Imprint 21
  Abdul Aziz ibn Saud Imprint 23
  Current Crisis 26
- *THE SAUDI GOVERNMENT* *28*
  Wahhabi Islam is the State 28
  The Al Saud-Wahhab Partnership Continues 32
- *CHAPTER ONE BIBLIOGRAPHY* *36*

CHAPTER 2   Al Qaeda's Ideological Origins, Its Next of Kin
And Arab-Muslim Problems 38

- *RADICAL MILITANT ISLAM* *41*
  The Muslim Brotherhood 42
  The Brotherhood Spreads to Saudi Arabia 45
  Al Qaeda's Next of Kin—Takfir Wal Hijra 47
  The Concept of Islamist Jihad 49
  Modern Wahhabi-Salafism or "Bin Ladenism" 50

- *PROBLEMS IN THE MODERN MUSLIM WORLD* *52*

  Radicalism is Only Part of the Problem 52

  Other Contemporary Arab-Muslim Problems 54
- *CHAPTER TWO BIBLIOGRAPHY* *63*

CHAPTER 3   Wahhabism and Its Threats to the Non-Muslim World 65

- *WAHHABISM IN THE WEST* *66*

  Wahhabism in America 66

  The European Problem 71
- *THE WEST'S RESPONSE TO TERRORISM AND WAHHABISM* *79*

  America, the Paper Tiger 80

  Inscrutable Saudis—Gullible Americans 89

  The Gulling of America by Saudi Arabia 93
- *DETERIORATING SAUDI-AMERICAN RELATIONS* *98*

  Impact of the First Gulf War 99

  Decade of the 1990s 100

  Beginning of an Arab Spring 101
- *RHETORICAL ROYAL REMARKS* *103*
- *CHAPTER THREE BIBLIOGRAPHY* *107*

CHAPTER 4   The Bush Doctrine: Raising the Cost to the Terrorists and Providing an Antidote 111

- *FORMULATING AND INITIATING A NEW FOREIGN POLICY* . . . *112*

  The Extension of Sovereignty 113

  Application in Afghanistan—A Learning Experience 114
- *COMPLETING THE BUSH DOCTRINE AND CONTINUING THE PURSUIT* *118*

  Expanding the Definition of Hostile Action and U.S. Defense Efforts 120

  Application to "Allied" Enemy Governments 122

  Putting the New Bush Doctrine Together 124
- *IMPLEMENTATION OF THE BUSH DOCTRINE* *131*

  Why Iraq? 132

  A Surrogate War in Iraq 134

  U.S. Diplomacy and Multilateralism 136

Immediate Benefits of Invading Iraq 139

- *DEMOCRATIZATION OF THE ARAB-MUSLIM WORLD*. *141*

The Afghan Experience. 142

The Iraqi Experience. 143

- *CONCLUSIONS ABOUT THE BUSH DOCTRINE*. *148*
- *CHAPTER FOUR BIBLIOGRAPHY* *151*

CHAPTER 5   The Iraq War—Where Nothing Met
Expectations 155

- *OFF TO AN APPARENTLY GOOD START*. *156*

The Easy Part 157

Failures to Adjust to the New Realities 161

- *THE OCCUPATION*. *163*

Failure to Plan. 163

The Abu Ghraib Prison Disaster 169

A Loss of Momentum and Confidence 173

- *AN INTERIM GOVERNMENT* *176*

Inability to Bring Factions Together 176

Fallujah—Round II. 178

Election Preparations 179

- *CONCLUSIONS AND PROGNOSTICATIONS ABOUT THE WAR*. . . *181*
- *CHAPTER FIVE BIBLIOGRAPHY* 184

CHAPTER 6   The War on Terror: Recapitulation, Prognosis,
and an Unfinished Agenda 187

- *THE EXPLOSIVE MIXTURE OF POLITICS AND RELIGION* *187*
- *THE SCORE AFTER FOUR: GOOD GUYS 9, BAD GUYS 3* *190*

Little Offense for al Qaeda 190

America on the Offense. 194

- *HOLDING ON TO THE LEAD* *199*

Back to Multilateralism. 200

Lessons Learned about Using Military Options. 203

The Carrot of Freedom and Democracy 206

- *SEEDS OF HOPE—ROOTS OF CHANGE*. *207*

Reform of Islam Needed 208

A Generation of Peace 209

Light Some Candles. 211

• *CHAPTER SIX BIBLIOGRAPHY* *212*

APPENDICES 214

• *APPENDIX A: CHRONOLOGY OF KEY EVENTS IN THE HISTORY OF SAUDI ARABIA* *215*

• *APPENDIX B: ABOUT THE AUTHORS.* *221*

Index 223

Authors' Preface

This book had an unusual genesis; it grew out of the authors' fiftieth high school reunion in 2004 when two classmates, who hadn't seen each other for at least 25 years, discovered a mutual interest in the subject of the war on terror. One of the authors had the opportunity, while serving in the United States Air Force and in a subsequent career in international investment banking, to develop a special thesis about the origins of the war on terror through a series of lectures and seminars that he developed and led following 9/11. The other, a retired college professor and health economist, was fascinated with the retired Air Force colonel's thesis and offered to assist in developing a full exposition of how the war started, how President Bush's new post-9/11 foreign policies responded to the challenges presented, and where the nation stands four years after 9/11 in its fight against radical, militant Islamists. Brief author biographies are included in the Appendix at the end of the book.

The authors believe that it is vital that people throughout the world understand the nature and origins of militant Islamist terrorism and identify credible solutions. It is also vital to comprehend and appreciate the strategy that America and its global partners have set in motion to win the global war on terror and recast the political landscape of the Middle East. Three years before 9/11, Osama bin Laden, al Qaeda's leader, declared in 1998:

> The ruling to kill the Americans and their allies—civilians and military—is an individual duty for every Muslim who can do it in any country in which it is possible to do it, in order to liberate the al-Aqsa Mosque and the holy mosque [Mecca] from their grip, and in order for their armies to move out of all the lands of Islam, defeated and unable to threaten any Muslim.

Since 9/11, the world has learned that radical, militant Islam is a deadly disease that must be stamped out because it is a perilous threat to the West and endangers Muslim societies of all types around the world. Militant Islamist leaders are not open to negotiation or reason as many in the West would hope, and their ideology goes far beyond classical Islam's concept of "just jihad," or righteous struggle. To most Muslims, Islam stands for peace, justice, equality, human dignity, rule of law—qualities demonstrated throughout Islam's history, and especially during its "Golden Age," while Europe was emerging from the Dark Ages of ignorance and poverty. Osama bin Laden's theology of hate, death and destruction, and the type of Islamic law that he contemptuously envisions for the world, would be catastrophic for the Islamist societies he hopes to create in the wake of destruction. Indeed, it is a formula for global disaster. The result would be failed Muslim states far worse than Afghanistan under the Taliban, producing violence, devastation, despotism, poverty, intolerance, suppression of women and all minorities, and the worst form of underachievement, mediocrity, and oppression the world has ever seen. Informed and rational people of all persuasions ultimately will not support such a theology of darkness and hate, and this is why bin Laden and his armies of terror are destined for failure and destruction.

The first three chapters discuss the causes of radical, militant Islam and why it erupted in barbarous violence in the name of God in the late 20th century. Also discussed is the enormous impact that vast Saudi oil wealth has had in spreading Wahhabi-Salafist ideology around the world for the last 25 years. Subsequent chapters address how success in the global war on terror will bring the broader Middle East into the world's family of nations politically, economically and socially. The book does not place blame on any one people or nation but rather focuses on how to collectively succeed in the war against the radical, militant Islamists, a war that is vital to the future of Islam, Western civilization, the greater Middle East, and the future of the world. The authors believe that ultimate victory over militant Islam's forces of darkness and armies of hate will herald a new 21st century era of peace, stability, and unprecedented global economic growth.

"Fundamentalism" is a term often used to define conservative American Protestantism, but it has recently gained general usage in describing religious faiths such as Saudi Arabian Wahhabism and other ultra-orthodox sects that rely on literal interpretations of their scriptures. However, because Wahhabism contradicts some of Islam's basic doctrine and tenets, it can be misleading to call Wahhabism "fundamentalist." We have tried to use the term "radical, militant Islamist," or some close variant, to more accurately define and depict the enemy—Bin Ladenism—although we occasionally use the term "fundamentalist" from time to time when its usefulness is appropriate.

In their violent past covering over 200 years, Saudi Arabian Wahhabis have had many Islamic religious decrees (fatwas) issued against them for their uncompromising ideology and brutal actions they had frequently taken against other Muslims. To deflect such criticism, Wahhabis have preferred to call themselves

"Salafists" as a way of describing their goal of returning society to the days of Mohammed in the 7th century. Throughout this book, we use the terms "Wahhabi" and "Salafist" interchangeably and refer to radical, militant Islamist ideology as "Bin Ladenism." Words and their definition are very important and even the difference between the words "Islamic" (the people and culture of Islam) and "Islamist" (political Islam espoused by militants) is necessary to point out because the great majority of the world's Muslims represented by the word "Islamic" are also victims of bin Laden's ideology of hate. The world, and especially the West, unfortunately ignored Wahhabism for decades, but the world was aroused in the aftermath of 9/11, realizing that the Saudis had opened Pandora's Box and let the genie of radical, militant fundamentalism escape, starting in the early 1980s, with their vast and unprecedented oil wealth.

With little recognition by the outside world, and with initial support of the American government during the waning days of the Cold War, the Saudis unleashed a lethal virus of dormant Islamist extremism and militancy upon the world—their form of reactionary Islamist fundamentalism called "Bin Ladenism"—that escaped to ravage the earth with death, destruction and suicide bombings. The lethal virus of Islamist extremism was adopted and molded by al Qaeda and its militant followers, people who are extreme in their primitive beliefs and devoted to an ultra-literal interpretation of the Holy Koran and Hadith—the deeds and sayings of the Prophet Mohammed. The Islamist militants are extreme in their belief that Islam was corrupted and contaminated by hated barbarians and unbelievers (infidels) and can only be purified by destroying the infidels and establishing a purely Islamic state based on God's law and divine instruction. The militants are extreme in their messianic and missionary zeal to convert the world to their way of thinking through intimidation, any type of force, savage violence, stealth, lies and false propaganda, and ultimately achieve martyrdom through their violent actions. Atrocities conducted by Muslim suicide bombers are irreverently called *"missions of sacred explosions"* by radical Islamists and are conducted with Koranic assurance of rewards in Paradise and supported by deeply held Muslim beliefs of the holy righteousness and duty of jihad and martyrdom. Unrestrained by voices of moderation and literally interpreted, the Holy Koran mandates violent action against nonbelievers (infidels) and under the caption, "You Shall Be Stern With the Disbelievers," provides extremists and scripturalists with justification for their militant beliefs and actions to die for the one true God:

> O you Prophet, strive against the disbelievers and the hypocrites, and be stern
> in dealing with them. Their destiny is Hell; what a miserable abode! [Holy
> Koran, Sura 9:73]

Could it be that man's religions are inherently violent and have within them
the seeds of their own destruction through the very violence they have prescribed?
Judaism, Christianity and Islam are the world's great monotheistic religions and
Islam accepts Christianity's Jesus as another agent of God in the long line of bib-
lical prophets from Abraham, Moses, Jesus, and Mohammed, God's latest voice
of divine revelation as a messenger for mankind.

> Say (O Muslims): We believe in Allah and that which is revealed to us and
> that which was revealed to Abraham, and Ishmael, and Isaac, and Jacob, and
> the tribes, and that which Moses and Jesus received, and that which the
> prophets received from their Lord. We make no distinction between any of
> them, and to Him we have surrendered." [Holy Koran 2:136]

All three great monotheistic religions trace their origins to the Old Testament
and the Prophet Abraham, and violence is well documented throughout the holy
texts. Why do Islamist extremists kill for their faith, and how can Allah, the one
true God—the God of Abraham—justify brutal and indiscriminate violence
against innocent men, women and children? How can any true religion support
political and military conquest as something intrinsic to its theological beliefs?
Yet Islam and the words of Mohammed exhort its followers to action and to martyrdom: "Jihad is your duty…Paradise is in the shadow of swords."

Literally interpreted, these words provide inspiration and motivation for
Islamist militants to kill nonbelievers and achieve martyrdom and a special place
in Heaven in the process. In its purist scripturalist form, the doctrine of Islam as
interpreted by militant Islamists such as bin Laden and his followers calls its
believers to spread the faith by converting, conquering, subjugating and, if necessary, killing all apostates and nonbelievers in the name of the Prophet Mohammed and Allah, the God of Abraham. Even though the Holy Koran says in Sura
2:256, "There shall be no compulsion in religion," extremist, militant Islamists
demand death for all nonbelievers, including those Muslims who do not accept
extremist interpretations of Mohammed's revelations in the Holy Koran and
Hadith sayings or who might convert to another religion.

The concept of jihad is deeply rooted in Islam, especially in the Arab world,
and is at the heart of the death cult of al Qaeda's Islamist terrorism. Throughout
the Holy Koran, like much of the Old Testament of the Bible, intolerance is

widely evident but the Muslim faith is inevitably linked to conflict because Muslims are instructed by the Holy Koran to despise nonbelievers and take up the call for religious conflict and violent jihad to defend and expand the faith. To the secular West, this sounds unreasonable, like something from Christianity's troubled and bloody past in the Middle Ages, or from the violence of the Reformation. However, the fact remains that Islam has a long history of violence and al Qaeda and its followers are merely a modern reincarnation of earlier Muslim religious fanatics and brutal killers who have appeared throughout the centuries, seeking Paradise and a permanent seat on the right hand of God for their radical and deadly beliefs.

The authors are confident that the United States is uniquely positioned in the first decade of the 21st century to lead the world in its victory over the *"global war on terror"* and bring about truly meaningful change in the Middle East as well as a new world order, with reinvigorated and reformed international institutions for the post Cold War era. The rapid globalization of the world economy over the past 25 years, fueled by the West's technological and business innovation, has led to unprecedented economic growth around the world. But such rapid progress and change come at a cost, as violent anti-globalization forces such as radical, militant Islam try to push back the clock of civilization in Luddite fashion by creating theocratic Islamist states and destroying Western culture and institutions. To achieve success in its global war against militant Islamist terrorism, the United States has assembled a coalition of over 100 nations and has implemented a revolutionary strategy to transform the Middle East and neutralize the devastating effect of the fanatical and archconservative strain of Sunni Islam that has inspired al Qaeda and its anti-Western Islamist terror network. This extreme version of Islam is derived from Saudi Arabian Wahhabi-Salafism, and it calls for Islam to reject everything modern and return to an ultra-fundamentalist, reactionary version of the Muslim faith, totalitarian Islamic law, traditional customs, and an idealized 7th century way of life.

Today we live in a rapidly changing and interconnected world, a truly remarkable historical era, with interdependent globalized economies and rapidly changing technological innovation. We are also engaged in a protracted and violent war against militant Islam, a truly global struggle, but as George Will recently remarked in *The Washington Post*, there is no guarantee that civilization as we know it will survive, for in the long history of the human race, democracy and human freedom are relatively recent and short-lived concepts. While the West faces uncertainties in the struggle against militant Islam's armies of darkness, and while it is true that we do not yet know precisely how it will end, what has become abundantly clear is that the world will succeed in defeating militant Islam because of the West's flexible, democratic institutions and its all-encompassing ideology of freedom.

The real strength of the West resides in its fundamental values of freedom and democracy. Liberal and open societies permit hate-filled, militant ideologues to speak out under constitutional safeguards, even as the militants advocate destruction of the West and its ideals. And in speaking out, they reveal their utter horror and terror even as alliances between Islamists and the political left have gradually developed in Europe and the United States since the end of the Cold War, fueled more recently by opposition to the Iraq war and America's uncontested and far-reaching military and economic power. Some liberals in the West have found it difficult to make fundamental moral distinctions between basic issues of right and wrong and many have defended Islamist militancy in a false belief that terrorism is simply the consequence of resentments caused by pervasive American cultural arrogance and growing American global hegemony. While every nation around the globe has problems, nothing can justify suicide bombings and beheadings in the name of God, or suicide airline attacks such as those against the World Trade Center in New York City and the Pentagon in Washington, DC, on September 11, 2001. The world's wakeup call to the threat of global terrorism was the attack on the United States on 9/11, and it is now clear that we live in a world where tolerance of Islamist extremism—"Bin Ladenism"—will ultimately lead to collective suicide for the West and for the world of Islam as well.

Moreover, dependence on foreign oil has grown to become a severe threat to American and Western security by promoting trade imbalance and providing billions in Western monetary support for regimes that have sponsored terrorism. During the many decades of the Cold War and up to 9/11, the United States and the West largely remained timid in addressing energy insecurity issues and learned to develop a tolerance for Middle Eastern autocrats and despots. The United States is the world's largest consumer of oil and today the entire world and its global economy are dependent on potentially unreliable sources of imported oil. Saudi Arabia and its neighbors along the Persian Gulf possess nearly two-thirds of the earth's known oil reserves and Saudi Arabia alone is the world's largest supplier of crude oil to the world and the supplier of last resort in times of global oil shortages. As the leader of the free world and engine of the global economy, the United States has a moral obligation to its own people and to the people of the world to ensure that Persian Gulf oil remains secure and does not fall under hostile forces that seek to destroy the West, its institutions, and the world's economy.

As the Bush Doctrine was formulated in the twelve months following 9/11, the United States recognized that it could no longer remain passive toward the Arab Middle East and that it desperately needed to formulate and implement a new American foreign policy for its global war on terror. From a strategic perspective, President Bush determined that the United States had to aggressively pursue al Qaeda and that the best defense against further terrorist attacks on the United States was to remain on the offensive. The first offensive effort, less than three months after 9/11, was the extremely popular invasion of Afghanistan, which resulted in chasing Osama bin Laden into a remote area of Pakistan, toppling the Islamist Taliban government, and putting Afghanistan on the road to its first democratically elected government in its long history. Over the next year, the United States made substantial progress through tough, behind the scenes negotiations with most countries that possessed nuclear capabilities to secure their nuclear weapons stockpiles and technology from terrorist hands.

In an equally tough set of negotiations with Saudi Arabia, the United States also attempted to obtain sensitive information about Saudi relationships with al Qaeda and to prevent the Saudis from providing further financial assistance to bin Laden and his terrorist network, an orphaned offspring of Saudi Arabia's Wahhabi state religion. After nearly 60 years of a joint preferential diplomatic relationship, both sides played hardball with each other and the Saudis demanded that American troops leave Saudi soil and even threatened to break off diplomatic relations with the United States if it did not resolve the Israeli-Palestinian dispute. The authors contend that motivation for the American invasion of Iraq was in large part a result of the recalcitrant behavior of the Saudis. For the first time since President Roosevelt's meeting with King Abdul Aziz ibn Saud in 1945, the Americans actually out-gulled the Saudis. And most important, the Saudis released sensitive information about al Qaeda to the United States and took immediate steps to discontinue funding from both public and private Saudi sources.

The war in Iraq unfortunately was not America's finest hour from a military, intelligence, or ethical standpoint, and these shortcomings are outlined in the last two chapters. Much was learned from the Iraq experience, however, and the free elections on January 30, 2005 literally saved the day for the United States by demonstrating the power of the Bush Doctrine's antidote of freedom and democracy and in America's commitment to that ideal. Indeed, the subtitle for the book, "A Triumph of American Values," came from America's Iraq experience where victory was reclaimed by America's reassertion of its democratic ideal, notwithstanding the major failure to follow American ideals and values in the Abu Ghraib prison scandal which provided a major propaganda victory for al Qaeda.

In the final chapter, we briefly recount answers to the question of the war's origins, describe how the United States has achieved an overwhelming lead in that war, recommend changes in the Bush foreign policy for the remainder of the President's term in office, and suggest issues between the West and Islam that will require longer term changes on both sides. The authors remain steadfast in their conclusion that the United States is far ahead in winning the war against militant Islamists and that holding true to American values of freedom and democracy paves the way for success. We end on an optimistic note with hope for the future and confidence that mainstream Muslims will find a resounding voice in countering Islamist extremism through the dignity of Islam, reason, educational reform, and democratic practices that will nullify the ideologies of hate and ensure that Bin Ladenism does not spread and take root.

For us personally, it has been a most enjoyable experience that has been accomplished through the wonders of email and the Internet. Separated by more than two thousand miles, we conferred only through our regular Internet communications, but knowing each other since childhood certainly made those communications easier. We hope that our readers will find the book equally fulfilling and informative. We wish to thank the following for their valuable comments and for reviewing our manuscript: Dr. James Forest, West Point Terrorism Center; Peter Huessy, Committee on the Present Danger; Professor Peter J. Bergerson, Florida Gulf Coast University; and Reverend Ralph A. Baumgartner, St. Paul Area Lutheran Synod. We also wish to thank all of our friends and supporters who have helped make this book possible and hope to update the book with an epilogue via our web page at http://www.bushwaronterror.com/ as events develop as well as a second edition on the fifth anniversary of 9/11.

May 1, 2005

B. Wayne Quist   David F. Drake

NOTE: Citations to books or articles are made through the use of brackets around the author's name and, if available, the page number, or by the year of publication following the author's name in the text. All references are listed in the bibliography at the end of each chapter.

1

The Saudi Kingdom and Its People

On September 11, 2001, extremist Muslim killers savagely attacked the American homeland. The attack was the culmination of a series of assaults against American interests by al Qaeda, which until 9/11 was a relatively obscure Islamist organization led by a wealthy Saudi Arabian named Osama bin Laden and his fanatical "Afghan Arabs" with ties to the al Saud royal family of Saudi Arabia and wealthy Saudi business leaders. Moreover, fifteen of the nineteen jihadist hijackers that attacked the United States on September 11 were from Saudi Arabia, mostly from the conservative, Wahhabi-dominated Asir region near Abha and Khamis Mushayt in the southwestern province of the desert kingdom.

The origins of al Qaeda and militant Islam—"Bin Ladenism"—started with the creation of modern Saudi Arabia and its marriage to Wahhabism, an ultra-conservative and puritanical sect of Sunni Islam born in the Arabian desert over 200 years ago. Saudi Arabian Wahhabis and members of al Qaeda are Sunni Muslims. The fault line between the divisions of Islam lies between the dominant Sunnis in the greater Middle East and South Asia, and the minority Shiites that are largely located in Iran, southern Iraq, Pakistan, and along the western shores of the Persian Gulf, including Saudi Arabia's Eastern Province. Mutual hatred and distrust runs deep between the two major Muslim factions, starting shortly after the death of the Prophet Mohammed in the year 632, and are based on historical disagreement over the succession of authority after Muhammad's death. Another fault line in the Muslim world lies between the 300 million people in the Arab world that represent about 20 percent of the world's Muslims and the billion or more that make up the remaining 80 percent around the world. A chronology of key Saudi Arabian historical events is contained in the Appendix at the end of the book.

1

Wahhabism played a central role in the creation of the Saudi kingdom in the early 20th century and has been utilized as a political instrument of the royal family to retain power ever since. However, the ruling al Saud family learned very early that using a firebrand religion for political purposes can be a two-edged sword and, as we shall see, it is both a lesson and a dilemma for the Saudi leaders that has never been clearer than today. This would have had little interest to the world except for the discovery of vast oil riches beneath the barren desert sands of the Arabian Peninsula soon after the nation of Saudi Arabia was established over 70 years ago. The combination of great wealth derived from oil and a conservative brand of Islam that was radicalized by militants from the Egyptian Muslim Brotherhood starting in the late 1960s resulted in the dramatic explosions of the 9/11 "day of fire."

THE DESERT KINGDOM

Saudi Arabia is a large and arid desert kingdom, over 1,000 miles north to south and 800 miles east to west, nearly the size of the United States east of the Mississippi. The people of Saudi Arabia have tribal roots going back to their ancient nomadic Bedouin origins and they are well known for their fierce fighting capabilities, abundant desert hospitality, genuine warmth, grandiose poetic expression, and noble graciousness. In many ways, Saudi Arabia in the 21st century is just now entering the modern world even though its significant oil wealth and financial strength have recently provided all of the external trappings of modern society. The problem the West faces with Saudi Arabia today is that underneath a thin veneer of modern shopping centers, advanced Western technology, and a costly social welfare system for its exploding population, is an all-pervading, severe, and absolute fundamentalist religious establishment that dominates every element of Saudi society in ways that appear medieval to Western observers and visitors.

If it was not for oil, and now radical Islamist terrorism, the West would probably not pay much attention to Saudi Arabia, but the fact remains that the United States is by far the world's largest consumer of oil, importing nearly 60 percent of all its oil from foreign sources. Saudi Arabia is the world's largest oil producer and exporter, with 25 percent of the earth's proven reserves in its Eastern Province along the Persian Gulf. Moreover, Europe and Asia are even more dependent on Persian Gulf oil, making the world's interconnected global economy hostage to Persian Gulf oil where nearly two-thirds of the earth's known oil reserves are located. China's gigantic thirst for oil alone accounts for well over half of the oil currently transported daily through the vulnerable Straits of Hormuz from the Persian Gulf.

Most importantly, Saudi Arabia is the home of Islam and its holiest cities, Mecca and Medina, located in the Western Province near the Red Sea. Mecca is the birthplace of the Prophet Mohammed where he received his first revelation from Allah in the year 610, and Medina is the burial site of the Prophet. Mecca is also the destination for the annual Hajj pilgrimage that brings more than two million Muslims from around the world to the Great Mosque, the site of the holy black stone given by God to the Prophet Abraham, the Kaaba ("the cube"). Significantly, the title of the king of Saudi Arabia is "Custodian of the Two Holy Mosques," the Great Mosque in Mecca and the Prophet's Mosque in Medina.

To understand Saudi Arabia is to appreciate the profound influence of the harsh Arabian Desert on the Saudi people and their culture and to understand that Islam is truly an all-encompassing way of life, totally integrated into government and personal affairs alike, because of the intermarriage decades ago between the large ruling al Saud family and the reactionary Wahhab families. Saudis, like many Arabs, generally believe that their conservative Islamic values are far superior to Western secular values and this belief is buttressed by the importance of the tribal nature or extended family structure of Saudi society, wherein old and trusted family loyalty and self-assurance can exceed allegiance even to the state, which is relatively new.

Another feature of Saudi society is its culture of consultation and consensus wherein, "the king is both chief consensus maker and chief executive" [Long]. Bedouin tribal democracy goes back centuries and calls for consensus among tribal leaders as well as the opportunity for tribal members to discuss grievances with their leaders. Many Westerners have attempted to categorize Saudi behavior based on years living and working with Saudis in the kingdom, but even then, the Saudi mindset can be an enigma:

> To Westerners, Saudi behavior appears that of a paranoid schizophrenic. This is because the Saudi mindset is based on Bedouin values, and feelings about the West are ambivalent. Saudi behavior patterns differ from those in the West in eight major, interrelated areas: pride, sensitivity, distrust, emotionality, vengefulness, perception of time, intentionality and dishonesty [Long].

A feature of the Saudi enigma is a character trait that may derive from Bedouin tribal culture and centuries of polygamy that predate Islam. Under Islamic law, men are permitted up to four wives, although members of the Saudi royal family appear to have taken many more than four over the course of their married lives. "Gulling," or deception and duplicity, is a Saudi character trait that may be tied to the difficulty of juggling family responsibilities between multiple wives and many children from each. Saudi men often complain about their "women problems" and the troubles that arise from multiple wives and large families, especially from female jealousies that arise from falsehoods and rumors.

Saudis have also exhibited an exceptional sense of insecurity because of historical perceptions of being surrounded by enemies on all sides and the on-going need to defend their unique form of Islam. Saudi beliefs are based on an ultraconservative Wahhabi interpretation of the Holy Koran that serves as the constitution of the country and a formal set of rules that guide every aspect of living in the desert kingdom. Under Saudi Arabia's harsh Islamic law, the state and religion are inseparable and no churches, synagogues, temples, or shrines of any religion other than the Saudi version of Islam known as "Wahhabism" or "Salafism" are permitted. Proselytizing by any other faith is prohibited by law in Saudi Arabia and even nonbelieving Muslims are persecuted, their books banned and sensitive government jobs denied, as with the approximately two million Muslim Shiites who live in the oil-rich Eastern Province of the Saudi kingdom.

THE FOUNDING OF SAUDI ARABIA

The Founder of the Kingdom

In 1902, a shrewd tribal chieftain and colorful desert warrior named Abdul Aziz ibn Saud, the "Falcon of the Peninsula" [Khaled bin Sultan], captured Riyadh, the capital of present-day Saudi Arabia, and embarked upon a 30-year campaign to unify the Arabian Peninsula under the rule of the House of Saud. Following the turmoil of the First World War and the demise of the Ottoman Empire, Abdul Aziz ibn Saud (1880-1953) established a theocratic monarchy with the support of the Wahhabi partnership created by an earlier marriage alliance between the al Saud and Wahhab (al Sheik) clans. Shortly after Abdul Aziz Ibn Saud captured Riyadh, he organized his loyal Bedouin tribesmen into the Wahhabi Ikhwan army, a precursor of al Qaeda and today's Saudi Arabian National Guard (SANG), and through severe discipline molded it into a fierce and loyal fighting force. The Wahhabis and Abdul Aziz ibn Saud exhibited exceptional hatred of Islamic minorities such as Shiites and Sufis (the mystical, spiritual dimension of Islam) and by 1927 they had captured the holy cities of Mecca and Medina in western Saudi Arabia. In 1932 Abdul Aziz ibn Saud proclaimed the Kingdom of Saudi Arabia and announced himself as first king, with succeeding rulers to come from direct lineal descendants [CIA]. The old desert chieftain and first king was wounded and scarred many times in battle and has been honored and commemorated in epic Saudi poetry for decades. Melodic Arabic verse is especially appealing to the people of the harsh Arabian Desert and the following tribute to their venerated founder and king is very moving when recited aloud around a desert campfire at night under clear skies and brilliant stars:

Abdul Aziz Ibn Saud and the Retaking of Riyadh

Banished was I from the heart of Arabia,
Riyadh, my home, had been stolen by others;
banished was I, and my father and mother,
brothers and sisters, deprived of our birthright.
Sadness we felt for the years that denied us
the feel of sand of the Nejd in our hands.
Kindness we found in Kuwait beyond measure,
but kindness alone could not cure the pain
of living in exile, a life without pleasure,
for pleasure, not nurtured in honor, will wither.
I knew from the earliest years of my living
that I must return to the place of my birth.
They told me that only my death would await me,
(but fear is a far harsher master than death);
they warned of the dangers of crossing the desert
but it was the desert had given me breath.
They asked how a lad could recapture a city,
when put to the sword what my pride would be worth;
I asked how the seed, lying dry in the sand,
at the first taste of rain can emerge from the earth.
"Who will ride at my side on this perilous venture?
Who will risk life and limb to expel Al Rashid?"
Sixty answered my call, young and brave, one and all.
"With all of our strength, we will give what you need;

we will stand by your side when the battle is joined
until each of us falls—or Riyadh is freed."
It was not for the glory we rode from Kuwait;
we held faith as our shield and justice our sword.
I sought to regain the land of my fathers
but in all I deferred to the will of the Lord.
We rode towards Riyadh with banners unfurled,
putting trust in the God who created the world.
Ramadan fasting was over, I summoned my kinsmen;
without hesitation they answered my call.
Like shadows that slip over sand dunes at sunset
we gathered in silence beneath Riyadh's wall.
On that night long ago, when the time came to act,
I knew in my heart what it was to be free;
the greatest good fortune in life for a man is
to know he has reached for the best he can be.
Whatever might follow that cold, moonless night
we would know we had fought for a cause that was right.
I chose from my band a mere handful of men;
each one read the risks from the look in my eyes.
We scaled the walls under cover of darkness;
we watched for the sun to put light in the skies.
Outnumbered, we knew that our hope of success
must depend in the end on our use of surprise.
In a fight it is true if you strike off the head of
a man or an army, the battle is won.
The fate of the Emir of Riyadh was sealed,
he must die for the wounds of Al Saud to be healed.
We struck as the lion descends on its prey,
forced open the fortress, brothers then joined the fray.
The garrison knew that resistance was futile;
Al Saud had returned to its home on that day.
Looking back through the decades,
the taking of Riyadh was but one step on a path,
building a nation, devout, proud and strong,
with justice its sword, faith as its shield,
in the land where the message of God was revealed
[Saudi Ministry of Culture and Information].

When Abdul Aziz ibn Saud proclaimed the monarchy and Kingdom of Saudi Arabia to the world in 1932, he linked the legitimacy of the Saudi royal family to the tenets of Wahhabi-Salafism and Islamic law. Today Wahhabi Islam is the basis of the Saudi royal family's internal and external legitimacy as a ruling family. Saudi Arabia's international standing in the Muslim world is derived from its role as the defender and protector of Mecca and Medina, the birthplace of Islam and its holiest places. To try to make amends for ostentatious living and in deference to powerful Wahhabi clerics and members of the al Sheik clan who hold senior government posts, King Fahd changed his title in 1986 to "Custodian of the Two Holy Mosques" in Mecca and Medina. By forming a pact with the Wahhabis to share power, the Saudi government gave ultra-conservative Wahhabi clerics control over the entire religious, judicial, and educational system, with senior Wahhabi leaders and clerics heading cabinet-level ministries.

The Role of Wahhabism

As Thomas Jefferson proclaimed self-government, freedom, and democracy for the United States in the 18th century, Wahhabism was taking root in the Arabian Peninsula. Preaching an ideology of hatred and a radically intolerant and violent digression from mainstream Islam, Wahhabism came into being under the leadership of Sheik Mohammed bin Abdul Wahhab, partly as a reaction to oppression from the Ottoman Empire and European imperialism, but more from his loathing of venerated shrines and ancestor worship practiced by contemporary Muslims. Sheikh Muhammad bin Abdul Wahhab was the son of a religious judge and when he was persecuted for calling Muslims to return to what he believed was the original form of "pure" Islam, he found protection in the central Nejd region of Saudi Arabia where Muhammad bin Saud ruled.

In 1744 the religious leader Sheik Muhammad bin Abdul Wahhab concluded an agreement with the tribal leader, Muhammad bin Saud, an ancestor of the first king, to bring so-called wayward Arabs of the Arabian Peninsula back to puritanical monotheism and the "true Muslim faith." The two leaders confirmed their arrangement with an oath and cemented the relationship with intermarriage pacts between the al Sheik (Wahhab) clan and the al Saud clan that continue to the present day. Through the descendants of the al Sheik and al Saud clans, the lasting partnership between these two large desert families eventually led to the establishment of the Kingdom of Saudi Arabia in the 20th century.

As a demonstration of their religious zealotry and pious iconoclasm, Wahhab's followers destroyed sacred tombs, graveyards, images, and even mosques in

Mecca, Medina and Iraq, much as the Taliban destroyed ancient Buddhist monuments and venerated religious icons in Afghanistan in the 1990s. The goal was to return Islam to the "purity" of the 7th century, but before long Wahhabism came to be seen as a deviant and violent Muslim cult, and several mainstream Islamic religious decrees (fatwas) condemned Wahhabism's narrow ultra-orthodoxy. These harsh criticisms caused followers of ibn Abdul Wahhab to call themselves "Salafists," or "Companions of the Prophet" and not "Wahhabis," a practice and preference followed to this day.

By the early 1800s the al Saud clan ruled much of the Arabian Peninsula from their stronghold in the isolated and central Nejd region. The power of the al Sauds and fanatical Wahhabis alarmed the Ottoman Empire and an Ottoman army was sent into the interior of the Arabian Desert to contain the influence of the al Saud clan. By 1824 the al Sauds had regained political control over central Arabia and ruled from Riyadh, but were forced into exile in 1891, living along the Rub al-Khali, the "Empty Quarter," before settling in Kuwait. In 1901, Abdul Aziz ibn Saud left Kuwait and recaptured Riyadh the following year. This event marked the beginning of the modern state of Saudi Arabia, and in 1912 Abdul Aziz ibn Saud organized his loyal Bedouin tribesmen into the fierce Wahhabi Ikhwan army.

Between 1924 and 1927, in the political vacuum that followed the collapse of the Ottoman Empire after the First World War, the Ikhwan army recaptured Mecca and Medina, the holiest places in the Muslim faith. To break traditional tribal allegiances and avoid family feuds, the Saudi leader settled members of the Ikhwan army and their families in colonies located around desert oases to promote agriculture, forcing the tribes to abandon their traditional nomadic way of life. Members of the Ikhwan army were provided arms and ammunition as well as living quarters, mosques, schools, agricultural equipment, training, and strict Wahhabi religious education. The Bedouin tribesmen that formed the Ikhwan were instructed in fundamentalist Wahhabi precepts and their obedience, zealotry, and xenophobia quickly created a disciplined army of dedicated and fierce arch-traditionalists willing to die for their extreme beliefs.

By the late 1920s the Ikhwan army had become difficult for Abdul Aziz Ibn Saud to control because of fanatical Ikhwan efforts to conquer traditional enemies such as Muslim Shiites and spread their Wahhabi-Salafist faith by the sword in the same way Islam converted infidels in the 7th and 8th centuries. Reactionary Wahhabi clerics even accused Abdul Aziz Ibn Saud of losing faith—backsliding—because of his support for western innovations such as telephones, telegraph, and automobiles, and for sending one of his many sons to school in Egypt, a country whose people the Ikhwan condemned and reviled as nonbelievers. To reassert his authority, Abdul Aziz Ibn Saud ruthlessly suppressed the Ikhwan army and beheaded many of the leaders, a memory that today's radical Wahhabi clerics do not forget, for merciless suppression of the Ikhwan solidified authority and neutralized dissent. On September 23, 1932, Abdul Aziz Ibn Saud proclaimed the Kingdom of Saudi Arabia as an Islamic state, naming himself as first king, Arabic as the national language, and the Holy Koran as the constitution.

Abdul Aziz ibn Saud founded a theocratic monarchy and the modern nation state of Saudi Arabia through an alliance of fanatical Wahhabi clerics and devout Bedouin tribesmen of the Arabian Desert. Through the compelling force of his personality, threats of violence and war, Abdul Aziz ibn Saud established strategic alliances with the various Bedouin tribes by taking as many as 17 wives and fathering 36 or more sons, including the subsequent rulers of the Kingdom of Saudi Arabia. When his forces captured the holy Muslim cities of Mecca and Medina in western Saudi Arabia, they displayed extraordinary hatred of nonbelievers and other Muslims, especially Shiite and Sufi Muslims. As a descendant of Mohammed bin Saud and a recognized Wahhabi leader with the title "Imam" (religious leader), Abdul Aziz ibn Saud successfully molded Wahhabi-Salafism into the framework of the new nation of Saudi Arabia by integrating the Bedouin tribes of the Arabian Peninsula into a modern state that was first recognized by Great Britain in 1927. By marrying into the many Bedouin tribes, Abdul Aziz ibn Saud consolidated his power and the Saud family proliferated, producing as many as 5,500 to 7,000 first tier royal princes today and tens of thousands of other members of the ruling royal family who are lavishly supported by Saudi Arabia's billions in oil income.

Over time, especially as modernization and the effects of globalization emerged and members of the Muslim Brotherhood from Egypt and Syria infected Saudi Wahhabis with their brand of militant and violent Islamist radicalism, Saudi Arabia's reactionary Wahhabi clerics reinstated the medieval concept of jihad, or "holy war," against nonbelievers and any type of progressive thinking. With an ideological motivation similar to the old king's Ikhwan army, the stepchild of Saudi Wahhabi-Salafist ideology—"Bin Ladenism"—seeks to convert infidels or, failing that, advocates the murder of innocent people, including women and children, and with guarantees of martyrdom and heavenly rewards in the afterlife for the fanatical perpetrators.

The cause of radical, militant Islamist terrorism is not mainstream Islam or Islam as a whole but rather the radicalized Wahhabi-Salafist religious creed practiced in Saudi Arabia. The fact remains that the 9/11 terrorists were indoctrinated in militant Wahhabism and were predominantly from Saudi Arabia. Osama bin Laden and fifteen of the nineteen hijackers were born and raised in Saudi Arabia and were profoundly influenced by militant Wahhabi-Salafism that is still taught in the Saudi Arabian school system and in Wahhabi schools in the United States, Europe, and around the world. Moreover, twelve of the fifteen martyred Saudi hijackers on 9/11 were from the conservative Khamis Mushayt region in Western Saudi Arabia near Abha where strong Wahhabi influence has existed since the early days of the kingdom.

Saudi Arabian citizens are al Qaeda's largest single nationality and according to reliable news reports, nearly one-quarter of the prisoners that have been held by American forces at Guantanamo Bay, Cuba were Saudis, mostly young men who had traveled to Afghanistan believing they would participate in some type of relief work for their Muslim brothers. In 2004, the United States and Saudi Arabia reached agreement whereby some of the younger Saudis incarcerated in Cuba were repatriated to Saudi custody for trial back home, but it remains to be seen if these young, hard-line terrorists actually faced trial in Saudi Arabia or were let loose to seek martyrdom as suicide bombers in Iraq. For even yet today the legacies of Abdul Aziz ibn Saud are still evident and at work throughout the vast oil empire that the old king skillfully and cunningly crafted in the early 20th century.

THE KINGDOM OF OIL AND ALLAH

The evidence of oil goes back many years in the Middle East where oil and tar were used for many purposes over the centuries. In 1871 a German group visited Iraq and reported abundant supplies of oil. In 1907 another German mission reported that Iraq was a "lake of petroleum" and the following year oil was found in Iran. Iraq began exporting oil in 1934, shortly after the major Iraqi oil field was discovered at Kirkuk in 1927. In 1932, the British discovered oil in Kuwait and Bahrain off the east coast of Saudi Arabia and in 1938 the Eastern Province of the Saudi kingdom gushed forth with "black gold." Today Saudi Arabia is a center of great wealth and a strategic world power with 25 percent of the earth's known oil reserves. It was not always so, for in the first years of the monarchy the principal revenues supporting the kingdom were fees or taxes collected from the annual flow of Muslim pilgrims to the holy cities of Mecca and Medina. Cash generated from the pilgrims was stored in a strongbox carried by the king's financial advisor and was used by Abdul Aziz ibn Saud as his private purse.

Discovery of Oil

That changed when oil was first discovered in 1938 in the Eastern Province of Saudi Arabia along the Persian Gulf. The beginning of Saudi oil wealth had actually started in 1933 when the King Abdul Aziz Ibn Saud granted exclusive rights to Standard Oil of California (SOCAL) to explore, extract and sell oil for 60 years. SOCAL was the first American company to enter into competition with the British for Middle East petroleum. The accumulation of vast Saudi oil wealth and the ultimate establishment of Saudi Arabia as the world's dominant oil player and manager of global oil prices began with the 60-year oil concession that King Abdul Aziz ibn Saud gave to Standard Oil of California in 1933. A few years later, American oil companies known today as Exxon, Chevron, Texaco, and Mobil formed the Arab American Oil Company (ARAMCO) in a unique partnership with the Saudi government. Oil was initially transported by barge to Bahrain, then by oil freighters, and in 1950 a pipeline was completed through the desert to Lebanon and the Mediterranean Sea. ARAMCO continued to explore for oil in the Arabian Peninsula, finding even larger fields in the 1950s, and liquefied petroleum gas processing started in Saudi Arabia a decade later.

Even before the oil concession was granted, the old Saudi king had been exposed to several prominent American doctors and missionaries in the Eastern Province of Saudi Arabia. He perceived the United States as non-threatening and manageable, particularly when compared with "untrustworthy" Europeans. Most importantly, the old king was fearful of European colonial ambitions, especially the British, and he was very adept at playing power politics as he had demonstrated with the Ottomans, British, and French during the First World War. The Americans were seen as being gullible, easy to work with and manipulate—easy infidels to "gull"—because they were so naïve in their willingness to do good and because they came from far away and had no special axe to grind regarding local or regional politics. Earlier, Kuwait had granted an oil concession to the British-Iranian Oil Company, known today as the British Petroleum Corporation, (BP) and the old king's trusted British advisor, Harry St. John Philby (1885-1960), was instrumental in assuring that Saudi Arabia's oil did not go to the British as in Kuwait. Philby was a dedicated Arabist and British civil servant who grew dissatisfied with British policy toward the Arabs following the First World War. In 1930 Philby left the British Foreign Service in Transjordan (predecessor of today's Jordan) after being accused of spying, joined the Saudi monarch in Riyadh, and converted to Islam with the name "Hajj Abdullah." During World War II, Philby's son, Kim, became an even more infamous British spy and it is ironic that an American company received the 60-year concession to the vast Saudi oil fields at the urging of a British advisor to the shrewd Saudi king.

Through the troubles of the Great Depression and global war in the 1930s and 1940s, Saudi Arabia stood apart from the rest of the world, guided by the shrewd and wise old desert warrior, King Abdul Aziz ibn Saud. Saudi oil had become important enough during the Second World War for President Roosevelt to hold a meeting in February 1945 with King Abdul Aziz ibn Saud shortly after his Yalta meeting with Stalin and Churchill. During the war, the United States desired to secure its access to Middle East petroleum supplies and acquire a base in the Middle East that could link aerial routes from the Mediterranean to Asia. Roosevelt's historical meeting aboard the presidential yacht "USS Quincy" in Egypt's Great Bitter Lake of the Suez Canal resulted in an agreement between the two countries that eventually established a major United States Air Force base at Dhahran in the Eastern Province and the U.S. Military Training Mission to Saudi Arabia (USMTM). The agreement was not formalized until the Eisenhower administration and has remained in effect to this day. The historic meeting between the Saudi king and President Roosevelt that resulted in an informal alliance between the two countries to protect the Saudi oil fields was important to both sides because nearly two-thirds of the earth's known oil reserves are located in the Persian Gulf region, from Iraq to the United Arab Emirates (UAE), and 25 percent of the world's oil reserves are in Saudi Arabia alone.

The old king died in Taif, Saudi Arabia on November 8, 1953, and was buried in an unmarked grave in Riyadh according to Wahhabi ritual and custom. As a devoted Arabist, Harry St. John Philby remained in Saudi Arabia even after the death of his friend the old king, and died there himself in 1960. Today Persian Gulf oil is the world's economic lifeline and is critical to the security and stability of the world's economy. After the Roosevelt meeting, little attention was subsequently paid to American relations with Saudi Arabia until the Arab oil embargo following the October 1973 Arab-Israeli war. The oil embargo resulted in the quadrupling of oil prices in the 1970s and provided a windfall of billions in Saudi oil income, the beginning of the Saudi oil bonanza. Because of Western dependence on Persian Gulf oil, President Jimmy Carter announced the "Carter Doctrine" to the world in 1980, declaring that the vast Persian Gulf oil reserves are vital to the United States and Western interests and that the United States would defend the Persian Gulf oil fields from aggression. Each succeeding president, Democrat and Republican administrations alike, has endorsed this presidential doctrine, culminating in the deployment of 550,000 American troops to Saudi

Arabia during the first Gulf War in 1990-1991 when Saddam Hussein invaded Kuwait.

Impact of Oil on the Kingdom and the World

Unprecedented oil wealth made it possible for the Saudi religious establishment to spread its radicalized form of Wahhabi Islam around the world over the last 25 years. Saudi Arabia is the world's largest and cheapest oil producer and exporter, controlling about 25 percent of the earth's proven oil reserves and there may be even far more oil and gas reserves in the vast "Empty Quarter," or Rub al-Khali, of the Arabian Desert, which has never been fully explored.

Saudi Arabia did not become a rich nation overnight but proceeds from its "black gold" soon made profound changes in the poor and arid desert kingdom. Oil generated only about $2 million in royalty payments in 1938 but by 1948 the Saudi king received nearly $50 million in annual royalties. In 1973, Abdul Aziz ibn Saud's son King Faisal, who was raised in a Wahhabi household and whose son is the current Saudi foreign minister, initiated the Arab oil embargo that resulted in the quadrupling of oil prices by the late 1970s.

By 1978 Saudi oil wealth had mushroomed to $50 billion and exceeded $100 hundred billion two years later. Global oil prices fell in the 1990s but Saudi oil revenues still averaged $70 billion from 1999 to 2003 and reached nearly $110 billion in 2004 when oil prices spiked to more than $55 per barrel in the fall. Today Saudi Arabia has the largest known petroleum reserves in the world, ranks as the world's largest producer and exporter of petroleum, and is a leading member of the Organization of Petroleum Exporting Countries (OPEC). It has also served as the only oil producer willing and able to pick up slack in global oil production when demand peaks or supply problems develop elsewhere in the world's oil network. Saudi Arabia's "swing capacity" of nearly two million barrels per day has made it a key American ally in maintaining price stability for global oil markets, independent of OPEC, but the Saudi "swing capacity" is diminishing. Saudi Arabia has an oil-based economy with the central government controlling over 25 percent of the earth's proven reserves as well as the country's major economic activities. Petroleum accounts for about 75 percent of Saudi Arabia's budget revenues, 45 percent of its gross domestic product (GDP), and 90 percent of exports [CIA].

After the quadrupling of oil prices in the 1970s due to the Arab oil embargo, the world witnessed the greatest transfer of wealth since Spain removed tons of gold from the New World in the 17th century. Many Saudis became overnight billionaires and the excesses of the Saudi royal family became legendary. To maintain internal stability and avoid criticism for their ostentatious lifestyles, the Saudi royal family and other wealthy Saudis started paying off the Saudi Wahhabi religious establishment with direct cash grants and through an intricate network of international Muslim charities.

In November 1979, Wahhabi extremists and members of the Muslim Brotherhood seized the Grand Mosque in Mecca in reaction to the excesses of the royal family. In response, King Fahd endeavored to bolster the royal family's tarnished reputation by using the new Saudi oil wealth. After the insurgency was put down and the leaders were publicly beheaded, King Fahd directed millions and ultimately billions into international Islamic charities that funded radical militant Islamist groups around the world and established Wahhabi-Salafist schools and mosques with hate-filled messages against Jews, Christians, and other nonbelievers. Saudi oil wealth was used to spread a fanatical and frightening form of ultra-conservative Islam across North Africa and Central Asia, and into Indonesia, the Philippines, Europe, and the United States. Between 1975 and 2002 it has been estimated that the Saudi government directed as much as $70 to $90 billion in Islamic aid projects around the world, far more than the Soviet Union spent on propaganda during the entire Cold War. This vast sum does not even include an unknown but very substantial amount of additional funding from private Saudi sources, providing aid to the families of suicide bombers and motivating young Muslims around the world to kill infidels and commit unspeakable acts of violence in the name of God. Regrettably, most of the suicide bombers in Iraq following the overthrow of Saddam Hussein were identified as young Saudis, many just teenagers who were exposed to a steady diet of Wahhabi propaganda during their impressionable and rigidly dogmatic school years. Oil wealth and the transfer of petrodollars to radicalized Saudi clerics let loose the genie of Wahhabi Islamist fundamentalism.

Whether we like it or not, oil—***imported oil***—is the lifeblood of Europe, Asia, the United States, and the entire global economy. Without imported oil, the world's economic engines would slow to an idle and grind to a halt in global economic depression. The source of the world's oil is predominantly from Muslim countries where Islam is struggling for its ideological heart and soul in what might someday be called the Muslim Reformation. Table 1.1 contains estimates of the world's crude oil reserves summarized by the top 15 countries with the highest reserves. Five of the first six countries are Persian Gulf states. Muslim states are indicated with a double asterisk.

Table 1.1
2004 Crude Oil Reserves by Country*

Rank	Country	Proven Reserves (billion barrels)
1	Saudi Arabia**	263
2	Canada	178
3	Iran**	130
4	Iraq**	115
5	United Arab Emirates (UAE)**	98
6	Kuwait**	97
7	Venezuela	78
8	Russia	69
9	Libya**	36
10	Nigeria**	34
11	United States	29
12	China	24
13	Mexico	16
14	Algeria**	11
15	Norway	10

*Multiple Sources: U.S. Energy Information Administration, *International Energy Annual Report*, March 4, 2005 http://www.eia.doe.gov/emeu/international/reserves.html; *World Oil*, Vol. 224, No. 8, Aug. 2003.
** Muslim countries

The Persian Gulf, or the Arabian Gulf as the Saudis prefer to call it, is a 600-mile-long body of water between Iran and the Arabian Peninsula. It is one of the world's strategic waterways because of oil, and at its narrowest in the Straits of Hormuz, the Gulf is only a few miles wide with limited navigation, a choke point that could easily bottle up the world's oil supply. Saudi Arabia leads the world in crude oil reserves by a long margin and by its ability to pump nearly 12 million barrels of oil per day and provide a surge capability during global shortages and crises.

Until 9/11, America's relationship with Saudi Arabia was nearly all about oil and little else, other than the offsetting effect of lucrative contracts for American companies to build the Saudi infrastructure and sell expensive weapons and other American products not on the Saudi blacklist. Saudi Arabia still tracks foreign companies that do business with Israel, based on an Arab League boycott that dates to 1951 shortly after the establishment of Israel. For years, the Saudis had boycotted companies like Ford and Coca-Cola for doing business with Israel but they were subsequently taken off the official blacklist as the Saudis amassed oil wealth. After 9/11, the Saudi-American equation became more complex and expanded from simply maintaining freely flowing Persian Gulf oil at moderate prices for the global economy to including cooperation with the United States in the global war on terrorism. But even the importance of the war on terrorism did not override oil as the central factor in the relationship between the two countries because Western dependence on Persian Gulf oil has steadily increased. In 1970, American crude oil production peaked and has declined steadily since, to the point that today the United States imports nearly 60 percent of its oil.

The world consumes about 82 million barrels of oil each day, with the United States accounting for about 25 percent of the world's total consumption, and the numbers are growing so rapidly that by 2030 it is estimated that global consumption will reach 120 million barrels per day, with 60 percent of the increase coming from Asian countries such as China, Japan, Korea and India. Each day, Americans burn about 45 percent of all gasoline that is refined in the world, so better mileage efficiency for automobiles can result in significant savings in the total amount of oil the United States imports. However, the Paris-based International Energy Agency (IEA) [2004] reports that there is no immediate fear that the world will run out of oil anytime soon, based on estimates of energy demand up to 2030. The report states in part, "The earth contains more than enough energy resources to meet demand for many decades to come." But global demand for oil in the past decade grew more rapidly than projected, especially from Asia, where dependence on imports is even higher than in the United States. The issue now is the reliability of oil suppliers.

Over the next 20 years it is expected that demand for energy from Asia will exceed North America because American energy demand will increase more slowly while Asia's is forecast to double. Though Asia has abundant coal reserves, it will import the majority of its natural gas and oil as demand doubles by 2025 or 2030. In 2004, Asian oil imports increased to 64 percent of total Asian consumption, an all-time high, and they are expected to rise to 69 percent by 2010, based on demand of more than 25 million barrels per day, up from 22 million today and nearly the same as American daily consumption. By 2010, the Asia-Pacific region will produce only about 30 percent of the oil it needs annually. The big drivers in Asian demand are Japan and China, now the second largest oil consumer in the world after the United States and importing about 50 percent of its oil directly from the Persian Gulf.

As China's top oil supplier, Saudi Arabia recently negotiated a stake in a Chinese refinery, and in 2003 China's SINOPEC won a Saudi contract to develop natural gas in the vast and barren Rub al Khali Empty Quarter of Saudi Arabia. Because of its severe energy shortage and dependence on Persian Gulf oil, China also signed a $70 billion oil and natural gas agreement with Iran in the fall of 2004 to supply China with 150,000 barrels of oil per day for 25 years. Japan and Korea are even more dependent on foreign oil, importing almost 100 percent of their oil, and nearly one-third of that from the Persian Gulf. That is why a large Japanese consortium consisting of major Japanese companies such as Mitsubishi, Mitsui, Marabena, Itochu, Tomen, Chiyoda, JGC, and Toyo, recently negotiated an agreement with Iraq for strategic claims to Iraqi oil fields.

European imports have also grown to the point where today Europe imports 80 percent of its oil, over one-third coming from the Persian Gulf. Second only to Saudi Arabia, Russia is also a major oil supplier and even with its domestic problems it has great potential from abundant oil reserves that rank sixth in the world, and Canada has vast reserves of retrievable oil sands. Emerging suppliers in Central Asia on both sides of the Caspian Sea as well as Iran are also significant players in the global oil calculus, and one of the world's largest undeveloped sources of crude oil lies underwater off the west coast of Africa in Nigeria. Finally, Iraq has significant oil reserves and its oil production has the potential of rivaling Saudi Arabia as additional fields are explored and neglected infrastructure are developed and improved. While there is little danger of the world running out of oil in this century, the crux of the issue for the United States and the West is the reliability of the sources of imported oil. The fact remains that most of the major oil-producing regions of the world are controlled by Muslim countries where suspicion of America's motives and disenchantment with American Middle East policies have increased since 9/11 due to the war on terror and American military action to liberate Afghanistan and Iraq.

As American domestic oil reserves peaked and then started a steady decline in the early 1970s, global oil prices quadrupled later in that decade as a result of the Arab oil embargo following the October 1973 Arab-Israeli Yom Kippur War and the formation of OPEC. That is when Saudi oil wealth began to mushroom and Western firms began implementing contracts worth billions of dollars in infrastructure development and weapons purchases in the kingdom. To counter the threat of further oil shortages and make a political statement, President Jimmy Carter put in place America's first conservation initiatives since the Second World War, mandating a 55 MPH speed limit on freeways and increased mileage standards for automobiles. In time, these initiatives took hold and the pace of American demand for oil lessened, eventually driving down global prices a decade later. President Carter laid the groundwork for another American initiative shortly after revolutionary Shiite Muslims overthrew the Shah of Iran in 1979 by announcing what became known as the "Carter Doctrine" in his State of the Union speech in January 1980, stressing that security of Persian Gulf oil was considered an American "vital interest" to be defended "by any means necessary, including military force." President Reagan confirmed this policy in the 1980s during the Iran-Iraq war (1980-89) and President George H. W. Bush invoked the Carter Doctrine when Saddam Hussein invaded Kuwait in 1990 and threatened Saudi Arabia and Persian Gulf oil facilities. The first President Bush formed a massive global coalition that drove Iraq from Kuwait and neutralized the Iraqi threat to the Persian Gulf oil fields. The Carter Doctrine remains in place to this day and the United States can be expected to invoke its terms again if Persian Gulf oil is once more threatened. American oil companies and their global partners have operated in the Persian Gulf for nearly 70 years. They know the region and its problems well, but have done little to help the United States lessen its dependence on imported oil. American energy security objectives have been based on the premise that oil demand is tied to the long-term health of the world economy, but successive American administrations since Carter have failed to meet their stated energy security goals:

U.S. ENERGY SECURITY GOALS

- Promote diversity of energy sources to avoid dependence on oil and lower American dependence on foreign suppliers

- Avoid dependence on a single supplier nation and reduce price volatility

- Protect national and economic security by promoting a diverse supply and delivery of reliable, affordable, and environmentally sound energy

- Protect national and economic security by providing world-class scientific research capacity and advancing scientific knowledge

- Protect the environment by resolving the environmental legacy of the Cold War and by providing for the permanent disposal of high-level radioactive waste [Dept. of Energy]

In fact, American energy independence has been a dismal failure on almost all counts, especially diversity of suppliers and flexibility, because OPEC possesses the only real flexibility. In the fall of 2004 oil peaked at more than $55 a barrel and by mid 2005 oil topped $60 per barrel, an all-time high, and American imports of foreign oil continued to rise to a record high of nearly 60 percent of total domestic consumption. The United States and the West have little flexibility in the global oil market because Muslim OPEC nations control most of the world's oil reserves and spare production capacity. For the next several years, almost all of the world's additional production lies along the Persian Gulf and most of that is in Saudi Arabia. When oil prices peaked in late 2004 and again in June 2005, OPEC spare capacity was only one million barrels per day and almost all of that was from Saudi Arabia, making the United States and the West hostage to the very country most responsible for fomenting radical, Islamist fundamentalism, hardly a successful energy security policy for the world's largest economy [Bremmer and Hawes].

While the Bush Administration has firmly pressured the Saudi government to take a more active role in fighting radical, militant Islamist terrorism, it continues to believe that the Saudis will remain a reliable "swing producer" of oil, but the degree of risk in that assessment is high. At the end of 2004, Saudi Oil Minister Ali al Naimi said that Saudi Arabia had surplus production of about two million barrels, "which could be used when needed," but that was the extent of OPEC's excess production. OPEC supplies more than one-third of the world's oil on a daily basis, and in early 2005 OPEC countries were pumping the most oil in 25 years in response to record global demand and increased demand from China and India, and because of disrupted supplies from Iraq, Venezuela, and Nigeria.

Since the 1973 Arab oil embargo, the American government has worked diligently with Saudi Arabia, as the supplier of last resort, and the other principal suppliers of crude oil to the world market to keep the global supply of crude oil in balance with constantly rising global demand. The primary basis for America's relationship with Saudi Arabia through successive administrations in Washington has been to ensure stable and relatively low energy costs to support global economic growth. But 9/11 created a new and overriding issue—combating terrorism and its ideological sources—and Saudi-American relationships became even more complex and vital.

Over the last 60 years, since President Roosevelt met Abdul Aziz ibn Saud in 1945, succeeding American administrations have come and gone, each reinforcing America's policy of maintaining stability in the world's oil supply. Moreover, over the last 30 years, American energy security policy has failed while former American ambassadors, retired generals and international businesspeople have made millions of dollars working for the Saudis, or for institutions funded by the Saudis, or for American companies doing business with the Saudis, or seeking to do business with the Saudi government. For the most part, these are intelligent and honorable people who understand the issues in the region and have an appreciation for the difficulty of doing business in Saudi Arabia—up to the limits of any Westerner's ability to know. Many of these distinguished Americans are registered as agents of a foreign government (Saudi Arabia) with the U.S. Justice Department and U.S. Congress as required by law and many others have been co-opted by the Saudis to promote and lobby Saudi issues in Washington, DC and European capitals. This type of collusion has been promoted as a deliberate pattern of Saudi "gulling" of America over the years.

The process of formally dealing with the Saudis while being openly "gulled" by Saudi leaders continues unabated today, as bureaucrats and political appointees often look to lucrative Saudi consulting jobs after retirement due to the huge volume of money available and the entrenched relationships that exist on both sides between people in government and the private sector. There has been a long-standing mutuality of interest between the United States and Saudi Arabia based on maintaining oil price stability for the sake of the global economy. The Saudis know and understand that oil demand is tied directly to the long-term health of the global economy and, to their credit, the Saudis have been good oil partners over the years, reliably playing their role in the partnership as the world's largest oil supplier to the market of the world's largest oil consumer.

After 9/11, however, Saudi-American relationships changed dramatically and people in leadership positions in the United States government finally began to comprehend the serious impact of American gullibility and culpability over the years as well as the complexities of Saudi Arabia as a 21st century nation just emerging from the Middle Ages. With great wealth from an underground treasure that the world relies upon, the complex Saudi-American relationship in the post-9/11 era developed an added dimension in addition to freely flowing oil and reduced pricing volatility—and that new dimension is the common goal of winning the war against radical, militant Islam. But the question remains: Is modern Saudi Arabia willing and capable?

MODERN SAUDI ARABIA

In less than three generations, Saudi Arabia literally vaulted from its 7th century Bedouin origins to approach a modern 21st century society, skipping intermediate phases of development that typically require centuries. What the West faces in Saudi Arabia today is the gigantic task of successfully moving a country with ultra-conservative medieval values into the 21st century. The United States created many of Saudi Arabia's governmental institutions in good faith to the point that today modern Saudi Arabia is largely an American creation but one that came back to haunt its creator on 9/11. The formation of the Saudi bureaucracy and establishment of modern governmental institutions started in earnest in the 1960s during the reign of King Faisal and accelerated with the advent of oil wealth and fallout from the 1979 Iranian Shiite revolution. Physically, organizationally, and economically, most Saudi Arabian bureaucratic institutions resemble agencies of the U.S. government—all funded by massive Saudi oil wealth from the 1980s. In a 2003 interview, Thomas Lippman described the humanitarian origin of United States-Saudi relationships that were initiated and cemented with the first king of Saudi Arabia, Abdul Aziz ibn Saud, by American medical missionaries in the 1930s:

> The relationship began not with the signing of the first oil contract but with the work of medical missionaries from the missionary hospital in Bahrain that was established at the beginning of the twentieth century by the Reformed Church in America. The first Americans that King Abdul Aziz met were doctors from the Bahrain missionary hospital, who requested to come into the kingdom, where medical conditions were terrible. People suffered from tuberculosis, malaria and all kinds of chronic diseases.
>
> The doctors would come for weeks or even a couple of months at a time and treat the people. They were not allowed to preach nor were they allowed to establish a permanent presence, but they did introduce the king to the notion of people who would come from across the sea and not be Muslims, and who would give, without taking, to the people of Saudi Arabia, and, in my opinion laid the groundwork for the king's favorable view of Americans that was partially responsible for granting of the oil concessions to American instead of British firms in the 1930s" [Lippman, 11/2003].

American Imprint

Beginning with President Roosevelt's commitments to the old king in 1945 and the gift of a DC-3 civilian airliner, President Truman's "Point Four Program" followed in the 1950s, and American support for Saudi Arabia continued under each successive American administration. The first American institution established in Saudi Arabia was the Arabian American Oil Company (ARAMCO) following the 60-year oil concession granted to Standard Oil in 1933. Before being nationalized by the Saudi government in 1982, ARAMCO had grown into a gigantic American presence in the Eastern Province and thousands of American expatriates and their families lived in secluded American housing compounds that resemble suburban America of the 1950s and 1960s. During the Roosevelt-Abdul Aziz meeting after the Yalta Conference with Allied leaders in 1945, the United States agreed to help protect the Saudi oil fields in return for an American air base in the Eastern Province. The emerging Cold War against atheistic communism following the Second World War caused the Saudis to side with America in the post-war environment and to place great value on the ARAMCO relationship that produced such unbelievable wealth for them.

Except for oil and ARAMCO, American involvement in Saudi Arabia evolved without fanfare and publicity until the 1973 Arab-Israeli war and the quadrupling of oil prices following the Saudi-led Arab oil embargo. That same year, the Saudi government acquired 25 percent ownership in ARAMCO and the British announced their intention to depart the Persian Gulf where they had been the dominant military force for decades. In 1974, President Nixon established the U.S.-Saudi Joint Economic Commission and American involvement in Saudi Arabia increased dramatically following the overthrow of the Shah of Iran in 1979 by Ayatollah Khomeini's Shiite Islamist fundamentalist revolutionaries. Nixon's "Twin Pillar" Persian Gulf policy had called for dual support of both Iran and Saudi Arabia, but that policy collapsed when the Shah and his family fled for their lives, greatly alarming the Saudi royal family and causing serious concern regarding the Shiite minority in the Saudi Eastern Province and proselytizing Iranian fundamentalists a few miles across the Persian Gulf.

With massive, new oil wealth and renewed concern for security against a radical Iranian Shiite threat, the Saudis contracted with American businesses and several branches of the U.S. government to create and transform its governmental agencies and develop a modern Saudi bureaucracy, with many agencies and departments becoming nearly identical to their American counterparts. Some of the American institutions and government agencies are listed below, along with their Saudi creations [Lippman, 2003]:

- U.S. Military Training Mission: Modernized Royal Saudi Air Force (RSAF) and Saudi Arabian National Guard (SANG)

- U.S. Treasury: Established Saudi Arabian Monetary Agency (SAMA)—the Saudi central bank

- U.S. Army Corps of Engineers: Construction of facilities worth billions of dollars

- Ford Foundation: Saudi Civil Service and Saudi Bureaucracy—established centralized personnel system, civil service, training programs, payroll, recruiting system for Saudi civil service

- U.S. Saudi Arabian Joint Commission on Economic Cooperation: Provided American expertise for economic development

- Trans World Airlines (TWA): Created Saudi Arabian Airlines (Saudia) from gift of DC-3 in 1945: American aircraft, pilots, administrators, maintenance personnel, training programs

- U.S. Geological Survey: Provided Saudi Irrigation and Agricultural Assistance

- American Universities and Hospitals: Created Saudi Universities, Hospitals and Practices

- U.S. National Park Service: Established First National Park in Saudi Arabia

Abdul Aziz ibn Saud Imprint

Modern Saudi Arabia in many ways reflects the indelible imprint of the United States government but the kingdom itself reflects the imprint of its founder, King Abdul Aziz ibn Saud, who by most counts had over 50 children from his many wives and whose sons have successively ruled the country since his death in 1953. Saud became king in 1953 when his father died but was deposed by members of the royal family 10 years later in favor of King Faisal who was assassinated in 1975 by a deranged, Wahhabi-influenced nephew seeking revenge for his brother who had been killed in a clash with Saudi security forces in 1966. King Khaled followed Faisal and died in 1982 from heart failure and King Fahd, the current king, assumed the throne. Fahd was born in 1921 but has been incapacitated since a series of strokes in 1995 and 1996. His half brother Crown Prince Abdullah, born in 1923 or 1924, is the de facto ruler today, having been ordained by the royal family as next in line for the throne.

Abdullah's full title is "His Royal Highness Crown Prince Abdullah Ibn Abdul Aziz, Deputy Prime Minister and Commander of the National Guard," but he is not one of the so-called "Sudairi Seven," sons of the old king's favorite wife, Hassa bint Ahmad Sudairi. King Fahd is a Sudairi and two other Sudairis, Prince Sultan and Prince Nayef, lie in waiting for their turn at the throne, as do younger generations of princes. The seven Sudairi brothers, listed below, are now in their 70s and 80s and confront the health problems of aging, but continue to control powerful government institutions:

The Sudairi Seven

Fahd bin Abdul Aziz ibn Saud	King & Prime Minister
Sultan bin Abdul Aziz ibn Saud	Second Vice Minister & Minister of Defense & Aviation
Abdul-Rahman bin Abdul Aziz ibn Saud	Vice Minister of Defense & Aviation
Nayef bin Abdul Aziz ibn Saud	Minister of Interior
Salman bin Abdul Aziz ibn Saud	Governor of Riyadh
Ahmad bin Abdul Aziz ibn Saud	Vice Minister of Interior
Turki (II) bin Abdul Aziz ibn Saud	Chairman, Arabian Cement Company, Ltd.

Through decades of extravagance, the West has criticized members of the royal family for their unrestrained self-indulgence, and it is widely known that King Fahd smoked, used alcohol excessively and lived extravagantly, especially at his villa in Marbella, Spain where decadence abounded. Fahd lived a life of ostentatious wealth and consistently demonstrated a belief that money could solve all problems, as he did after the seizure of the Great Mosque in Mecca in 1979 by Wahhabi extremists and members of the Muslim Brotherhood.

Abdullah, however, has a different reputation. He grew up in the desert among the remote northern tribes before the discovery of oil and raced horses and camels with his loyal Bedouin followers. By 1962 Abdullah was selected to command the Saudi Arabian National Guard (SANG) consisting of well over 50,000 loyal and highly-trained Bedouin tribesmen responsible for internal security. Today Abdullah's strengths rest with his reputation for integrity and hard work and the fact that the National Guard he has commanded for over 40 years is loyal to him personally. Abdullah's sons are also in senior positions in the National Guard where they have maintained strong Wahhabi and Bedouin tribal connections. The modern Saudi Arabian National Guard is a direct descendant of the Wahhabi Ikhwan militia and was formed for internal security purposes as a counterweight to the more traditional military forces under Prince Sultan, one of the Sudairis and a full brother of King Fahd. In many ways al Qaeda is also a reincarnation of the Ikhwan with many similar characteristics. Abdullah and his family have close family ties to the northern Saudi Arabian Shamar confederation, a powerful and ubiquitous Wahhabi tribe that reaches from Iraq into Syria and Saudi Arabia. Iraqi Wahhabis have been some of the fiercest insurgents fighting American forces in the Sunni Triangle northwest of Baghdad and most are from the Shamar confederation. Abdullah's family also controls the tribal council that rules Mecca and Medina and he maintains strong relationships with the Ulama, the powerful Saudi Wahhabi religious hierarchy that controls the influential Ministry of Religious Affairs, Ministry of Justice, and Ministry of Education. Abdullah has spent little time outside Saudi Arabia and has been critical of America and the West in the past, but he has recently taken steps to appear more moderate, as in a 2002 interview with *New York Times* reporter, Tom Friedman, when he offered a Saudi solution to the Arab-Israeli stalemate. But even as late as the spring of 2004, Abdullah was quoted saying:

> It became clear for us and I say it, not 100 percent but 95 percent, that Zionists' hands are behind what is going on now. Unfortunately, they deceived some of our sons. The Devil made them daring and they are supporters of the Devil and colonialism.

Abdullah's Sudairi rivals are Prince Sultan, born in 1924, and Prince Nayef, born in 1934. Sultan's official title is "His Royal Highness Prince Sultan Ibn Abdul Aziz, Second Deputy Prime Minister, Minister of Defense and Aviation and Inspector General." As Minister of Defense, Sultan controls the entire Saudi military establishment except for Abdullah's countervailing National Guard. Sultan and his Sudairi brother, Abdul-Rahman, and Sultan's son Khaled control the traditional Army, Navy and Air Force. Another of Sultan's sons, Bandar, has been the influential and popular Saudi ambassador to the United States in Washington, DC since 1983. Until 9/11, Bandar was a highly effective Washington power broker with close personal connections to high-ranking Republicans and Democrats alike for over two decades. Since 9/11, however, Bandar has appeared less frequently in public and Abdullah seems to have installed his own people to guide Saudi relationships in Washington while keeping Bandar more in the background. Sultan and Bandar tend to tilt toward the West, but Sultan is a loyal family member and supporter of the existing Wahhabi power structure while having grown extremely wealthy from years of large commissions on military contracts that he controls through the Ministry of Defense and Aviation (MODA).

Prince Nayef is Minister of Interior where he and his full Sudairi brother, Ahmad, are in charge of internal security and control the secret police and religious police, the Mattawa. Saudi Arabia is a tightly controlled oligarchy and Prince Nayef is a strong Wahhabi supporter with close ties to prominent Wahhabi clerics in the ministries that report to him. Prince Nayef has headed the interior ministry and its secret and religious police since the early 1970s. His ministry is responsible for enforcing Islamic law and it is well documented that torture is commonly used to obtain confessions. Executions are sanctioned for capital crimes and offences other than murder such as witchcraft, adultery, sodomy, robbery, sabotage, apostasy (renunciation of Islam), and a catchall charge of "corruption on earth." In early December 2002, Prince Nayef told a Kuwaiti magazine, "Who committed the events of September 11?...I think they [the Zionists] are behind these events" and questions abound regarding corruption at high levels and royal family support of al Qaeda [Bergen].

Current Crisis

Competition has always existed among the princes, but today outward signs point to a growing battle between Abdullah, Sultan and Nayef. Few Western observers really know what goes on within the inner workings of the royal family that rules the inscrutable desert kingdom. Many experienced observers believe that the serious problems caused by al Qaeda attacks in the kingdom, hard pressure from the United States for reform, and the strength of the Wahhabis within the government, have placed the royal family in the most serious crisis of its existence and with a diminishing chance of compromise. The outlook for the survival of the royal family as an institution is less than favorable because its very existence requires rapid change to become a true constitutional monarchy with a broadly representative government.

With 5,800–7,000 first tier princes and tens of thousands of other members of the Saudi royal family dependent on overly generous oil stipends that feed expensive tastes, there is a strong potential for a bloody struggle within the Saudi royal family after King Fahd dies. Many younger members of the royal family and influential Saudi businessmen have been educated in the West and understand the problems faced by the ruling family and the need for reform. Many of these good people are working hard for reform, but in the final analysis, the tale of the Saudi royal family is an ancient story replete in the annals of history. The struggle within the Saudi royal family today is symptomatic of failing absolute monarchies throughout history and is today reminiscent of the final years of the Shah of Iran.

In 2004 Osama bin Laden warned that the Saudi royal family is destined to meet the same fate as the Shah due to corruption, ostentatious living and wayward policies. It is well to remember that the first and primary goal of al Qaeda is the overthrow of the Saudi monarchy, followed by restoration of the Sunni

Caliphate and installation of a Taliban-like regime with a rigid Wahhabi legal system in Saudi Arabia and around the world. Any suggestion of reform by the Saudi monarchy looks like weakness to al Qaeda, inviting even more al Qaeda-inspired violence.

If the Saudi royal family falls to radical, militant forces in the near future, world markets will tremble, the price of oil could soar to $300 per barrel or more, and the world economy will sink into global depression. The only alternative for the West at that time would be to unite behind U.S.-led NATO forces in Iraq to secure the Saudi oil fields in the Eastern Province and help mainstream, moderate Muslims internationalize the holy cities of Islam in Mecca and Medina. The Saudi rulers are faced with daunting challenges of uncertain royal family succession as well as the monumental task of bringing the desert kingdom, its people, and its ultra-conservative religious clerics and culture into the 21st century while facing rapid and enormous change.

The royal family has had a long history of peacefully accommodating and then violently smashing the Wahhabi religious clerics when they defy authority, and that is what might happen again if the royal family is pushed further into a corner. When the Wahhabi Ikhwan rose up against Abdul Aziz ibn Saud in 1928-30, he publicly beheaded the leaders, and when Wahhabi extremists seized the Great Mosque in Mecca during a 1979 religious rampage, the Saudi regime executed over 60 of the extremists, with public beheadings throughout the country as an example [Lippman, 2004].

Besides the problems of its religious clerics, the Saudis also face dramatic population growth, fluctuating oil revenues, continued deficit spending, as well as the difficulty of accommodating the incessant forces of globalization and modernization. The future portends many problems relating to social dislocation caused by rapid modernization and runaway population growth rate that will double the number of Saudis in 20 years. High wages and an uncompetitive economy in the global market are the result of a poor Saudi work ethic, high salary expectations and a failed public school system that does not provide needed job skills or training. Unless the royal family is successful in quickly implementing critically needed reforms, these conditions could result in the overthrow of the monarchy by a radical Islamist government dominated by the military and with little hope of a Western-style democracy.

Other developments are also disturbing. The Saudis are wedded to huge levels of defense spending and corruption, with about 13 percent of Saudi GDP devoted to defense versus 4.3 percent for China and 3.2 percent for the United States by way of comparison. Moreover, the Saudis acquired 50 ballistic missiles from China a few years ago with a range of 2,000 miles and they recently negotiated an arms-for-oil exchange to upgrade the missiles with the latest Chinese technology. China is motivated to secure its sources of oil because it imports nearly two-thirds of what it consumes and has recently negotiated large deals with both the Saudis and Iran. Meanwhile, it has been widely reported in the press that the Saudis had funded as much as $7 billion for nuclear weapons programs in Iraq under Saddam Hussein and in Pakistan. It is further alleged that the Saudis have an agreement with Pakistan to receive nuclear warheads for the upgraded Saudi missiles that will be used as a deterrent to Israeli and potential Iranian nuclear capability across the Persian Gulf.

All in all, trouble lies ahead for the absolute monarchy that could be dubbed the kingdom of "intolerance swaddled in faith" [Cohen]. The reality after 9/11 is that the United States can no longer take Saudi Arabia for granted as it has in the past, and as many desert warriors have observed, "desert winds are blowing"—change is in the wind—but it is also well to remember that, "nothing is easy in the desert."

THE SAUDI GOVERNMENT

The Arabian Peninsula was never colonized during the 18th, 19th and 20th centuries like most Arab countries in the region, and for countless centuries, nomadic Bedouin tribes wandered the open Arabian Peninsula, well known for their insular, traditional, and xenophobic Bedouin culture and rigid "code of the desert" required for survival. The barren heartland in the center of Saudi Arabia around the capital, Riyadh, formed a natural barrier to the Ottoman Turks, Portuguese, British, and other European colonial powers. Since its inception in 1932, Saudi Arabia has been an absolute monarchy—a true authoritarian oligarchy—without elected representative institutions or political parties until partial municipal elections in February 2005.

Wahhabi Islam is the State

Legitimacy of the monarchy comes from its relationship with the Wahhabi religious leaders. Wahhabism is the most fundamentalist Muslim sect in Islam and the Wahhabi clerics prefer to call themselves "Salafists" for advocating an ultra-conservative version of Islam that demands Islamist states, Islamic law, and a return to the "pure" days of 7th century Islam. Saudi Arabia is a uniquely Islamic country where church and state are a single entity with no separation possible because it would be contrary to the Wahhabi interpretation of Islam. To Wahhabi believers, separation of church and state as in America, Europe, or Muslim Turkey cannot be tolerated because it would undermine Islam's doctrine of church and state as an integrated entity. According to Wahhabi thinking, secular states are governed by man-made laws and Islamic states like Saudi Arabia are governed by what they believe to be God's laws as revealed in the Holy Koran and writings of the Prophet Mohammed. Disfavored Muslim sects such as Shiites and Sufis, Christianity, Judaism, and all other religions are banned in Saudi Arabia, and Saudi Wahhabis have been especially virulent in their persecution and discrimination against the Shiite minority in the Eastern Province near the oil fields that makes up nearly 15 percent of the Saudi population.

The Wahhabi-controlled Commission for Promotion of Virtue and Prevention of Vice under Prince Nayef's Ministry of the Interior has cabinet rank in the government, and strict Wahhabi Islamist norms are enforced by the Commission's Muttawa religious police who operate much like the severe Taliban Islamist fundamentalist regime in Afghanistan that was overthrown by the United States in November 2001. Saudi Arabia is governed by Islamic law (shariah) derived from the teachings of the Holy Koran, which is believed to be the Word of God, and from the Sunna, the words and deeds of the prophet Muhammad as recorded in the Hadith. The term "shariah" in Arabic literally means "the path to the watering hole" and as Islamic religious law, it serves as a religious code for living, similar to the moral system of the Bible for Christians. However, Saudi Arabia has the strictest interpretation of shariah in the world.

The judicial system in Saudi Arabia is closed to the public and the government does not permit demonstrations or criticism, although there has been some loosening because the advent of the Internet and satellite television has changed the ability of the Saudi government to control what people think. Moreover, the Iraqi national elections in January 2005 served as a driving force for reform throughout the Middle East, including Saudi Arabia. Yet, if people do demonstrate or criticize the government today they risk detention or torture. Until recently, defendants have not had the right to representation by a lawyer, are poorly informed of the status of legal proceedings against them, and trials are generally held behind closed doors. When individuals are brought to trial before an Islamic court, the proceedings do not meet accepted international standards for fairness and punishments are medieval and brutal. The consumption of alcohol is punished by whipping, theft by the amputation of limbs, and under full implementation of Islamic law, 100 lashes and death by stoning are mandated for married women convicted of adultery or fornication. Beheading and stoning for "sorcery" and nonbelief are routine under Saudi law, ranking Saudi Arabia first in the world for beheadings and second only to China for the number of deaths by capital punishment. "Executions by the law of God" (Iaqmet al-Had in Arabic) is a weekly public beheading spectacle held after noon prayers each Friday, either in the court of the main mosque or in a square in front of the regional governor's palace. For crimes like robbery accompanied by premeditated murder, crucifixion for 24 hours is adjudged, followed by swift public beheading using a long, curved scimitar. A State Department report released in February 2004 stated that Saudi Arabian security forces and religious police have been guilty of serious human rights abuses, conduct closed trials, provide no legal counsel for defendants, and implement barbarous punishment such as beheading, amputation and stoning for "sorcery," nonbelief and blasphemy [State Department] .

Sayyid Qutb, intellectual theoretician of the Egyptian Muslim Brotherhood, admired the Saudi legal system and commended it as the basis for other Islamist states and a solution to the world's ills. The country is governed day-to-day by the king as head of state and a Council of Ministers that was established by King Abdul Aziz Ibn Saud in 1953. The Council of Ministers consists of 29 cabinet-level members and is responsible for all affairs of state. The Council meets weekly and is presided over by the king or his deputy, the crown prince. Various ministries and government agencies serve under the Under the Council of Ministers and most are located in the capital, Riyadh. Regional governors, who are senior members of the royal family with cabinet-level rank, head 13 regional provinces. The governors are responsible to the Minister of Interior for regional governance matters, hold power over the local tribal leaders, and are authorized to carry out capital punishment.

Saudi legislation called the "Basic Law" was implemented in 1993. The Basic Law was an attempt for the first time to formalize a written constitution and it further defined the government's rights and responsibilities to Saudi citizens and established a Consultative Council called the "Majlis Al Shura," the Saudi form of democracy. Initially 60 members and now 120, all appointed by the king, the Majlis was established to bring together distinguished Saudi representatives from a mixture of clans, religious and business leaders and professionals to serve four-year terms and advise the king on matters effecting the country. The concept of a tribal council is well established in Bedouin culture and the Saudi Majlis resembles its earlier Bedouin models. Members are appointed by the king and not elected, and the king is the final arbiter on all issues. The Majlis is unique in that it is an extension of centuries old Bedouin tradition permitting any member of the clan or tribe to appeal to the local sheik or leader to express the nature of a problem and seek redress for a perceived wrong, regardless of how small or trivial. The Saudis implemented the Majlis as their own version of representative government and they went out of their way to declare that the Majlis is not a step toward Western-style democracy but rather an extension of Saudi tradition that goes back to the days of the Prophet Mohammed.

The Saudi Basic Law lays out the ground rules for the Majlis, or Consultative Council, the structure and organization of the Saudi government, and what the Saudis call their "Bill of Rights for Saudi Citizens," as summarized below [Saudi Ministry of Culture and Information]:

SAUDI "BASIC LAW"

Article 5: The system of government in Saudi Arabia shall be monarchical. The dynasty right shall be confined to the sons of the Founder, King Abdul Aziz bin Abdul Rahman Al Saud (Abdul Aziz Ibn Saud), and the sons of sons. The King names the Crown Prince and may relieve him of his duties by Royal Order. The Crown Prince shall assume the powers of the king on the latter's death.

Article 6: Citizens shall pledge allegiance to the King on the basis of the Book of God and the Prophet's Sunnah, as well as on the principle of "hearing is obeying" both in prosperity and adversity, in situations pleasant and unpleasant.

Article 7: The regime derives its power from the Holy Koran and the Prophet's Sunnah, which rule over this and all other State Laws.

Article 8: The system of government in the Kingdom of Saudi Arabia is established on the foundation of justice, "Shura" and equality in compliance with the Islamic Shariah (the revealed law of Islam).

Article 23: The State shall protect the Islamic Creed and shall cater to the application of Shariah. The State shall enjoin good and forbid evil, and shall undertake the duties of the call to Islam.

Article 24: The State shall maintain and serve the Two Holy Mosques (in Mecca & Medina). It shall ensure the security and safety of all those who call at the Two Holy Mosques so that they may be able to visit or perform the pilgrimage and "Umrah" (minor pilgrimage) in comfort and ease.

Article 26: The State shall protect human rights in accordance with Islamic Shariah.

Article 28: The State shall provide job opportunities to all able-bodied people and shall enact laws to protect both the employee and the employer.

Article 30: The State shall provide public education and shall commit itself to the eradication of illiteracy.

Article 33: The State shall build and equip the armed forces to defend the Islamic faith, the Two Holy Mosques, the society and the homeland.

Article 36: The State shall ensure the security of all its citizens and expatriates living within its domains. No individual shall be detained, imprisoned or have actions restricted except under the provisions of law.

Article 37: Houses are inviolable. They shall not be entered without the permission of their owners, nor shall they be searched except in cases specified by the law.

Article 41: Foreign residents in the Kingdom of Saudi Arabia shall abide by its regulations and shall show respect for Saudi social traditions, values and feelings.

Article 43: The "Majlis" of the King and the "Majlis" of the Crown Prince shall be open to all citizens and to anyone who may have a complaint or a grievance. Every individual shall have the right to communicate with public authorities regarding any topic he may wish to discuss.

Article 45: The source of Ifta (religious ruling) in the Kingdom of Saudi Arabia is the Holy Koran and the Prophet's Sunnah. The law shall specify the composition of the Senior Ulama Board and of the Administration of Religious Research and Ifta and its jurisdictions.

Article 46: The judicial authority is an independent power. In discharging their duties, the judges bow to no authority other than that of Islamic Shariah.

The Al Saud-Wahhab Partnership Continues

Wahhabi religious leaders form the Ulama, which has a long and significant history that started in 1744 with the political and religious alliance between the al Saud family and Mohammed bin Abdul Wahhab [Saudi Ministry of Culture and Information]. The Saudi Ulama enforces the rigid standards of Wahhabism, controls the Ministry of Religious Affairs, Ministry of Education, and Ministry of Justice in the Saudi government. In this capacity, the Ulama implements Islamic law and jurisprudence (shariah), judges all legal cases in the courts according to Islamic law, administers public education at all levels, supervises the mosques including what is preached both at home and abroad, and controls international funding and support for mosques and schools in foreign countries. As strict Wahhabi religious leaders, the Ulama has played a key role in the country from its inception and continues to control all divisions of the Saudi government that have any remote relationship to religion, including the preaching of Islam abroad.

The present-day Saudi royal family cemented its covenant with the Wahhabis when Mohammed ibn Saud, local Arab chieftain and ancestor of the present ruling family, married the daughter of Ibn Abdul Wahhab (1703-1791), the founder of Wahhabism. This linked the al Saud and al Sheik (Wahhab) families with the obscure Wahhabi Sunni cult, which was unique to the harsh Arabian desert and by all standards, then or now, a perversion of mainstream Islamic teachings. Wahhabis were ruthless with their enemies, especially the Shiites, and their puritan zeal resulted in the destruction of sacred Islamic tombs, graveyards, paintings, and mosque adornments wherever their Ikhwan army rampaged in an attempt to return the people of the desert to the "purity" of Mohammed's 7th century Islam. Natana J. DeLong-Bas [2004] has contrasted Wahhabism with Bin Ladenism:

> The real Muhammad Ibn Abd al-Wahhab, as revealed in his written works, was a well-trained and widely traveled scholar and jurist, as well as a prolific writer. His extant written works fill fourteen large volumes, including a collection of *Hadith*; a biography of the Prophet Muhammad; a collection of *fatwa* (juridical opinions); a series of exegetical commentaries on the Holy Koran; several volumes of Islamic jurisprudence (*fiqh*), numerous theological treatises; and other varied works, including detailed discussions of jihad and the status of women. The scope of his scholarship stands in marked contrast to the few legal rulings (*fatwa*) issued by Osama bin Laden. More importantly, his insistence on adherence to Koranic values, like the maximum preservation of human life even in the midst of jihad as holy war, tolerance for other religions, and support for a balance of rights between men and women, results in a very different worldview from that of contemporary militant extremists. The absence of the xenophobia, militantism, misogyny, extremism, and literalism typically associated with Wahhabism raises serious questions about whether such themes are "inherent" to Wahhabism and whether extremists like Osama bin Laden are truly "representative" of Wahhabism and Wahhabi beliefs.

Treatment of women is especially harsh in the Saudi kingdom. Women's rights as known in the West are virtually nonexistent in Saudi Arabia because of the Ulama's ultra-strict and literal interpretation of Islamic law. Stoning, amputation, and public beheading for capital crime are common and Saudi cultural taboos create immense problems for Saudi women in their efforts to enter the 21st century. Other Muslim countries differ significantly from Saudi Arabia in their interpretation of the Holy Koran, which shows that it is not Islam, as a whole, but rather the strict Saudi interpretation of the Holy Koran and sayings of the Prophet Mohammed that has failed to adapt to the modern world.

The plight of women under strict Islamic law in Saudi Arabia seems medieval and barbaric by Western standards, both in interpretation and practice. As laid out in the Holy Koran in the 7th century, Islamic law governs women's activities and all aspects of behavior outside the home. The list of female restrictions and prohibitions is lengthy, starting with rigid segregation of the sexes, even to the point that Saudi women have separate entrances to their homes. Outside the home, women must be fully covered in black, including a black facial veil that must be worn even in oppressive desert heat, and when they leave their homes, a male family member who can wear cooler white robes, must escort them. Social customs and tribal taboos are so formidable in some remote and especially conservative parts of Saudi Arabia such as the Al Kharj region south of Riyadh that not even a woman's husband or children are permitted to see her face until she dies [Qusti, 9/3/03]. A 5,000-man Wahhabi religious police force called the Muttawa strictly enforce Islamic law, calling the faithful to prayer five times a day and arresting violators of rigid Wahhabi rules for fraternization between the sexes and violation of the rigid female dress code. In 2004 the Muttawa was strengthened to pacify senior Wahhabi clerics in the government in the wake of the government crackdown on extremists following successive al Qaeda attacks within the kingdom. Different standards prevail for women in Saudi Arabia, as in almost everything, and capital punishment is even more extreme for women.

Under Islamic law, a woman may be stoned to death if she has been raped or convicted of extramarital sex, but most capital punishment for women is by firing squad, while men are beheaded with a sword slightly longer than one meter. Under the law, women are treated as chattel and are the personal property of the husband or father, while men may practice polygamy and are permitted to have up to four wives. Women are prohibited from driving cars and are frequently forced into arranged marriages as early teenagers. Inheritance rights favor men over women—two shares for men and one for women—and divorce and child custody are strictly male prerogatives, legally ordered upon peremptory demand by the husband with no objection permitted by the wife. Under Islamic law the right of revenge belongs to the heir of the victim, and in cases of murder or other wrongful death, the heir can exchange this right for a cash compensation amount called the "blood-price." In the death of a woman, however, the heir receives only half the blood-price of a man and the same discount formula applies to the death of a Jew or a Christian. Female obesity is a problem in much of the Arab world because men consider heavyset, overweight Arab women attractive. Young girls are frequently force-fed to make them gain weight at an early age and increase their marketability for marriage, a practice that often leads to early health problems. Evidence in court from a woman is only valid if a male member of her family accompanies the woman and even then, evidence from a female counts as only half of a man's testimony. Women also have limited career opportunities and are generally restricted to teaching and medicine, although some women have recently been attracted to businesses they can operate within the limitations of Islamic law. To travel outside the country requires permission from a male family member, and the many restrictions on women caused by rigorous interpretation of Islamic law and Saudi cultural taboos are pervasive, as liberal Saudi writer Raid Qusti [9/17/2003] has observed:

> Uttering a woman's name is still a social taboo here. How in the world can we expect women to get behind the wheel of a car?" From the first second you set foot in King Abdul Al-Aziz International Airport in Jeddah or King Khaled International Airport in Riyadh you see only men. The airport staff is male; the people at the Saudi Arabian Airlines counters are all male; the passport officials are all male; and the car rental employees are all male. I would not blame a first-time visitor for thinking that creatures from outer space had zapped all the women. But sadly, the fact is that women have no public presence whatsoever in Saudi Arabia. They exist only behind closed doors. The idea that our society sees a public female presence as a threat to its customs is utterly misplaced and wrong in the 21st century. For too long we have been a handicapped society, a society which relied on only half the country's human resources—the male half...How do you get people to change their mentality? Where do we start? Currently the prevailing custom in Saudi Arabia is that women and men should never mix, in any way, in public or at work. The other part of this custom is that women are limited to roles in education and teaching.

So, the question remains: Is modern Saudi Arabia prepared to join the rest of the world in the 21st century or will it remain mired in clerical hatred and continue to propagate the world with Islamist terrorists bent on returning to a violent and primitive past? As Raid Qusti observed, where do the people of Saudi Arabia begin their efforts to initiate reform, and how do people and institutions change their basic outlook when religious ideology seems so opposed to everything modern and the rapid pace of change.

With this in mind, the next chapter looks at al Qaeda and its ideological origins to further identify the underpinnings of Saudi Arabian Wahhabism and its impact on the world today, as today's "Bin Ladenism" takes Saudi Arabian Wahhabism to a new level of violence, intolerance, and xenophobia.

CHAPTER ONE BIBLIOGRAPHY

Abdullah bin Abdul Aziz ibn Saud, Crown Prince, "Press Release of May 3, 2004," Riyadh, Saudi Arabia: Saudi Press Agency, May 3, 2004.

Bergen, Peter, "The Al Qaeda Connection, Try Riyadh, Not Baghdad," December 18, 2002, www.thenation.com.

Bremmer, Ian, and Hawes, Crispin, "An Insatiable Thirst for Oil," *National Interest*, Fall 2003. http://www.inthenationalinterest.com/Articles/October2004/October2004Bremmer.html.

Central Intelligence Agency, *The World Fact Book*, Washington, DC: Government Printing Office, 2004.

Cohen, Richard, "Intolerance Swaddled in Faith," *Washington Post*, May 1, 2003.

Delong-Bas, Natana J., *Wahhabi Islam: From Revival and Reform to Global Jihad*, Oxford, England: Oxford University Press, June 2004.

International Energy Agency (IEA), *World Energy Outlook, 2004*, Paris: IEA, 2004.

Khaled bin Sultan bin Abdul Aziz, Prince and General, *Desert Warrior: A Personal View of the Gulf War by the Joint Forces Commander*, New York: HarperCollins, 1995.

Lindsey, Gene, *Saudi Arabia*, New York: Hippocrene Books, 1991.

Lippman, Thomas, *Inside the Mirage: America's Fragile Partnership with Saudi Arabia*, Boulder, CO: Westview Press, 2003.

___, *"Comments"on Saudi—U.S. Relations*, Washington DC: School of the Advanced International Studies (SAIS), Johns Hopkins University, November 7, 2003, http://www.saudi-us-relations.org/newsletter/saudi-relations-interest-12-16.html.

___, "The Crisis Within—In Saudi Arabia, Rebellion, and Reform Seize Center Stage," *Washington Post*, June 13, 2004, http://www.washingtonpost.com/wp-dyn/articles/A35988-2004Jun11.html.

Long, David E., *The Kingdom of Saudi Arabia*, Gainesville: University Press of Florida: 1997.

Qusti, Raid, "Criticism of the Saudi Custom Forbidding Women to Show Their Faces in Public," *Arab News*, September 3, 2003.

___, "Saudi Arabia is a Male-Dominated Country," *Arab News*, September 17, 2003.

Saudi Ministry of Culture and Information, *The Saudi Arabia Information Resource*, Riyadh, Arabia: Kingdom of Saudi Arabia, 2004.

U.S. Department of Energy, *Department of Energy Strategic Plan: Protecting National Energy and Economic Security with Advanced Science and Technology and Ensuring Environmental Cleanup*, Washington DC: Government Printing Office, September 30, 2003, http://www.doe.gov/engine/content.do?BT_CODE=ABOUTDOE.

U.S. Department of State, *Country Reports on Human Rights Practices 2003 Saudi Arabia*, Washington, DC: Government Printing Office, February 25, 2004.

2

Al Qaeda's Ideological Origins, Its Next of Kin And Arab-Muslim Problems

Al Qaeda was formed in the late 1980s and early 1990s after bin Laden's "Afghan Arabs" helped defeat the Soviet Union in Afghanistan. It is, however, a descendent of a long line of radical Islamic movements that have been offshoots of militant Islamist thought over the centuries. The chapter begins by briefly reviewing the history of mainstream Islam and then outlines the radical offshoots and their relationship to al Qaeda. It concludes by discussing the problems of the modern Arab-Muslim world.

Islam, Christianity, and Judaism share the same theological roots and the same religious texts that go all the way back to Abraham and the Old Testament prophets. The Holy Koran refers to Jews and Christians as "People of the Book," for the adherents of all three great religions are truly children of the same God, recipients of earlier revelations, and literally brothers and sisters in the family of the same father, Abraham, alike in all things. Shylock's emotional appeal in Shakespeare's "The Merchant of Venice" still resonates with resounding clarity even today:

> Do we not have…"eyes, hands, organs, dimensions, senses, affectations, passions?" Are we not…"fed with the same food, hurt with the same weapons, subject to the same diseases, healed by the same means, warmed and cooled by the same winter and summer…If you prick us, do we not bleed? If you tickle us, do we not laugh? If you poison us, do we not die? And if you wrong us, shall we not revenge? If we are like you in the rest, we will resemble you in that.

As both the Bible and Koran warn and as Galatians, chapter six, points out, "Whatsoever a man soweth, that shall he also reap." The origins of Islam go back to the early 7th century in the year 610 when an Arabian businessman named Mohammed began receiving what he believed were divine revelations that became the text of the Holy Koran, the sacred book of Islam. In Arabic the word "Islam" means peace, purity, submission, and obedience. In religious terms, Islam means submission to the will of God and obedience to God's law, following a true and pure way of life. The Arabic language of the Holy Koran has great poetic beauty and splendor, especially when read aloud, and it has forceful linguistic power capable of moving and inspiring listeners for centuries. Memorization of the entire Holy Koran is a frequent assignment in fundamentalist Islamist schools and Wahhabi religion classes in Saudi Arabia. Lying under the clear desert firmament at night, as giant stars dot the black sky like marshmallows, the rhythms of ancient Arabic poetry, and the vastness of space itself, are as mesmerizing today as they were centuries ago in the time of the Prophet. Mohammed's divine revelations started in 610 and by the year 629 he was able to raise an army of loyal believers in his newly proclaimed faith and take control of Mecca and Medina, the holiest cities in the world of Islam. Mohammed died in 632 at the age 63, having produced four surviving daughters from his eleven wives and the Arabian Peninsula was united for the first time in recorded history.

In the decades following Mohammed's death, Islam spread rapidly east and west by means of violent jihad, or "holy war," throughout the Middle East and Iran, and into North Africa, Spain and southern France in the 700s, and from Southwest and Central Asia through India into Malaysia, the southern Philippines, and eventually the Indonesian archipelago. Today Islam is the world's fastest growing religion and accounts for nearly a quarter of the world population with almost 1.5 billion believers. After its rapid expansion into Europe and Asia, Islam advanced for nearly a thousand years as the Christian West retreated. The Arab-Muslim world fought off invading European Crusaders for nearly two centuries from 1099 to 1244.

The victorious Muslim forces under Saladin, a Kurdish general from present-day Iraq, defeated the Crusaders and were able to retake the holy city of Jerusalem in 1187 from rampaging French Crusaders—the "Franks"—who had earlier captured Jerusalem and massacred thousands of Muslims, an event vividly remembered in the Arab world today. In 1258 invading Mongols from Asia destroyed Baghdad, and in 1453 the Ottoman Turks took Constantinople, renamed the old city Istanbul, and established the Ottoman Empire that lasted until the First World War and extended throughout the entire Arab-speaking world from the Persian Gulf across Africa and into Europe.

During Europe's Middle Ages, and under successive Muslim leaders, cities such as Damascus and Baghdad were far ahead of their European counterparts and well known during the "Golden Age" of Islam for their advanced universities and learning centers, fine libraries, countless book dealers, the first hospitals, opulent public baths, and generous support for the arts and sciences. Ancient Greek and Roman texts were translated into Arabic, saving priceless manuscripts for future generations. Local Islamic governments admired and supported inquiry into philosophy, higher mathematics, and science, and the medieval Arab-Muslim world made major significant contributions to civilization in the fields of theology, astronomy, chemistry, geology, metallurgy, botany, and poetry.

The Ottoman Empire lasted from 1453 until the end of the First World War when representatives of the victorious British and French drew present Middle East geographical boundaries while sitting around Winston Churchill's dinner table. The Ottomans had sided with Germany in World War I and most Arab nations supported the losing German Nazis and its racial theories of hateful anti-Semitism during the Second World War. The Ottoman Empire was multi-ethnic, pluralistic and generally tolerant of other religions and ethnic groups, but in the aftermath of the First World War and the demise of the Muslim Caliphate under the Ottomans, the newly created Arab-Muslim states were impoverished and impotent, paving the way for corrupt and oppressive governments and radical Islamist terrorism. In a recent interview, Dore Gold [2003], Israel's former ambassador to the UN stated:

> It is important to remember for perspective that Islam, while relegating no Muslims to a second class status, nonetheless showed a remarkable degree of tolerance at times, especially to the Jewish people: the Ottoman Empire opened its doors to Jewish refugees from the Spanish Inquisition in the 15th century and provided land grants for Jewish resettlement in the Land of Israel, well before the British. The Ottoman Sultans were the caliphs of all Sunni Islam, yet this background of limited inter-religious tolerance has been wiped out entirely by the new Islamic militancy, that has been fed by the Wahhabis of Saudi Arabia and the Egyptian Muslim Brotherhood.

RADICAL MILITANT ISLAM

Some observers have called the Middle East countries that were created after the First World War "tribes with flags," because they lacked the typical national-istic cohesion associated with the development of other countries around the world. What bound them together, however, was Islam and for centuries, the Muslim Caliph had been the guardian of Islamic law and the Sunni Islamic state. The loss of the Caliphate and a cohesive Islamic religious leader following the First World War was devastating to the world's Sunni Muslims, especially in the newly created Arab states. Today the restoration of the Sunni Islamic Caliphate is one of Osama bin Laden's major goals and is an emotional issue that resonates loudly and widely throughout the entire Muslim world as an issue all Sunni Arabs can support.

The history of Islam includes a bloody account of a long line of Muslim extremists and ideologues that deeply influenced today's radical Islamist mili-tants. Ibn Abdul Wahhab (1703-1791), the religious fanatic and zealot who founded Saudi Arabia's Wahhabi-Salafist movement in the 18th century, and Sayyid Qutb (1906-1966), the Egyptian Muslim Brotherhood polemicist and theoretician executed by Nasser in 1966, both emphasized a puritanical and mili-tant form of Sunni Islam as a reactionary "reformation" of the religion to bring it back to is earliest profile. Many years before Wahhab and Qutb, the 7th century Kharijites, followed by the 11th century "Assassins," paved the way as violent Islamist terrorists with tactics and ideology reminiscent of today's militant Islam-ists. After the death of Mohammed, the Kharijites emerged as ultra-strict, radical fundamentalists with revolutionary zeal and their example has inspired extreme Islamist groups like al Qaeda, Takfir wal Hijra and Islamic Jihad. The 11th–13th century Assassins, from whom the English word "assassin" is derived, murdered their enemies as a religious duty. The Arabic name means "hashish smoker" and refers to the Assassins' use of hashish to promote visions of paradise before attack-ing their victims.

Another radical Islamist ideologist was Ibn Taymiyah (1263-1328), a fierce theologian and religious leader who became the model for the Saudi Wahhabis, Muslim Brotherhood, and Osama bin Laden. A new mosque in Los Angeles, funded by the Saudi government, is named in honor of Ibn Taymiyah but few California Muslims know what the name really implies. Hassan al-Banna (1906-1949), was the influential Egyptian teacher and neo-fundamentalist who estab-lished the radical, Islamist Egyptian Muslim Brotherhood, and Sayyid Mawdudi

(1903-1979) was a renowned Muslim journalist, reformer and neo-fundamentalist who founded the radical Islamist party Jamaat-i-Islami in Pakistan.

The long succession of Islamist extremists who preceded Osama bin Laden for many centuries shared a core belief that is common to most Muslims today: that Islam is a total, all-encompassing way of life and the Holy Koran is God's revelation and foundation of Muslim life, including Islamic law, which conflicts with man-made law in democratic countries. The radical extremists insist that religion, the state, and society are a single, integrated entity and that separation of church and state is therefore not possible. They insist without compromise that Islamic law (shariah) provides the sole, ideal legal foundation for modern Muslim society and that departure from Islam and reliance on the West are the causes for the decline of the Muslim world since the "Golden Age of Islam."

Today's radical extremists are generally well educated, use modern innovations such as computers, email and the Internet, and argue that science and technology must be harnessed and used effectively to pursue the will of God. They also argue that personal and violent jihad are necessary and justified by the Holy Koran to solve problems in the Arab world by Islamizing society and eventually the entire world. Long legal arguments have been developed by Muslim scholars making the case for violent jihad and justifying the use of nuclear weapons against the West because of perceived damages that go back to the Crusades. Ultimately, the arguments of today's radical Islamist militants call for death to all nonbelievers or conversion to an extremist form of Islam with no compromise or tolerance for other beliefs whatsoever. Finally, the goal of Osama bin Laden and other extremists is to restore the Islamic Caliphate, a goal that has broad support throughout the Muslim world.

The Muslim Brotherhood

Al Qaeda is the product of the merger of two Egyptian Islamist fundamentalist factions, the Islamic Group and Egyptian Islamic Jihad. Al Qaeda's top philosopher and theoretician, Dr. Ayman Al Zawahiri, founded the Egyptian Islamic Jihad and has long-standing ties to Takfir wal Hijra, the most aggressive Islamist terror organization in the world today, operating in the Middle East, Europe, and America. Bin Laden's dynamic and self-funding al Qaeda terrorist organization is a transnational movement that gained strength as the result of a marriage between Zawahiri's Egyptian killers and bin Laden's fanatical Saudi "Afghan Arabs" who, after the Afghanistan war against the Soviet Union, had become professional jihadists and were no longer welcome back home in ultra-conservative, theocratic Saudi Arabia. The Saudi-Egyptian marriage joined bin Laden's "Afghan Arabs" and their radicalized Saudi Wahhabi ideology with Zawahiri's Egyptian terrorists and their long-standing radical, militant ideological background. Their common ground was Saudi Arabian Wahhabism as influenced by the writings of Sayyid Qutb and radical members of the Muslim Brotherhood.

Al Qaeda's Egyptian factions had evolved from Egypt's Wahhabi-influenced, fundamentalist, Islamist movement, the Muslim Brotherhood, called "al-Ikhwan al-Muslimun" in Arabic, and were guided by the principle Islamist philosopher and theoretician, Sayyid Qutb (pronounced "Kuh-tahb"). Osama bin Laden was profoundly influenced by the writings of Qutb (1907-1966) as well as from the strict Saudi Arabian Wahhabi interpretation of Islam that he absorbed during his impressionable and formative years in the Saudi Arabian educational system.

The Muslim Brotherhood was founded in Egypt in the late 1920s by Hassan al-Banna (1905-1949) and has distinct Wahhabi-Salafist ideological roots that emanate from an influential Egyptian intellectual writer early in the 20th century who was on the payroll of the first Saudi King, Abdul Aziz ibn Saud [Gold, 54-5]. This early Saudi effort to buy intellectual influence marked the beginning of a consistent Saudi effort over the years to "gull" its friends and "manage" its problems by silencing critics with money and buying endorsements from international scholars and politicians. Saudi lobbying behavior continues to this day, especially in American and European capitals and prestigious universities that have received large Saudi endowments for their Middle East studies departments in Faustian bargains that typically result in the loss of academic independence and objectivity and the promotion of Saudi propaganda.

Having extended itself far beyond Egypt, the Muslim Brotherhood today is a secretive, militant society, active in more than 70 countries and with well-documented links to terrorism [Mintz and Farah, 2004]. The Muslim Brotherhood has devoted followers around the world, including the United States, but especially in Europe where it is the dominant movement among the large European Muslim communities. The Muslim Brotherhood extends throughout the Muslim world today and has gained legitimacy in many places because of continued strong financial support from the government of Saudi Arabia and its billions in oil revenue. The message of the Muslim Brotherhood is very clear and marks the way for today's terrorists and suicide bombers:

> God is our objective; the Holy Koran is our constitution; the Prophet is our leader; struggle is our way; and death for the sake of God is the highest of our aspirations.

Sayyid Qutb's sharp intellect and prolific penmanship helped him to rise quickly as the leading writer, spokesperson, and intellectual for the Muslim Brotherhood. Qutb advocated classical Wahhabi tenets such as strict Islamic law (shariah) and a return to the so-called purity of the early days of Islam as a counter to what he believed were the devastating effects of America and the modern world. When Gamal Abdel Nasser overthrew Egypt's King Farouk in 1952 and formed the Egyptian Republic, Qutb collaborated with Nasser's pan-Arab socialist movement and appealed for Islamic law as the only basis for a new Egyptian Islamic state. Qutb's loud initiatives were rejected by the new Egyptian government, and after the Muslim Brotherhood attempted to assassinate Nasser, Qutb was imprisoned and subsequently executed in 1966 for his uncompromising rigidity and outspoken radical, fundamentalist Islamist beliefs. Even while enduring painful torture in prison Sayyid Qutb wrote voluminously, focusing on the plight of the Arab-Muslim world in the 20th century. He posed fundamentalist Islamist solutions to the many heathen problems he envisioned when he lived in the United States in 1948-1949 and articulated sharp theological criticism of modern Western life that in his view demanded violent jihad against imperialistic Western interests and corrupt Muslim regimes. Qutb wrote that the human condition had become unbearable not only in America, but around the world, because humanity had lost its soul and lost touch with God.

Many of the problems that Qutb envisioned in modern Western society are similar to those deplored by conservative Christians in America today: Godlessness, permissive attitudes toward sex, unfettered female freedom, declining moral standards, pornography, homosexuality, adultery, divorce, corruption, corporate larceny, violence, obscenity, profanity, gluttony, sloth, obesity, unchecked gambling, and people saying, "Since there is no Hell, let's enjoy ourselves here on earth, indulge our appetites, without fear of punishment after death."

Most conservative Christians in the United States would agree with Qutb that the spread of wealth in the West had weakened the religious and ethical base of societies that had originated in fear and poverty. They would also agree that sin had grown as wealth increased, that so-called "modern" people had come to resent old-fashioned ethics because modern life was to be enjoyed, that the sources of immorality—wealth, falling moral standards, political strife, war—had left people unanchored in a global sea of violence. They would agree that when society declared the Ten Commandments to be man-made and not divine, the moral code lost its effectiveness, taboos disappeared, and expediency and pleasure reigned supreme. Guilt and fear of sin were diminished, conscience was free to take the easy path, people no longer yearned to be good, for the ends would justify the means, and immorality became another form of individualism.

This is what Qutb saw when he lived in the United States following the Second World War. He observed that man's inspiration, intelligence and morality had degenerated, especially in the infidel West, and that sexual relations between men and women had deteriorated "to a level lower than beasts." He stated further that humanity had become anxious and skeptical, causing spiritually unhappy people to turn to drugs, crime, and alcohol and away from religion. The solution according to Qutb was a rigidly fundamentalist version of Islam that rejected modernism and the secular West's separation of church and state that advocates according to the Christian Bible, "Render unto Caesar what is Caesar's and unto God what is God's."

The Brotherhood Spreads to Saudi Arabia

Followers of Qutb and the late Abdullah Azzam who greatly influenced Osama bin Laden, believe that Islam has been under attack from the globalizing, imperialistic, capitalist West for centuries and that the mission of true Muslim believers today is to preserve Islam from extinction by the West's rampant forces of globalization through any tactic necessary, including murder, terrorist bombings, beheadings, and the destruction of sinful societies in North America, Western Europe, and Asia. Bin Laden's followers are not concerned about dying in their effort to change the world, for death and immortality are seen as the culmination of righteous struggle or "jihad" in the name of Islam, and this type of struggle means ultimate martyrdom for their cause and a special place in Heaven.

After the execution of Sayyid Qutb by Nasser in 1966 and the disastrous Six-Day Arab-Israeli war that followed the next year, Sayyid Qutb's brother Mohammed and many other members of the Muslim Brotherhood were expelled from Egypt and Syria and found highly sympathetic refuge among ultra-orthodox Wahhabi clerics in Saudi Arabian universities in Jeddah and the two holy cities. As early as 1961 the Saudi royal family had permitted the Muslim Brotherhood to start the Islamic University in Medina, and following the 1967 Six-Day War with Israel, the Muslim Brotherhood splintered into a radical movement that further penetrated the Saudi educational system. Mohammed Qutb became a distinguished professor of fundamentalist Wahhabi Islamist studies at King Abdul Aziz University in Jedda and was later one of Osama bin Laden's influential teachers. It was during this turbulent time in Egypt following the 1967 Arab-Israeli war that Saudi Arabia and its Wahhabi clerics became a magnet for leading Egyptian and Syrian Islamist fundamentalists and theoreticians who ultimately became leading professors at Wahhabi fundamentalist universities in Mecca and Medina, Islam's holiest cities in Saudi Arabia. In his statement to the 9/11 Commission, Mamoun Fandy [2003], senior fellow at the United States Institute of Peace, outlined the role of the Muslim Brotherhood in Saudi Arabia:

> The Muslim Brotherhood movement was born in the Egyptian coastal city of Ismaeliya in 1928. After they were thrown out of Egypt during the Arab cold war between Nasser and King Faisal of Saudi Arabia, the Muslim Brothers went to Saudi Arabia. There they worked in the field of education. They were responsible for radicalizing Saudi students who were raised in the strict but quietist Wahhabi tradition. Although many people in America have come to see Wahhabis as the source of all evil in Islam, in fact the Wahhabi doctrine developed over the years in Saudi Arabia has been status quo oriented rather than radical. When the Saudis welcomed the members of the Muslim brotherhood they did so naively—not thinking that they were giving them a chance to influence young Saudis. It is the "brothers" who were responsible for development of certain radical teachings in the Saudi education system and for the spread of the radical *madrasas* (religious schools) throughout the Middle East and South Asia. And, while some Saudis influenced by the teachings of the Muslim brothers remained faithful to that organization, others developed even more radical versions of its doctrines, creating the new organizations that gave us Osama bin Laden and al Qaeda. This was in part because many Saudis felt that this originally Egyptian organization was trying to steal the mantle of Islam from Saudi Arabia. Saudis felt that to compete with a global organization such as the brotherhood, they too would have to establish similarly wide-reaching networks of influence. This is what led to the rise of the Muslim league and the Muslim youth organization and many other charities that we know now have been directly or indirectly linked to terrorism.

The Arab world faced another disastrous defeat by Israel in the October 1973 Yom Kippur War, and as oil prices quadrupled in the 1970s because of the Arab oil embargo, Saudi Arabia's Wahhabi religious leaders now had access to hundreds of millions in hard cash and began exporting the writings of Sayyid Qutb and their version of radical Wahhabi Islam around the world. The Saudis formed the Muslim World League in 1962 as well as several international Islamic charities and began endowing professorships and funding entire departments at prominent universities such as Al-Azhar University in Cairo, the oldest and most distinguished university in the Muslim world. Forty years later, nearly all Al-Azhari professors had received Saudi stipends and the Saudis soon followed a similar process in Europe and the United States, establishing Middle East Studies departments in distinguished universities and buying off academicians and the rigor of academic independence. Al Qaeda received much of its strength and legitimacy throughout the Arab world from Saudi funding and the influence and inspiration of Sayyid Qutb and the fierce rhetoric of Abdullah Azzam, making the organization popular and well funded today, with powerful ideas, global capabilities, and a level of sophistication and resiliency that has surprised and confounded its enemies.

Al Qaeda's Next of Kin—Takfir Wal Hijra

Al Qaeda has many links to other extremist Islamist terrorist operations around the world. Significant among these is the Takfir wal Hijra, the most brutally violent Islamist terrorist operation in the world today. Takfir ideology is an extreme extension of Saudi Arabian Wahhabi-Salafist doctrine. It expresses unrestrained hatred of Shiite Muslims and, like Osama bin Laden, calls for restoring the Sunni Caliph, the Islamic political and religious leader of prior Muslim empires. Abu Musab al Zarqawi is an exceptionally fierce Takfiri fighter who gained notoriety in 2004 by leading Sunni terrorists in a holy war of true believers against infidel American and coalition forces in Iraq. Zarqawi is a Jordanian-born Palestinian and in late 2004 Osama bin Laden announced that Zarqawi had officially aligned his terrorist forces in Iraq with al Qaeda. Prior to the American invasion of Iraq in 2003, Zarqawi had operated without notice in Iraq but with Saddam Hussein's knowledge and support, and he even established a terrorist training camp in Afghanistan with bin Laden's assistance. Today Zarqawi's organization consists of some of the most violent and dedicated jihadists in the world, most notorious for their gruesome videotaped beheadings in Iraq.

The principle al Qaeda theoretician, Dr. Ayman Al Zawahiri, is the most prominent Takfiri. He is also the founder of the Egyptian Islamic Jihad organization and a long-standing member of the Muslim Brotherhood. His prominent role and influence within al Qaeda helped spread Takfir's radical and violent ultra-orthodoxy in the belief that all non-Muslim leaders in the world must be overthrown by any means possible, including assassination and violence. In Zawahiri's view, all infidels as well as all Muslims who do not fit the Takfir ideal are subject to sanctions including death. The ideology of Takfir—accusing other Muslims of apostasy—has also been identified as the incubator of extremism in the Saudi school system that created thousands of young, radical Saudi followers of bin Laden and teenage suicide bombers in Iraq. Takfir is active in Europe and the United States, and its origins, like so many terrorist groups, trace back to

Egypt with Salafist and Saudi Wahhabi-Salafist ideological underpinnings. In fact, it is safe to say that wherever a Salafist movement exists in the world, the fingerprints of Saudi funding and Wahhabi ideology are evident. This type of radical Islamist ideology has spread rapidly to thousands of young European Muslims through Internet sites and online chat rooms, resulting in grotesque throat-slitting murders in the United States and Europe by Islamists in 2004.

Takfir is exceptionally capable in its ability to infiltrate Western societies and uses clever subterfuge by permitting members to disregard the normally strict injunctions of Islamic law against alcohol and illicit sex to help them blend into infidel societies and advance their specific terrorist mission. Mohammed Atta, the leader of the 9/11 airline hijackers, was a Takfiri. Atta and his 9/11 accomplices dressed as Westerners and rationalized going to bars and discos, using alcohol and calling prostitutes to their hotel rooms because they believed such activities supported their mission against the infidel America. In 2002, the United States Justice Department charged four Takfiri men in Michigan for planning shoe bombings, airline attacks, and conspiring to attack Disneyland, a Las Vegas casino, and the American Embassy in Jordan. Takfiri groups are guided by influential radicals like al Qaeda's Dr. Ayman Al Zawahiri and Sheik Omar Abdel Rahman, the exiled Egyptian cleric now imprisoned in the United States for conspiring to bomb New York City landmarks, and who issued the following fatwa in 1998:

> Cut all links with the [United States]. Destroy them thoroughly and erase them from the face of the earth. Ruin their economies, set their companies on fire, turn their conspiracies to powder and dust. Sink their ships, bring their planes down. Slay them in the air, on land, on water. And [with the Command of Allah] kill them wherever you find them. Catch them and put them in prison. Lie in wait for them and kill these infidels. They will surely get great oppression from you. God will make you the means of wreaking a terrible revenge upon them, of degrading them. He will support you against them. He will cure the afflicted hearts of the faithful and take all anger out of their hearts.

Even bin Laden was not pure enough and became a Takfir target during a 1996 assassination attempt in Sudan but in the final analysis, al Qaeda and its Bin Ladenism ideology serve as an umbrella organization for many Islamist terrorist operations around the world with varying degrees of ferociousness. What they all share in common is a hate-filled ideological framework that predates all of their organizations and is directly influenced by violence-inspiring Saudi Arabian

Wahhabism and its interconnected relationship with the Muslim Brotherhood and Sayyid Qutb's philosophy of violent jihad.

The Concept of Islamist Jihad

Jihad has had many interpretations throughout the history of Islam and confusion continues today with various interpretations of the meaning of jihad by Muslim and Western apologists for Islamist terrorism. Radical militant Muslims, many mainstream Muslims, and some Western apologists do not consider bin Laden and Islamist warriors as terrorists but see them as mujahadeen—"warriors of jihad"—fighting for the Muslim faith and defending it against attack. In Islam, the world is uncompromisingly divided into the House of Islam (the faithful) and the House of War (infidels who have not yet been surrendered to Islam) and there are two types of jihad. "Greater jihad" is defined as personal and of a spiritual nature, while "lesser jihad" is justified for violent and militant actions to expand the faith and defend Islam when the religion is threatened. When Saudi Wahhabis started exporting their version of Islam they reintroduced the concept of violent jihad to the Muslim world. The basic concept of jihad is found in the Holy Koran's seemingly reasonable command for believers to "struggle" in the path of God, striving to lead a good life and create a just society in the name of God. But in practice jihad goes far beyond a personal struggle to lead the good life. The mission of jihad has been defined as expanding Islam through personal "struggle" as well as by creating conditions where Muslims rule and Islam ultimately prevails. It calls for believers to spread the message of Islam through struggle in support of oppressed people, defending the faith, and violently overthrowing governments that threaten Islam, calling for death to nonbelievers if required to preserve the pure Muslim faith.

Jihad has been present throughout Islam's history and the goal of jihad is to spread the Muslim faith, either by conversion or by submission. Islamic history and jurisprudence have traditionally established only three choices for non-Muslims facing jihad: conversion to Islam, death, or submission under Islamic rule and accepting second-class citizen status. In the 7th century, jihad was ordered against Christians in Egypt and Syria and the practice of violent jihad continued throughout the spread of Islam, culminating in 1683 at the gates of Vienna when Islam's march into Europe was halted and violent jihad became less common, reappearing once again with Wahhabism in Saudi Arabia and its recent offshoot, "Bin Ladenism." The problem today is that most moderate Muslims are silent and fail to take a stand against violent jihad because the basic concept of jihad has such deep roots in Islam's history and is easily exploited by Islamist terrorists. Bernard Lewis describes the Muslim duty of jihad: "…the presumption is that the duty of jihad will continue, interrupted only by truces, until all the world either adopts the Muslim faith or submits to Muslim rule" [Lewis].

Modern Wahhabi-Salafism or "Bin Ladenism"

Saudi Arabia's Wahhabis are a virulent minority sect of Islam intricately entrenched into the autocratic monarchy and theocratic government that rule Saudi Arabia. Before becoming infected with the teachings of Sayyid Qutb and the Egyptian Muslim Brotherhood in the early 1960s, Saudi Wahhabis were a cloistered and seemingly harmless fundamentalist fringe movement within Sunni Islam and few in the West took them seriously. However, with their relatively recent oil riches, Saudi Arabian Wahhabis and their worldwide missionary movement sponsored international terrorist organizations such as al Qaeda and Hamas and spread deep hatred for the basic values of Western civilization such as freedom, democracy, religious tolerance, separation of religion from government, universal suffrage, women's rights, free press, free trade, free unions, and free political parties. Wahhabi-Bin Ladenism also displays unusually venomous attacks against perceived American and Western imperialism and justifies violence and stirs hatred by blaming others for persistent Arab failures. Wahhabism as practiced by ultraconservative clerics in Saudi Arabia is a distortion of the mainstream teachings of Islam and is manifested in conflicting Saudi government policies of rigid religious intolerance on the one hand and the promotion of modernization and Westernization on the other.

Well-educated Saudis and members of the Saudi royal family frequently blame others, especially the United States and Israel, for endemic and systematic problems in the Arab-Muslim world. Prince Khaled bin Sultan bin Abdul Aziz ibn Saud [1995] is the son of the Minister of Defense and nephew of King Fahd and a graduate of Sandhurst, England's West Point. Khaled has a master's degree from Auburn University and is a graduate of the U.S. Army Command and General Staff College and the U.S. Air Force Air War College, a training ground for future generals and senior allied officers. Prince Khaled was General Normal Schwarzkopf's Saudi counterpart during the Gulf War of 1990-1991 and he states the following in his memoirs of the Gulf War:

...all Arab dictators [talking about Saddam Hussein]...have been products of the Palestinian question: Israeli aggression has undoubtedly contributed to the rise of Arab militarism.

This type of thinking is part of a mindset that refuses to admit the nature of systemic problems and is quick to advance the Wahhabi state religion of Saudi Arabia around the world as a solution.

Saudi Arabian leaders are well known for "double-dealing" and "gulling" the West, trading oil for security as the old king did in the early days and as the Saudis are doing now, buying supporters in prestigious universities, while also permitting its state religion to spread hatred for the West and death threats to nonbelievers. As a result, there is growing agreement in the West that Saudi Arabia cannot be trusted and is no longer a reliable ally and may in fact have become an unpredictable antagonist in the war on terrorism. However, since the May 12, 2003 terrorist attacks in the Saudi capital Riyadh and several subsequent attacks in 2004 and early 2005, Crown Prince Abdullah and the Saudi royal family have taken decisive steps against homegrown terrorists that have attempted to destroy the increasingly dysfunctional and corrupt Saudi government. Crown Prince Abdullah has indicated some willingness to consider reform that would serve to provide a more open government, but not all observers agree that reform is possible. The Saudi government has been a key backer of the international Islamist terror network and has been active at multiple levels of international terrorism for well over 20 years. Senior members of the royal family, like Interior Minister Prince Nayef, have stated their belief that 9/11 was a Zionist plot involving the CIA and many remain wedded to the reactionary belief that Wahhabi-Salafism must continue to be promoted around the world as the solution for the world's problems. As a result, the events of September 11th and a significant lack of subsequent Saudi cooperation after 9/11 forced the Bush administration to reassess Saudi Arabia's reliability as a credible regional ally and to develop a new grand strategy for American policy and strategic relationships in the region. That strategy became codified in the post-9/11 Bush Doctrine and is unfolding in the Middle East, as chapter 4 describes.

The answer to how the Saudis could have opened Pandora's Box and released the genie of radical, militant Wahhabism into the world lies in the tangled history of Saudi Arabia's development as a theocracy. Wahhabism started in the Arabian Peninsula 250 years ago while American revolutionary leaders were developing their radical ideas and principles of freedom and democracy that are antithetical to Wahhabi principles that have promoted violence throughout its 250-year history. From the beginning of its origins as a desert nation of nomadic Bedouin tribes, Wahhabism has been the state religion of Saudi Arabia. Wahhabis control the Ministry of Education, Ministry of Religious Affairs, and Ministry of Justice where harsh Islamic Law is implemented with exacting cruelty. Saudi Arabia's Islamic law, shariah, is based on the Holy Koran, and is the same Islamic legal system that the world witnessed in Afghanistan under the Taliban with routine public executions and rigid oppression of women. Before 9/11, the West either ignored Saudi Arabia's Wahhabis or viewed the sect as a lunatic fringe of Sunni Islam, even though Saudi Arabia's vast oil wealth had permitted the export of Wahhabi-Salafism and promoted death to infidels and nonbelievers for many years. But even then, few in the West took note or were able to penetrate the complexities of the Byzantine desert kingdom.

PROBLEMS IN THE MODERN MUSLIM WORLD

Radicalism is Only Part of the Problem

The Muslim world is wide and diverse and it is important to remember that the "bad guys"—the militant Islamists—are a distinct though growing minority that represent a small fraction of the world's nearly 1.5 billion Muslims. There are several classifications of the various representations of Islam in addition to the major Sunni and Shiite divisions and it is clear that the "bad guys," the enemy, are the radical, militant Sunni fundamentalists like the Taliban, al Qaeda, Hamas and Palestinian Islamic Jihad who resort to violence in an attempt to create total-itarian Islamist states. It has been said that in recent years, "Not all Muslims are terrorists, but all terrorists are Muslims." A corollary reads, "Not all Salafists are terrorists, but all terrorists are Salafists." These are the "bad guys"—the radical, militant Bin Ladenists—the terrorists. There are also traditional fundamentalists in the Muslim world, like perhaps 70 percent or more of the population of Saudi Arabia and its ultra-orthodox Wahhabi religious establishment that support bin Laden's goals and provide funding for al Qaeda and other radical militant Islam-ists. Another group consists of more traditional Muslims that would include the moderate-conservative Shiite mullahs in Iran or Grand Ayatollah al-Sistani in Iraq who wish to preserve orthodox Shiite norms and old-fashioned behavior, while more liberal Shiite reformists in Iran and Iraq have traditional goals but are more flexible and innovative in compromising with modernity. Though their governments are not democratic by any means, Sunni leaders of Egypt, Jordan and Libya could be called modernists in the sense that they accept the fact that Islam can be compatible with the modern world, while secularists such as Attaturkists in Turkey go even further and clearly separate religion from the public sector by law.

Turkey is unique in that it is Muslim yet not Arab, straddles both Asia and Europe, and sits astride the Arab-Muslim world with its historical Ottoman legacy. Turkey and its 70 million people provide a natural partner for helping stabilize the region because Turkey is a long-standing member of the North Atlantic Treaty Organization (NATO) and the only Muslim member. Moreover, Turkey could become the first Muslim member nation of the European Union (EU) as early as 2015. With the fall of Saddam Hussein in Iraq, the world's only remaining fascist-oriented Baathist Party is in Syria, where along with a sprinkling of reactionary Socialists and Communists, religion is generally discarded and used to its own advantage, as Saddam Hussein did in Iraq.

Al Qaeda's prolific propagandist, the late Yusuf al Ayyiri, asserted visceral hated of the United States and the West, stating that the United States and Israel must be destroyed because they are leaders of a global anti-Islamic movement. The goal of what Ayyiri called "Zio-Crusaderism" is to destroy "true Islam" and achieve dominion over the Middle East and its valuable oil resources. The enemies are Jews, Christians, Shiites, lax Sunnis, and secularists, but to the al Qaeda extremists, America's most fearful weapon is the export of Western concepts of freedom and democracy. Democracy and popular sovereignty separate church and state which in turn disembowel "true Islam." Because religion and the state are one and the same, only God's laws can be implemented and not the man-made laws of secular democratic states. The logical result of democracy and unbridled freedom in al Qaeda's way of thinking is anarchy and destruction of Muslim society and its moral standards. Al Ayyiri condemned cable television and the Internet for unleashing torrents of filth and idolatry. He detested the United States because of its support for Israel and pervasive Jewish influence on the American government and because the West inspires godlessness, permissive attitudes toward sex and female freedom, and permits moral standards to decline. In Ayyiri's view, the result is fatal erosion of pure Arab-Muslim culture from within and therefore all enemies, including women and children, must be destroyed through violent jihad and by any means possible.

Other Contemporary Arab-Muslim Problems

The area of the Arab-Muslim world extends from the Persian Gulf across the Middle East to North Africa, and today encompasses 22 Arab nations and over 300 million people, with Arabic as a common language in varying accents. Although Muslim, Turkey and Iran with populations of about 70 million each are not ethnically Arab and are not included among the 22 Arab League countries in the greater Middle East and North Africa. Cairo has been a traditional seat of Arab knowledge and learning and a venerated center of Arab culture for many years. But since the end of the First World War and the demise of the ruling Ottoman Empire and the Muslim Caliphate, the Middle East has been a hotbed of Islamist militancy and radicalism with declining economic influence and corrupt, oppressive governments. Reasons for the political and economic decline of the Arab-Muslim world and the subsequent rise of Islamist militancy are many and complex. They include remaining vestiges of European imperialism, the creation of artificial Arab states following World War I, the establishment of Israel at the end of World War II, and a yearning by modern day Islamist fundamentalists to return to the glory days of Islam when Saladin defeated the Christian Crusaders and recaptured Jerusalem in 1187 or to the "pure" days of Mohammed. But the unfortunate fact remains that the 22 Arab nations today have a collective gross domestic product (GDP) that is less than Spain's, even with vast Arab oil riches. If oil income is subtracted, combined Arab GDP is less than the market capitalization value of a public company such as Nokia, the Finnish public telecommunications company [United Nations].

As noted earlier, the victorious French and British established present-day Middle Eastern boundaries, quite arbitrarily, after defeating and dismantling the Ottoman Empire that had sided with the Germans during the First World War. In the 1930s and 1940s, Arab nations supported Fascism and Nazism that produced harsh and vitriolic anti-American and anti-Semitic propaganda still present in many Arab schoolbooks today and now augmented with Wahhabi ideology exported by the Saudis in free textbooks printed in Arabic that include instructions on how to cut off the heads of infidels and statements such as the following:

> …everywhere you meet Jews, kill them…it is forbidden to have mercy on a Jew…beware of Jews, they are treacherous and disloyal…Muslims are commanded to kill non-Muslims…anyone supporting Western methods of government deserves excommunication from God's mercy, from Islam.

Most Arab nations of the Middle East had sided with the Germans against the Allies during the Second World War and once again witnessed humiliating defeat. Hajj Amin al-Husseini, the grand mufti of Jerusalem and leader of the Palestinians during the war years, was an advisor to Hitler and the Nazis, visited Auschwitz with Heinrich Himmler, and made plans to open a Palestinian death camp for Jews following anticipated German victory over the Allies. But that did not happen and after the war, as Soviet Communism rose over the ashes of Eastern Europe, a new Cold War emerged that pitted the Soviet Union's Warsaw Pact against the West's North Atlantic Treaty Organization (NATO). The result was even more rabid anti-American and anti-Semitic propaganda that was spread throughout the Middle East by the Soviet Union as the Communist monolith attempted to gather allies in the oil-rich Arab world. Years of Western neglect and post-World War II concern for oil, stability, and a rigid anti-Soviet status quo created a vacuum of freedom in the Middle East and a sense of hopelessness among people in the region facing oppression and corruption from their governments.

For the last 50 years or more, political, economic and social stagnation, oppressive governments, tyranny, autocracy, and terrorism have been the norm in the Arab-Muslim world. Even the quadrupling of oil prices in the 1970s had little impact in pulling the region out of its misery as had been hoped at the time. The Arab-Muslim world unfortunately did not enjoy a liberating political evolution that energized other parts of the world over the last 50 years, especially after the collapse of the Soviet Union in 1991. The result was even greater stagnation and dependence, pulling the region down further when compared with the rest of the world. State-controlled economies, often on the Soviet model, failed to attract foreign investment due to corruption, bureaucratic meddling, and high investor risk, and even wealthy Arabs preferred to invest in Europe and the United States for higher returns and less risk. During this time, the only political alternatives in the region were limited to: (1) an autocratic model based on absolute monarchy like Saudi Arabia and other Arab countries; (2) a Baathist model like Assad's Syria or Saddam Hussein's Iraq based on fascist, Nazi, or Communist ideology; (3) a socialist model with a rubber-stamp parliament and military dictator as in Egypt; or (4) a theocratic model such as the Iranian Shiite Ayatollahs and a return to harsh and uncompromising Islamic law.

The Arab nations have a long way to go to catch up with the rest of the world because of inherent problems caused by repressive, autocratic regimes whose primary goal has been and remains political survival for the rulers. From 1980–2000 Arab nations had combined earnings of about $2.5 trillion, 90 percent from oil, and they employed fewer than one million of their 300 million people in the oil, refining or petro-chemical sectors. Since 1980, Arab oil revenues and foreign aid made up virtually all income and it went either to the state or directly to corrupt rulers who doled out government subsidies to the people through bloated, non-productive bureaucracies [Rivilin and Even].

To bolster their power and prestige, repressive Arab regimes have focused on security and the result has been massive and excessive expenditures on weapons. Together, the 22 Arab states of the Arab League spent nearly $50 billion on armaments in 2002, in addition to billions of dollars in military aid provided by the United States to Jordan and Egypt. Arab armed forces also tend to operate in centralized, authoritarian political systems and as a result use outmoded, bureaucratic and top-heavy military organizational models and doctrine inherited from the Soviet Union. This causes them to be overly cumbersome and rigid on the battlefield, made worse with poor training, especially for unmotivated enlisted men with limited education. Nearly 70 percent of Arab military expenditures were by Persian Gulf states that have questionable needs for such massive weapons programs and much of what they acquired has not been operated or maintained effectively, resulting in enormous waste and corruption. Even with the billions Saudi Arabia spent on its weapons systems, the Saudi army was no match for Saddam Hussein's forces during the first Gulf War and needed massive international assistance to oust the invading Iraqi forces. The most significant Saudi military investments were for air defense systems and military infrastructure that proved very effective in hosting hundreds of thousands of coalition forces in 1990-1991.

In 2001 six Arab states spent more on arms than they did on health or education, and even with such massive expenditure on weapons, Arab states have performed poorly in battle with their expensive arms. Egypt is an important example. With a population that has doubled in the last 30 years to more than 75 million today, Egypt is the largest country in the Arab world and is a very important and influential Arab country for historical, political, cultural, and social reasons. Egypt is highly Westernized and urbane and desires to be recognized as a major factor in regional development matters and wishes to strengthen the importance of its relationship with the United States. But even in a country as relatively open and modern as Egypt, there is no real democracy and important decisions are made centrally by a rubber-stamp parliament and not through the open discussion of a democratic decision-making process. Large bureaucracies and oversized armed forces, as in Egypt, ensure political survivability for Arab rulers who often threaten force against their own populations. A glimmer of hope emerged in 2005 when President Mubarak announced that the government of Egypt would permit multiple candidates in the 2005 presidential election, but most Arab regimes permit few checks and balances to challenge government actions and provide little accountability to the people.

Throughout the Arab world, the government or a single political party frequently controls newspapers, television, and radio, and open participation in the political process is limited to party leaders or other insiders, resulting in enormous insider benefits from ingrained corruption throughout the system. The consequence is that a viable Arab middle class has failed to develop due to a minimal role for the private sector and a lack of public debate in the political process. This in turn has caused economic stagnation and few political alternatives except for Islamist fundamentalism that has been ruthlessly put down in countries like Egypt and Algeria, while latent fundamentalism smolders menacingly throughout the entire Arab world due to lack of hope among the people and the overriding tenets of Islam that mandate struggle—jihad—against unjust rulers and nonbelievers. The cycle of hope and repression has repeated itself nearly every generation during the last century and Arab states have remained desperately trapped in a closed system designed to provide political survival for autocratic Arab rulers, despite a high number of political assassinations, but without basic economic, political, and social reform for the people.

Moreover, the legal system in most Arab countries is a disaster, causing high risk for invested capital and little incentive to attract foreign investment from Europe, Asia, or the United States. Decrepit, command economies are vestiges of socialism that failed and even the wealthiest Saudis, for example, invest their billions outside the Arab world, mainly in the United States and Europe, instead of in Arab economies because of high risks and poor returns. Anti-Semitic and anti-American propaganda dating to the Nazi and Soviet eras are endemic throughout the Middle East and have been so effective that wildly concocted Arab propaganda continually distorts reality, causing totally uncorroborated stories to be accepted as truth, as in the claim that the 9/11 attackers were Jews and CIA agents. Arabs are well known as the world's greatest conspiracy theorists and they tend to be overly suspicious, even of each other, often out of fear from living under oppressive governments and within violent environments. State-controlled Arab media frequently blame Israel and the American CIA as conspirators intent on the destruction of Islam and as reasons and excuses for long-festering social and economic problems. To this day, many Arab people do not believe that 9/11 was an Arab-led act of terrorism but rather an Israeli-CIA conspiracy designed to place blame on Arabs and Islam.

Unfortunately, the voices of moderation in the Arab-Muslim world are few and often muted due to intimidation and fear, most frequently because of the blare of Saudi-funded propaganda aired on mass media such as Al Jazeerah and Al Arabiya, both funded and controlled by the Saudi royal family and fed with odious Wahhabi-Salafist propaganda. This does not mean to say that there are no moderate Arabs, for there are many, and they have the same aspirations for a better life as other people around the world. But high birth rates in the Arab-Muslim world have resulted in rapidly growing, youthful, and restive populations, creating a large base of young people who are deeply angry and frustrated with their dispossessed state of affairs and poor prospect for opportunity in the future. And the young people have been further hampered by a failed educational system that recycles Nazi, Soviet, and Wahhabi-Salafist propaganda in hate-filled textbooks. The result, at best, has been poorly trained young people and a brain drain of the brightest young Arab people to the United States and Europe for those fortunate enough and with the means to escape the cycle of poverty, oppression, and violence.

In the case of Saudi Arabia, its failed higher educational system produces more degrees in religion than any other discipline, with two thirds of all Ph.D.'s awarded in Islamic studies. Few if any useful practical skills are taught in Saudi schools controlled by ultraconservative Wahhabi clerics and the Wahhabi-controlled Ministry of Education, resulting in high unemployment for young people with limited skill sets. Even though Saudi Arabia is the world's largest oil producer and still possesses vast oil wealth, the country has, until recently, run a large budget deficit for more than a decade. The Saudis, like most Arabs, have a fixation on security and the cost of massive Saudi arms purchases has outpaced the country's ability to pay. Moreover, the Saudi royal family routinely skims billions from the flow of petrodollars, and these illegal proceeds wind up in private international bank accounts of family members and the funds rarely reach Saudi Arabia. Evidence of widespread corruption and excessive government spending has been well documented over the years, and it does not stop, even with new and stricter rules of the game. Members of the Saudi royal family prefer to deal directly with American, British, and other companies to facilitate payment of illegal commissions through complex subcontract arrangements as opposed to using the Unites States or British government as an intermediary to manage large arms sales.

Powerful demographic forces are also operating, especially in the Middle East. Today there are over six billion people in the world, up from three billion only 30 years ago, and demographers forecast that world population will peak at about 9 billion between 2050 and 2070 and then begin a period of global decline due to falling birth rates. Of the more than six billion people currently in the world, there are approximately two billion Christians (33%); nearly 1.5 billion Muslims (23%); and 1.2 billion Hindus and Buddhists (22%).

In sharp contrast, there are only 14 million Jews in the world, with 40 percent of the world's Jews living in the United States and only 35 percent in Israel, all with low birth rates. Islam, which is about 90 percent Sunni, is the fastest growing religion in the world, with impoverished people and corrupt, repressive governments especially among the Arab nations. Estimates of Muslim populations vary widely due to lack of reliable census information and in some cases deliberately inflated statistics. In Lebanon, for example, there has been no official census since the 1932 census was conducted under the French League of Nations mandate and in Saudi Arabia the official census has always been kept as a state secret. Population estimates in the tables below were developed from the CIA [2004] and other independent sources.

Table 2.1
World & Muslim Population (2004) – Millions

Continent	Total Population	Muslim Population	Muslim %
Asia	3,830.1	1,010.7	26.4
Africa	861.2	414.3	48.1
Europe	727.4	51.2	7.0
North America	323.1	6.6	2.0
South America	539.8	1.6	.03
Oceania	32.3	.4	1.2
Total	6,313.9	1,484.8	23.5

Source: Central Intelligence Agency, *The World Fact Book*, Washington, DC: Government Printing Office, 2004.

Table 2.2
Population Summary
League of Arab States (Arab League) *

Country	Population (Millions)	Growth Rate (Percent)
Algeria	32.0	1.3
Bahrain	0.7	1.5
Comoros	0.7	3.0
Djibouti	0.5	2.1
Egypt	76.0	1.8
Iraq	25.0	2.7
Jordan	5.6	2.7
Kuwait	2.2	3.4
Lebanon	3.8	1.3
Libya	5.7	2.4
Mauritania	3.0	2.9
Morocco	32.0	1.6
Oman	2.9	3.4
Palestine	3.6	3.5
Qatar	0.8	2.7
Saudi Arabia**	26.0	3.5
Somalia	8.0	3.4
Sudan	39.0	2.6
Syria	18.0	2.4
Tunisia	10.0	1.0
United Arab Emirates (UAE)	2.5	1.6
Yemen	20.0	3.5
Total	**318.0**	

* Source: Central Intelligence Agency (CIA), *World Factbook 2004,* Washington, DC, Government Printing Office: 2004
** Includes approximately 6.5 million foreign guest workers

The Muslim world is not only blighted with overpopulation, but unemployment, authoritarianism, suicidal terrorism, and opposition to new ideas by conservative religious clerics, which have combined to stifle progress. The Muslim world has the highest unemployment rates in the world today and the highest rate of population growth in the world during the last half century. One-third of the Arab population is under the age of 15 and these teenagers will soon enter a bleak job market during their childbearing years. Saudi Arabia has always closely guarded its population statistics because of the embarrassingly small numbers of Saudis in contrast with its large number of foreign workers. With an annual 3 to 4 percent growth rate, the Saudi population has exploded from about 3 million in 1970 to 17 to 20 million Saudi citizens today, not counting the 6 to 7 million expatriate foreign workers in Saudi Arabia. At this growth rate, one of the highest in the world, the population of Saudi Arabia will double in 20 years to about 40 million people. Table 2.2 reports these demographic facts for the 22 countries that make up the Arab League.

Expatriate workers in Saudi Arabia make up about two-thirds of the total Saudi workforce and 95 percent of the labor force in the private sector, but half of the expatriate jobs are drivers and maids to support a large and growing female population that is prevented from driving or working in most jobs. Nearly 70 percent of the Saudi population is under the age of 25, creating a pool of millions of potentially radicalized and restive young Saudis, trained only in Saudi-funded Wahhabi schools, and many willing to die in battle against the perceived "Great Satan," the United States of America, with the blessings of Allah and their parents. In typical Bedouin fashion, Crown Prince Abdullah bin Abdul Aziz, acting regent and head of state, has said that Saudi Arabia must continue to increase its population and does not have an excessive birthrate, even though the Saudi population is projected to double in 20 years. The current generation of Saudi leaders in the royal family has been exceptionally sensitive about Saudi Arabia's true population and in the past has even inflated its census statistics, but the fact remains that the Saudi population has mushroomed in the last 30 years, creating a serious unemployment problem for its large number of restive, young people. How will the Saudi economy support so many people and how will the Saudi culture accommodate the impending changes that result from such rapid growth?

On the other hand, fertility rates are declining globally and except for Saudi Arabia they are falling faster in the Middle East than anywhere else on earth, changing the demographic dynamics over the next generation. This is a global phenomenon and even populous China will face huge problems due to its "4-2-1" problem (four living grandparents and two living parents for each worker), and by 2050, Mexico will be an older society, on average, than the United States. As a result, global demographic trends hold some promise for optimism, as Phillip Longman [2004] recently observed:

> Over the next decade, the Middle East could benefit from a similar "demographic dividend." Birthrates fell in every single Middle Eastern country during the 1990s, often dramatically. The resulting "middle aging" of the region will lower the overall dependency ratio over the next 10 to 20 years, freeing up more resources for infrastructure and industrial development. The appeal of radicalism could also diminish as young adults make up less of the population and Middle Eastern societies become increasingly dominated by middle-aged people concerned with such practical issues as health care and retirement savings. Just as population aging in the West during the 1980s was accompanied

by the disappearance of youthful indigenous terrorist groups such as the Red Brigades and the Weather Underground, falling birthrates in the Middle East could well produce societies far less prone to political violence.

The task, then, is to establish a generation of peace through ideas, jobs, and hope for the young people of the Middle East because the war on terrorism is a generational battle of ideology. The United States and the West need to aggressively start this process by working with the every country in the region to help establish a generation of peace and opportunity by creating meaningful jobs for the young and angry Arab population that is growing far faster than the native populations in Europe or in the United States. Wahhabi propaganda, fueled by Saudi oil wealth, has made Saudi Arabia a major destabilizing force in the world, with an ideology of intolerance that underlies a ruthless, hate-filled religious faith championed by reactionary clerics. The West must overcome this propaganda assault with its own ideas of freedom and democracy and actions to shine light into the darkness of Wahhabi-Bin Ladenism and its deadly creed.

Since the late 1970s, oil wealth has created a huge pool of Saudi capital, with hundreds of thousands of Saudi citizens investing billions of dollars in the American economy through investments in public and private companies, although several millions in Saudi investments have been repatriated from the United States since 9/11. With offices in Bahrain, New York, London, and Atlanta, Investcorp and Crescent Capital (now called Arcapita) invested billions in Saudi royal family funds through the First Islamic Bank of Bahrain and acquired dozens of well-known brands ranging from Gucci in Italy, Saks Fifth Avenue and Tiffany's in New York, to Caribou Coffee and Jostens in Minnesota. These prestigious investment firms made many other strategic acquisitions throughout the United States and Europe, following strict Islamic prohibitions regarding payment of interest or ownership in non-Islamic activities that sell alcohol or promote gambling, but many other investments by private Saudi citizens have been far more liberal and less Islamic. Robert Kaiser [2002] has observed:

> After nearly three decades of accumulating this wealth, the group referred to by bankers as "high net-worth Saudi individuals" holds $500 billion to $1 trillion abroad, most of it in European and American investments. Raymond Seitz, vice chairman of Lehman Brothers in London and a former U.S. ambassador to Britain, said Saudis typically put about three-quarters of their money into the United States, the rest in Europe and Asia. That would mean Saudi nationals have invested perhaps $500 billion to $700 billion in the American economy. That is a huge sea of fungible assets supporting the American economy and belonging to a relatively small group of people. Managing these hun-

dreds of billions can be a lucrative business for brokers and bankers in London, Geneva and New York. Which financial institutions get the business? When that question was put to Robert Hormats, a vice chairman of Goldman Sachs in New York, he paused for a moment, then answered: 'Every major financial institution in the world has some links with Saudi money.'

The problem Western civilization faces with militant Islam today has its antecedents within Islam itself and more specifically in Saudi Arabia. As we have seen, the Saudi kingdom is a vast and barren, oil-rich, desert oligarchy that was isolated for centuries and is ruled by an aging and corrupt theocratic monarchy with a medieval legal system that is based on the Holy Koran and dominated by ultra-conservative Wahhabi religious leaders. It is in Saudi Arabia that some answers to vexing questions can be found regarding the nature of militant Islam's 21st century warriors and their fanatical, totalitarian ideology.

The next chapter discusses the impact of the spread of Wahhabism around the world, especially into the United States and Europe. With billions in oil wealth, the Saudi government and wealthy Saudi citizens pumped unprecedented amounts of money into Islamic charities that funded mosques, schools and Wahhabi religious materials, while most Americans and Europeans had no idea they were contributing to a Wahhabi-Salafist mosque and Wahhabi-Salafist propaganda each time they filled their car with gasoline.

CHAPTER TWO BIBLIOGRAPHY

Berman, Paul, "The Philosopher of Islamic Terror," *New York Times*, March 23, 2003.

Central Intelligence Agency, *The World Fact Book*, Washington, DC: Government Printing Office, 2004.

Fandy, Mamoun, "Avoiding the Next Generation of al Qaeda," Statement to the third public hearing of The National Commission on Terrorist Attacks Upon the United States, July 9, 2003.

Gold, Dore, *Hatred's Kingdom: How Saudi Arabia Supports the New Global Terrorism*, Washington, DC: Regency Publishing, Inc., 2003.

Kaiser, Robert G., "Enormous Wealth Spilled into American Coffers," *Washington Post*, Page A17, February 11, 2002.

Khaled bin Sultan bin Abdul Aziz ibn Saud, Prince and General, *Desert Warrior: A Personal View of the Gulf War by the Joint Forces Commander*, New York: HarperCollins, 1995.

Lewis, Bernard, *The Crisis of Islam: Holy War and Unholy Terror*, New York: Modern Library, 2003.

Longman, Phillip, "The Global Baby Bust," *Foreign Affairs*, May/June, 2004, http:// www.foreignaffairs.org/20040501faessay83307//phillip-longman/ the-global-baby-bust.html.

Mintz, John, and Farah, Douglas, "In Search Of Friends Among the Foes; U.S. Hopes to Work With Diverse Group," *Washington Post*, Page A01, September 11, 2004.

Rivlin, Paul, and Even, Shmuel, "Political Stability in Arab States: Economic Causes and Consequences," *Memorandum 74*, The Jaffe Center for Strategic Studies, Tel Aviv University, December 2004, http://www.tau.ac.il/jcss/memorandum/memo74.pdf.

Shakespeare, William, *Merchant of Venice*, Act II, Scene 1, Shylock's "revenge speech."

United Nations, *Arab Human Development Report*, New York: United Nations, 2002.

3

Wahhabism and Its Threats to the Non-Muslim World

Of the nearly 1.5 billion Muslims living in 57 countries around the world, several million are sufficiently radicalized to actively support militancy and an ideology derived from Wahhabism that is deeply antithetical to basic Western values of freedom and democracy. The radicals are generally young and impoverished, especially in the Middle East where nearly two-thirds of the population is under the age of 24. A majority of the world's Muslims lives under oppressive governments and the young radical militants have had little hope for the future except for a religious faith that rejects traditional Islam in favor of a deadly and literalist interpretation of the Holy Koran.

Their numbers extend from the Persian Gulf across North Africa and into Europe, through Southwest and Southeast Asia, and into North America. The extremists among the young radicals are prepared to die for their beliefs. For many years, thousands of Wahhabi-Salafist missionaries have been funded by Saudi Arabia while promoting hatred of the West. They have identified America as the "Great Satan," and demanded the overthrow of elected democracies and installation of totalitarian Islamist governments with Islamic law like the Taliban and Saudi Arabian Wahhabi-style shariah.

The world of Islam is now struggling for its very heart and soul in a deadly tug of war between forces of moderation and radical, militant Islamists who, like the Wahhabi-Bin Ladenists and the Taliban, wish to turn back the clock to the 7th century and the time of the Prophet. In fact, historians will likely document the early 21st century as the period of the start of the Muslim Reformation, driven by new technology—satellite TV and the Internet—much as the Christian Reformation in the 16th century was enabled by the new technology of its age, the printing press, that unleashed the genie of freedom and human expression.

Driven by Saudi money, the message of the radical, militant Wahhabi-Salafists has been exported around the world and into the United States and Europe. In the last 20 years, approximately half of the 1,500 mosques and Muslim schools in the United States were built with Saudi money distributed through Saudi-controlled Islamic charities that control 80 percent of the mosques in the United States.

The fingerprints of Saudi Wahhabi funding of Salafist groups in the United States and Europe with ties to the Muslim Brotherhood movement are undeniable. American and European mosques have routinely received weekly faxed messages, directly from conservative Wahhabi clerics in Saudi Arabia, containing hate-filled sermons that call for death to Jews, Christians, and other nonbelievers and victory in the jihadist struggle against American and allied forces in Afghanistan and Iraq. The Saudi-funded Wahhabi lobby in the United States also routinely exploits American weaknesses through the generally pro-Palestinian orientation that exists among the political left and on campuses of American colleges and universities.

WAHHABISM IN THE WEST

Wahhabism in America

According to a recent survey, two million American Muslims say they are associated with a mosque, while the number of mosques in the United States has increased 25 percent since 1994 to about 1,500 today [Hartford Seminary]. Nearly two-thirds of all American mosques were founded since 1980 and there are about 1,625 Muslims associated with each American mosque, which translates to nearly 2.5 million active Muslims in the United States, a reasonable estimate. Of that number, according to the poll, about 30 percent are converts to Islam and nearly 90 percent of American mosques have Asian, African-American, and Arab members. The ethnic origin of regular participants in American mosques and the percentage of the American Muslim population for each group are shown in Table 3.1 below:

Table 3.1
Ethnic Origin of Mosque Participants in the U.S.

Region of Origin	Percent of Total
South Asian (Pakistani, Indian, Bangladeshi, Afghani)	33.0
African-American	30.0
Middle East/Arab	25.0
Sub-Saharan African	3.4
European (Bosnian, Tartar, Kosovar, etc.)	2.1
White American	1.6
Southeast Asian (Malaysian, Indonesian, Filipino)	1.3
Caribbean	1.2
Turkish	1.1
Iranian	0.7
Hispanic/Latino	0.6
Total	100.0

Source: Hartford Seminary "Mosque in America: A National Portrait," *Faith Communities Today,* April 2001.

About 90 percent of American mosques say that they strictly follow the Holy Koran and Sunnah (sayings and teachings of Mohammed) and over 70 percent report that the Holy Koran should be interpreted in a manner that reflects modern life. Finally, the poll indicates that 20 percent of American mosques operate a full-time school that is associated with the mosque. Radical Islamists coming into the United States often use mosques as a base of operation and exploit American qualities of openness, fairness, and helpfulness when aiding and assisting immigrants from foreign cultures and religions. When identified in the press as Wahhabis or Wahhabi-inspired and supported Salafists, American Muslim groups often claim to be victims of slander while at the same time slandering their critics and demanding government protection under the freedom of religion clause of the American Constitution. These groups do not typically identify the sources or amounts of their financial support, especially foreign funding.

In early 2005, the *Boston Herald* reported that a particularly violent East Boston-based street gang called MS-13 with roots in El Salvador consisted of alleged rapists and violent, machete-wielding criminals with links to the al Qaeda terrorist network [McPhee]. Raed Hijazi, an al Qaeda operative charged with training the suicide bombers in the attack on the USS Cole, lived and worked in East Boston and allegedly was tied to MS-13. The commercial jet airliners that destroyed the World Trade Center towers in New York City on 9/11 were hijacked from Logan International Airport in Boston, leading investigators to track the possible role of MS-13 in aiding the 9/11 hijackers.

Zacharias Moussaoui, a 9/11 conspirator captured in Minnesota shortly before 9/11, was an al Qaeda Takfiri who was inspired by Wahhabi teachings and operated from Minnesota because of Wahhabi-funded support that he was able to receive from the large Muslim Somali community in Minnesota and proximity to the porous Minnesota-Canadian border. Wahhabis have also actively recruited prison convicts in the American federal prison system, especially black and Hispanic prisoners. Chuck Colson [2002] commented: "Alienated, disenfranchised people are prime targets for radical Islamists who preach a religion of violence, of overcoming oppression by jihad." Al Qaeda training manuals specifically identify American prisoners as candidates for conversion because they may be disenchanted with their country's policies. Wahhabi-affiliated American organizations such as the American Muslim Council (AMC) actively proselytize, but they have a tendency to look down on Black American Muslims as deviants from true Islam. Yet the AMC readily counts Black Americans in their numbers to inflate the size of the American Muslim population for political influence and as a potential resource for future terrorist operations.

Muslims in the American armed forces are even more problematic. Unknowingly, the Pentagon has used Wahhabi-backed organizations in the United States to select and train Muslim imams (prayer leaders) for the U.S. Army chaplain corps. Chaplains are in a unique position to indoctrinate and influence converts about their faith, placing U.S military officials in a difficult position if Wahhabi clerics were to preach subversive sermons or incite vulnerable, new converts to violence in private talks with Muslim members of the American military. The best estimate is that there are as many as 15,000 Muslims in the American military, but no one knows for sure because Muslims do not commonly declare their religious affiliation and the military does not require them to do so. Some military personnel are Muslim by birth but most are converts, the majority black, with a sprinkling of Hispanics.

The American military first addressed the issue of conversion to Islam in Saudi Arabia during the first Gulf War in 1990-1991 and, since then, has had serious problems with the way Muslim military chaplains are selected and trained. In March 2002, a Customs Service task force raided a Muslim chaplain school and network of Islamic nonprofit organizations and businesses in suburban Virginia outside Washington, DC. The raid established evidence that Saudi-funded organizations funneled money to al Qaeda, Palestinian Islamic Jihad and other groups that support radical, militant Islam.

Moreover, in the aftermath of the first Gulf War, ultra-conservative Saudi Wahhabi clerics aggressively tried to recruit U.S. service members stationed in

Saudi Arabia, especially American Blacks and Hispanics. Under the guise of lectures on Saudi Arabian culture, American troops were forced by their commanders to sit through many hours of Wahhabi propaganda. An article by Mintz and Vistica in *The Washington Post* on November 2, 2003 summarized Saudi Wahhabi missionary efforts:

> Just after the 1991 Persian Gulf War against Iraq, huge tents were erected in Saudi Arabia near the barracks of U.S. military personnel. Inside, day and night, Saudi imams [Wahhabi prayer leaders] sent by their government lectured the GIs about Islam and made aggressive pitches to convert them. Saudi officials had promised that the discussions would touch only on Arab culture. But within months, about 1,000 soldiers, and perhaps as many as 3,000, converted to Islam—the largest surge of Muslims ever into the U.S. armed forces. 'It was quite aggressive,' said David Peterson, then the military's top chaplain in the region. 'In retrospect,' he said, 'there was reason for concern that foreign clerics had gained influence over the troops, but military officials were slow to grasp the implications,' he said [Mintz and Vistica].

Sitting in the audience with his fellow American soldiers was Timothy McVeigh, the convicted bomber of the Oklahoma City Federal Building, who served in Saudi Arabia during the first Gulf War. It is conceivable but unproved that Wahhabi ideology may have influenced and motivated McVeigh's violence, for he was alienated toward his country and an ideal ally for radical, nihilistic, Wahhabism and especially al Qaeda-inspired Takfirism. Recent circumstantial evidence has revealed intriguing evidence of a possible Wahhabi connection to McVeigh and his accomplice, Terry Nichols. Directly after the Oklahoma City atrocity, unsubstantiated reports indicated possible involvement of Middle Easterners in Oklahoma City in the days leading up to the bombing. Next was an unusual trip to the Philippines by McVeigh's co-conspirator Terry Nichols, who may have met with members of the al Qaeda-linked Islamist extremist group Abu Sayaff. Richard Clarke, former member of the White House National Security Staff in the Clinton administration, summarized his suspicions regarding Nichols' trip to the Philippines as follows:

> Another Conspiracy Theory intrigued me because I could never disprove it. The theory seemed unlikely on its face: Ramzi Yousef or Khaled Sheik Muhammad had taught Terry Nichols how to blow up the Oklahoma Federal Building. The problem was that, upon investigation, we established that both Ramzi Yousef and Nichols had been in the city of Cebu on the same days…on an island in the central Philippines. Yousef and Khaled Sheik Muhammad had

gone there to help create an al Qaeda spin-off, a Philippine affiliate chapter, named after a hero of the Afghan war against the Soviets, Abu Sayaff.

Could the al Qaeda explosives expert have been introduced to the angry American who proclaimed his hatred for the U.S. Government? We do not know, despite some FBI investigation. We do know that Nichols's bombs did not work before his Philippine stay and were deadly when he returned. We also know that Nichols continued to call Cebu long after his wife returned to the United States. The final coincidence is that several al Qaeda operatives had attended a radical Islamic conference a few years earlier in, of all places, Oklahoma City" [Clarke, 127].

Clarke's theory regarding the Oklahoma City bombing and a possible connection to al Qaeda is intriguing and plausible, made even more so because of the aggressive Saudi missionary efforts to convert American soldiers to Wahhabism. What we know for certain on the Saudi side is that shortly after the Gulf War senior Saudi military and religious leaders were directed to identify and assess potential American military converts to Islam. We also know that McVeigh was in Saudi Arabia at the time, was exposed to the Wahhabi lectures, and would have made a prime candidate for conversion, meeting the ideal profile of a dissenter desiring to undermine and discredit his country and make war against its policies.

In his memoirs of the Gulf War, Prince Khaled bin Sultan [1995], American General Norman Schwarzkopf's Saudi counterpart during the war, refers to his religious aide, a senior Wahhabi cleric. It is common practice for conservative Wahhabi clerics to be assigned to the staffs of Saudi military commanders to enforce Wahhabi doctrine among the troops, similar to the way the KGB operated at every level of the Soviet Union military structure to enforce Communist Party discipline at all levels of command and in the ranks. Wahhabi clerics are assigned and operate at every level of the Saudi military command structure for religious purposes, but one of the primary tasks during the Gulf War was missionary work to proselytize infidel allies, especially Blacks and Hispanics and disaffected American soldiers like McVeigh. Recruitment included expensive gifts as well as the long-standing Saudi practice of providing cash grants for new converts to travel to Mecca for the annual Hajj pilgrimage. Prince Khaled and his Wahhabi religious advisors deliberately gulled their American military partners, led by General Schwarzkopf, into permitting these unusual activities during the long redeployment phase of the Gulf War after hostilities had finished. In the American tradition of freedom of religion, American military leaders felt that the Wahhabi lectures would please their Saudi hosts while benefiting the educational and religious needs of American soldiers who were bored with time on their hands while waiting to return home. These unusual Saudi missionary efforts resulted in hundreds of American converts to Wahhabi Islam and additional military converts have come from Wahhabi-funded mosques located in the United States.

Unless Terry Nichols sheds additional light on the subject, it is doubtful if we will ever know for certain if Timothy McVeigh was motivated and inspired by Wahhabi brainwashing to bomb the Federal Building in Oklahoma City. But what we do know is that Muslims in the American military pose a unique problem of trust and risk, as evidenced by Sergeant Hasan Akbar. Prior to joining the U.S. Army as a Muslim soldier, Sergeant Akbar attended the University of California Davis and a nearby radicalized Wahhabi-funded California mosque. Akbar threw hand grenades that exploded in an American command center in Kuwait on March 22, 2003 just as American forces were about to launch their attack into Iraq. After tossing the grenades into the command tents, Akbar shot several soldiers with an automatic weapon as they ran from their tents, killing two officers, an American Air Force major and Army captain, and wounding fourteen others.

Massive Saudi propaganda efforts, extensive missionary work, and nearly inexhaustible Saudi funding for mosques and Islamic schools have created extraordinary problems unimaginable before 9/11 and have served to intimidate much of the mainstream American Muslim community into silence, although encouraging signs began to emerge in 2004 and 2005 when the North American Muslim community started to react to promising developments in the Middle East and to the vulgar beheadings, atrocities and utter horror that were perpetrated by bin Laden's followers in Europe and Saudi Arabia and by Zarqawi in Iraq.

The European Problem

Another problem that the West faces is the so-called "European Problem" because radical, militant Islam supported by Saudi Arabian Wahhabi theology now resides in the heart of modern Europe, making Europe not only a base of militant Islamist operations but also a prized target. The Arab-Muslim world spans Europe's soft underbelly and Europe's demographic pressures have resulted in Muslims leading the wave of immigration into Europe from the more than 300 million Muslims that reside along Europe's Mediterranean southern rim, with a rapidly expanding population. The majority are under age 20 and 40 percent are below the age of 14. At the same time, native European populations are aging and shrinking, making immigration an economic necessity, but Europe has utterly failed to integrate its large Muslim population into the broader social fabric.

Europeans have a different perspective than the United States regarding Muslims and terrorism, largely because Europe has such a large Muslim population and is geographically closer to the Arab-Muslim world than North America, and because Europe has such a long history of active involvement in the Arab-Muslim world due to its recent colonial past. Europeans in general, and certainly the French and Germans, believe that Americans do not understand the problems of the Arab-Muslim world because the United States is relatively young as a nation and is situated so far away from the Muslim world and Europe, where it is literally driving distance from France or Germany to Chechnya and Iraq. Moreover, Europeans have believed that Americans, as relative newcomers to the Middle East, exaggerate the problem of radical, militant Islam and the threat of global terrorism. While European attitudes began to change in 2005, many Europeans believe that the United States lacks the type of "old world" patience required to solve problems the "Arab" way because Americans are so naive on the one hand and such rash bullies on the other, and lack experience in the Arab world.

As the dominant colonial power for many decades, the United Kingdom has had long experience in Iraq, Jordan, Egypt, Oman, India, Pakistan, and elsewhere in the world. France feels that it knows and understands the people, culture and history in Syria, Lebanon, Algeria, and Morocco from its colonial past, just as the Netherlands is particularly knowledgeable in the complexities of the world's largest Muslim country, Indonesia. Germany believes that it understands Turkey and Iran better than other nations due to its large Turkish "gast arbeiter" population stemming from well-established relationships with the Ottoman Empire and ventures like the Berlin to Baghdad railroad in the 19th and early 20th centuries. Because of these historical ties, large Muslim populations range throughout Europe, from Italy in the south to Sweden in the north.

While there are few reliable Muslim population statistics, it is generally accepted that more than 50 million Muslims live in greater Western and Eastern Europe. Approximately 18 million Muslims, as summarized in table 3.2 below, live in the 25 countries of the European Union (EU), several times more than the relatively small Muslim population in the United States.

Table 3.2
Western Europe Muslim Population (Millions)

Country	Total Population	Muslims	% Muslim	# Mosques
Austria	8.2	0.5	6.1	-
Belgium	10.4	0.6	5.8	380
Denmark	5.4	0.2	3.7	-
France	60.4	5.9	9.8	1,500
Germany	82.4	4.2	5.1	2,400
Italy	58.1	1.1	1.9	250
Netherlands	16.3	1.1	6.7	400
Norway	4.6	0.1	2.2	10
Spain	40.3	1.1	2.7	400
Sweden	9.0	0.5	5.6	-
Switzerland	7.5	0.4	5.3	-
United Kingdom	60.3	1.8	3.0	1,600
TOTAL	**362.9**	**17.5**	**4.8**	**5,340**

Source: Central Intelligence Agency, *The World Fact Book*, Washington, DC: Government Printing Office, 2004.

A majority of Europe's Muslims live in the Balkans and southeastern Europe, areas once part of the Ottoman Empire. In Western Europe, the largest numbers of Muslims live in France, Germany, and the United Kingdom, with many immigrants coming from Turkey, Algeria, Morocco, Tunisia, and Pakistan, having remained in their European host countries as "guest workers." Their children are now native-born EU citizens with EU passports and there is a growing number of European converts to Islam. The presence of Islam is readily seen throughout Western Europe where there are about 2,400 mosques in Germany, 1,500 in France and 1,600 in England, most built with money from Saudi Arabian Wahhabi-Salafist sources.

In Great Britain, there are nearly two million Muslims and in 2004, the name "Mohammed" was listed for the first time in the top 20 most commonly chosen names of baby boys, according to the British Office for National Statistics. In England, more Muslims attend mosque each week than Anglicans attend church, and Oxford University's Center for Islamic Studies has established a lavish new center for Islamic studies, funded by the Saudis, with a large prayer hall, traditional Muslim dome, and minaret tower [Ferguson].

In Germany there are over four million Muslims but the native German population is projected to decline from 82 million in 2004 to about 67 million in 2050 while its Muslim population explodes. Saudi-funded Muslim institutions have become the spiritual home to Islamist terrorists, as evidenced by the 9/11 investigations into the al Qaeda cells that operated freely in Hamburg, Germany prior to the al Qaeda attacks against the American homeland on September 11,

2001. Similar cells now operate with relative ease throughout Europe, primarily due to open borders resulting from liberal and relatively unrestricted EU travel policies that have eliminated the requirement to show passports at borders. Today Muslim extremists can move freely through Europe and travel largely undetected all the way to Iraq through Turkey.

The King Fahd Academy was recently established in Bonn, Germany, the former capital, as a personal gift from King Fahd. Currently, German-Muslim children of Turkish guest workers are taught the same hate-filled curriculum used in Wahhabi schools in Saudi Arabia. The German public was recently shocked by surreptitiously taped radical Islamist sermons in a German mosque that revealed calls for holy war against Jews and infidels. Testifying before the U.S. Senate Subcommittee on Terrorism, Technology and Homeland Security, Dr. Alex Alexiev, Senior Fellow, Center for Security Policy, stated:

> The typical modus operandi in taking over a mosque or similar institution follows approximately the following pattern: Saudi representatives offer a community to subsidize the building of a new mosque, which usually includes an Islamic school and a community center. After completion of the project an annual maintenance subsidy is offered making the community dependent on Saudi largess in perpetuity. Saudi chosen board members are installed, a Wahhabi imam [prayer leader] and free Wahhabi literature are brought in and the curriculum changed in accordance with Wahhabi precepts. Visiting speakers of extremist views are then regularly invited to lead Friday night prayers and further radicalize the members. The most promising candidates are selected for further religious education and indoctrination in Saudi Arabia to be sent back as Wahhabi missionaries as the circle is completed" [Alexiev].

A German television report on June 30, 2004 indicated that Germany has 2,400 mosques compared with 1,500 to 2,000 in the much larger United States, and that the state of North Rhine-Westphalia announced the results of a study of textbooks used in the private Islamic school that the Saudi government established in Bonn. According to the report, Muslim children were taught that, "...the Muslim people's existence has been threatened by Jews and Christians since the Crusades, and it is the first duty of every Muslim to prepare to fight against these enemies."

In France there are over six million Muslims although the number might be as high as eight million. According to a French undercover police study reported in the French daily *Le Monde*, there has been a marked increase in the number of Islamist radicals taking over mosques in the greater Paris area, with 32 out of 373 Paris mosques reported to be now under the control of extremists in 2004:

According to the police, extremists take over by first criticizing the older generation's interpretation of holy texts and then bringing up political issues such as the ban of Muslim headscarves in French public schools, the Israeli-Palestinian conflict, and discrimination against Arabs. To maintain and increase community support, the radicals open day-care centers and nursery schools associated with the mosques and undertake the teaching of Arabic and the Holy Koran. Some Salafist radicals [Takfirs] are linked to al Qaeda and other terror groups and the increase of radical-controlled mosques is regarded as a threat to security in France and Europe [CNS News].

French researchers believe that the radicalization of mosques is a result of the growing Salafist movement in Europe inspired by Saudi Wahhabism. It appeals to young, second-generation Arabs who feel rejected by Western society and alienated from their immigrant family culture and traditional Islam, which they reject. The increase of this radical form of Islam has also occurred in other urban areas of France, Germany, and Britain. The radicals target young people and gradually take over by isolating older clerics who have practiced moderate Islam in their mosques. Stephen Schwarz [2002] has described the danger of Wahhabi-funded mosques:

What makes a Wahhabi mosque so dangerous? First, Wahhabi preaching and teaching to such a congregation will be fundamentalist, indoctrinating young and old in hatred, contempt, and distrust of Jews, Christians, and non-Wahhabi Muslims. Second, it will propagandize in favor of violence in places such as Iraq, Israel, and Chechnya. Wahhabi mosques serve as centers for the dissemination of extremist literature, including the "Saudi edition of the Holy Koran," a revised version of the Islamic scripture with insertions and distortions that make it an extremist document. The collection of money and the distribution of videos extolling jihad combatants also take place in these mosques. The step from such activities to direct recruitment of these combatants is small, as evidenced by the enlistment of British subjects to fight in Chechnya and American citizens who become al Qaeda operatives [Schwartz, 2002].

While there are fewer than 750,000 Jews in France and Germany combined, disturbing and growing trends of malevolent anti-Semitism are now present in Europe, and especially in France, mostly driven by militant Islamists. European anti-Semitism has reemerged because European Muslims share a common and unified hatred of Israel and support of the Palestinians. They also share a deep distrust of the United States, fed by daily Al Jazeerah television news, because of unswerving American support of democratic Israel and the American-led war in

Iraq. According to an officially commissioned EU study in 2003, almost all neo anti-Semitism in Europe comes from Muslim groups:

> Muslims and Palestinian groups were behind many of the [anti-Semitism] incidents it examined...Physical attacks on Jews and the desecration and destruction of synagogues and cemeteries were acts often committed by young Muslim perpetrators...radical Islamist circles were responsible for placing anti-Semitic propaganda [Benoit, 2003].

What is particularly disturbing is Europe's reluctance to address the problem of European anti-Semitism and its causes, especially Wahhabi-Salafist funding and support provided to anti-Semitic activities by Islamic charities. In many circles in Europe, Saudi funding for Europe's poor and isolated Muslim community is seen as benign, but there is well-documented proof that Saudi money and radical Wahhabi ideology in Saudi-backed schools, mosques, and foundations have caused increased support for terrorism among Europe's young and disaffected Muslims.

In Spain, Europe's largest mosque is located near Madrid, built by the government of Saudi Arabia, and with typical strings attached in directing what will be preached at Friday's call to prayer and how funds may be spent. In Greece, the King Fahd Foundation of Saudi Arabia financed an Islamic Center in suburban Athens. The Greek government recently donated the land for a large mosque that will be built by a Saudi Arabian Wahhabi foundation to accommodate the approximately 120,000 Muslims in the greater metropolitan area of Athens. The Muslim phenomenon in Europe is driven by changing demographics that are rapidly transforming the European landscape:

> Today, the Muslim birth rate in Europe is three times higher than the non-Muslim one. If current trends continue, the Muslim population of Europe will nearly double by 2015, while the non-Muslim population will shrink by 3.5 percent [Taspinar].

While population trends mean that European Muslims will soon have proportionally more influence in elections, European Muslims are even more alienated and distrustful following 9/11 and with recent exposure of al Qaeda-Takfir cells in Germany, Italy, France, Belgium, Spain, and the Netherlands. Al Qaeda's March 11, 2004 attack in Spain was a resounding victory for bin Laden, with near simultaneous bombings of four trains that killed nearly 200 people. Moreover, the attack in Spain knocked a major American ally out of the Iraq war. The world reacted in horror to successive 2004 al Qaeda beheadings in Iraq and Saudi Arabia and then later to the savage and violent murder of Theo Van Gogh in Amsterdam on November 2, 2004 by a Muslim militant who had connections to an al Qaeda-Takfir terrorist cell and a radical, Wahhabi-inspired Salafist mosque in Amsterdam. An encouraging development in March 2005 came from Spanish Muslim leaders when they announced a fatwa (religious ruling) against Osama bin Laden on the anniversary of the Madrid train bombings saying that according to the Koran, "the terrorist acts of Osama bin Laden and his organization al Qaeda...are totally banned and must be roundly condemned as part of Islam" [CNN].

An early casualty of these developments is Europe's widely accepted doctrine of multiculturalism, where all cultures are considered equal. France banned students and teachers from wearing headscarves in state schools in 2004, igniting fierce criticism from Muslim groups that claimed banning Muslim headscarves is a form of discrimination against the religion of Islam. Five German states also introduced headscarf bans for teachers in 2004 but Germany restricts only teachers and does not prevent students from wearing Islamic headscarves. Bavaria's culture minister was quoted as saying, "The veil is widely abused by Islamic fundamentalist groups as a political symbol." The Social Democratic Party (SPD) and Greens, both left-of-center parties that rule in a coalition at the national level in Germany, voted against the ban in the regional parliament and sided with Muslim groups, a trend that shows the European and American political left aligning with Muslim interests in Europe and the United States. It is likely that France will have a French Muslim majority at the national level within 25 years. The problem of militant Islamists in France is becoming acute due to extreme isolation, alienation, and discrimination against Europe's Muslim population and an uncertain future for young Muslims—a trend that is redefining Europe from Sweden and Norway in the north to Italy and Spain in the south. Caroline Wyatt, Paris correspondent for the BBC, recently noted: "Women in black chadors and abayas make Burgundy feel more like Barbary." She went on to say that family members, asylum seekers, and illegal immigrants add to the growing immigrant population who live in bleak French public housing, causing resentments of young Muslims to grow, while their French classmates move on to better positions in society [Wyatt]. Germany, with Europe's second largest Muslim population and ultra liberal political asylum policies, has also failed to integrate its largely Turkish Muslim population into Germany society. Germany's large Turkish population generally lives in isolated ghettos and the result is alienation and anger among Germany's large and youthful Muslim population, a trend witnessed throughout Europe. Moreover, the Muslim Brotherhood, with Saudi funding, has deeply penetrated Germany's large and increasingly hostile Muslim community with its radical agenda.

Because of their large Muslim populations, it should come as no surprise that most European politicians, especially in France and Germany, had difficulty supporting the United States in the Iraq war. What this means for the future of the EU is alarming, but positive developments in the Middle East in the spring of 2005 increased European support for the Bush Doctrine of freedom and democracy as the antidote to Bin Ladenism. Cells of young al Qaeda-Takfiris have embedded themselves into European societies, gulling their trusting infidel hosts while posing as moderate and mainstream Muslims, and waiting patiently to strike lethal and often fatal suicide blows against the heathen West.

French intellectuals are often humorous in their criticisms of the United States, but it is important to point out some of their recurrent absurdities because they often receive disproportionate importance and are a frequent source of disinformation in the press. Laurent Murawiec [2002] observed that it is popular today in some French intellectual circles to cite the "American way of life" as the greatest threat to civilization and to call "unbearable America" a totalitarian democracy that has "launched a war against the Old World." This is a popular theme with wide appeal among the French intelligentsia and some in the U.S., where the United States is seen as the world's last empire, that it orchestrated the Asian financial crisis in 1998 to bring down its rival Japan, and that it uses NATO to control Europe against Europe's own interests. Wedded for years to utopian Marxism, and mindful of their failure to achieve a communist utopia, many French intellectuals now support the goals of radical, militant Islamism. They have replaced their Marxist utopia with an Islamist transnational ideology of a utopian global Caliphate governing under Islamic shariah law instead of Marxist law. But most bizarre is the French claim that the CIA conspired with Saudi Arabian Wahhabis and their oil money in a "grand conspiracy" to secure the world's oil reserves for global capitalism in return for permitting Saudi Wahhabis and the Saudi royal family to establish and support dictatorships throughout the Arab-Muslim world [Murawiec]!

While 21st century French intellectuals may be amusing, there are also many voices of sanity and prudence in France who understand that the problem of radical, militant Islam in the heart of Western Europe is a sobering phenomenon, growing and festering in ways that are bound to spell trouble for the fledgling EU that remains paralyzed and unable to effectively address the threat. Meanwhile, new potential members like Muslim Turkey are knocking at the EU door, hoping for membership and the benefits it can bring to a poor Muslim country like Turkey that sits astride Europe and Asia. Turkey is a special case because of its secular makeup that resulted from Kemal Attaturk's revolution following the breakup of the Ottoman Empire after the First World War, and because Turkey is also a long-standing member of NATO. The United States government has supported Turkey's desire to join the EU, but not all European countries welcome a Muslim nation into the European Union because it is seen as a Muslim "Trojan horse." Even though Turkey is a non-Arab country and is highly Westernized, the world will have to wait until 2015 so to see how Turkey's prospects develop for EU membership.

Europe's problems with its large and growing Muslim population will continue to grow, but Turkey's strategic position in the Middle East and active membership status in NATO, the world's longest lasting and most successful international security structure in history, can provide a linchpin for logically extending NATO to the southeast into the countries of the Persian Gulf and the world's richest supply of oil. Such an initiative could create what might be called "SENATO," for Southeast NATO, extending NATO's security guarantees to the perennially unstable countries of the region and their oil fields that are vital to the world's economy.

THE WEST'S RESPONSE TO TERRORISM AND WAHHABISM

For over 30 years the West consistently failed to respond credibly to critical events in the Middle East, even in the face of increasingly violent terrorist attacks against American facilities in the Muslim world. Radical Islamist extremists concluded that the United States was a paper tiger as a result of its experience in Vietnam and long record of failure in the Middle East. Successive bombings of American targets in Lebanon, Saudi Arabia, Somalia, Africa, and Yemen emboldened Osama bin Laden and in the twisted logic of Wahhabi-Bin Ladenism, al Qaeda arrogantly declared open war against Saudi Arabia, the "the Great Satan" infidel United States, and Western civilization.

America, the Paper Tiger

The watershed year was 1979. The fall of the Shah of Iran and establishment of a Muslim Shiite theocracy under the Ayatollah Khomeini, the seizure of the Grand Mosque in Mecca by Wahhabi extremists in November 1979, and the Soviet invasion of Afghanistan in December of that year were earth-shattering events that profoundly affected the young Osama bin Laden and Saudi thinking at the time. The Iranian Shiite revolution in 1979 occurred as the Saudis were amassing their vast oil wealth. While the Iranian revolution spread concern in the West, the collapse of the Shah's regime created utter panic in Saudi Arabia, especially among the members of the royal family who feared that they might meet the same fate as the Shah. Saudi Wahhabis harbored historical hatred of Muslim Shiites and the Saudi royal family was deeply distrustful of the intentions of the new theocratic government in Iran.

Moreover, American President Jimmy Carter appeared weak and ineffective and the Saudis openly questioned America's reliability as an ally to stand up to the Iranian revolutionary leaders, let alone the atheistic Soviets. This Saudi attitude was reinforced by the inability of the Carter administration to resolve the Iranian hostage crisis and respond effectively to Saudi security concerns. And when Carter ordered two AWACS command and control aircraft and six unarmed American F-15 fighter aircraft into Saudi Arabia in 1980 in response to a Yemeni border incursion, the Saudis openly ridiculed President Carter for the futile American response and Carter's failure to comprehend the seriousness of Saudi security concerns.

Fear of Shiite Iran has always been a primary Saudi security issue, made even more alarming to the Saudi ruling family in 1979 because most of the residents of the oil-rich Eastern Province were Shiites and their loyalty to the Saudi government was questionable in the face of the Iranian Shiite revolution that ousted the ruling Reza Pahlavi family from Iranian power. Wahhabi hatred for Shiites is extreme and goes back to the earliest days of Islam and the schism following the death of the Prophet Mohammed. A majority of the world's Shiites live in Iran and in the southern two-thirds of present-day Iraq where the two holiest Shiite cities, Karbala and Najaf, are located. During an anti-Shiite rampage in 1802, an Ikhwan force of 12,000 Saudi Wahhabis attacked and massacred approximately 4,000 Shiites in Karbala, Iraq and destroyed holy Shiite shrines, including the tomb of Hussein, the sainted Shiite grandson of the Prophet Mohammed. The following year, Wahhabi Ikhwan forces, already allied with the al Saud clan, attacked and desecrated the holy Shiite city of Najaf, Iraq, the burial site of the sainted and highly revered Ali, son-in-law of the Prophet Mohammed.

As the Saudis assessed the impact of the 1979 Iranian revolution, they were also forced to deal with the seizure of the Grand Mosque in Mecca by Wahhabi militants in November 1979 and the Soviet Union invasion of Afghanistan in December. On November 20, 1979 several hundred Wahhabi extremists and members of the Muslim Brotherhood seized control of the Kaaba, Islam's most sacred place, in the Grand Mosque of Mecca. The leader was the grandson of one of the original Ikhwan who had ridden with the old Saudi king, Abdul Aziz ibn Saud, and called for the overthrow of the royal family and a return to the strict Islamic practices of an earlier age. Justification for their extreme actions was a belief, with some justification, that the royal family had lost its legitimacy due to corruption, ostentatious living, and imitation of the West, the same charges made by the Ikhwan against the old king in the late 1920s and similar to bin Laden's charges today. And like the old king, Saudi reaction to the Mecca incident was rapid and severe. More than 200 Saudi troops and militants were killed and the Saudi government later publicly beheaded over 60 extremists.

To the royal family in 1979, the world seemed to be spinning out of control and King Fahd, in predictable fashion, threw money at the problem with millions of petrodollars earmarked for domestic religious education and a conservative Wahhabi Islamist agenda inspired by Muslim Brotherhood educators at Saudi universities in Mecca, Medina, and Jeddah. With the support and encouragement from the American government, the Saudis also began pouring millions of dollars of their newly acquired oil wealth into Pakistan, Afghanistan, and North Africa for anti-Soviet and anti Iranian Wahhabi propaganda, Islamist schools, and Wahhabi mosques. This was an especially desperate effort to counter the threat of the spread of Iran's violent, revolutionary Shiite fundamentalism throughout the region and around the world, and especially in Saudi Arabia's own backyard with its large Shiite minority living along the Persian Gulf oil fields—as many as 2-3 million potentially unstable Saudi Shiites who suffered decades of Wahhabi discrimination, persecution, and second class status. Saudi government funding for Islamist schools in Western Pakistan and the subsequent formation of bin Laden's Arab brigade to fight against Soviet atheism in Afghanistan later gave rise to al Qaeda in the late 1980s and early 1990s and a new wave of extremely violent Islamist terrorism exploded upon the world scene based on Wahhabi-Muslim Brotherhood ideology and objectives.

Four subsequent events erupted during the waning years of the late 20th century, starting with the end of the Iran-Iraq War that had lasted from 1980 to

1988. In rippling effect, the dramatic fall of the Berlin War in 1989, the Iraqi invasion of Kuwait in 1990, and the sudden demise of the Soviet Union and atheistic Communism in 1991, cascaded upon the world and bewildered the Saudis, causing joy in some quarters and deep dismay and unsettlement in others. During the Iran-Iraq War, the Saudis provided direct support and aid to the secular Iraqi Sunni leader, Saddam Hussein, against the Iranian theocratic Shiite regime, but the Saudis were surprised and bewildered by Saddam Hussein's invasion of Kuwait in 1990, only a year after the long and bloody Iran-Iraq War ended. The subsequent 1991 first Gulf War against Iraq and the demise of the Soviet Union in the same year ended a decade of international and regional tumult that set in motion a renewed bid by the Saudis to use their oil wealth with devastating effect to spread Wahhabism around the world. With the assistance of Saudi oil money, the decades of the 1980s and 1990s resulted in a rekindling of Islamist fundamentalism and a fueling of rampant anti-Americanism and anti-Semitism.

The 1990s caused other problems relating to the rapid globalization of the world economy and from excesses brought on by the computer-telecommunications revolution, growth of the Internet, and the U.S. stock market bubble that finally burst in the crash of early 2000. In the Muslim world, and especially among Saudi Arabia's conservative population, these unprecedented economic events were underscored by President Clinton's sex scandals that shocked and horrified the entire Muslim world and deflected the attention of the American administration away from al Qaeda and bin Laden. These factors, coupled with a general lack of concern for foreign affairs by the American public and the Clinton administration in the 1990s, convinced militant Islamist terrorists such as Osama bin laden and his emerging al Qaeda global terrorist organization that the United States and other Western democracies were decadent, immoral, corrupt, and impotent.

Then came September 11, 2001 and al Qaeda's terrorist attacks against the World Trade Center in New York and the Pentagon in Washington, DC. The attacks on 9/11 were a direct result of perceived American weakness in the Arab-Muslim world because of consistent American failure to respond vigorously to militant Islamist attacks against American facilities and interests going back some 30 years.

The United States had lost a number of diplomats in isolated Middle Eastern terrorist incidents in the 1970s, but the first significant attack on the West by violent radical Islamists was by Ayatollah Khomeini's Iranian Shiite Muslims who seized 52 Americans in the American Embassy in Tehran in 1979. Held as prisoners for 444 days, the Carter administration lost credibility in the eyes of the world with its failed and aborted rescue attempt. Fearful of Reagan's threats during the presidential election campaign, the Iranian mullahs released the American hostages on January 20, 1981, the day Ronald Reagan was inaugurated and President Carter left office. The United States had unfortunately suffered serious loss of face in the Muslim world by its inability to mount an effective rescue attempt and free its embassy staff.

Two years later in 1983, Hezbollah, a Shiite-Iranian-sponsored Palestinian group, launched two suicide bombing attacks on Americans in Lebanon, first on the American Embassy in Beirut, killing 63 embassy employees and wounding 120, and then on the U.S. Marine barracks at the Beirut airport, killing 241 marines and wounding 81. President Reagan did not retaliate against these deliberate acts of terrorist warfare because his Defense Secretary, Caspar Weinberger, expressed concern about damaging American relations in the Middle East. Instead, Reagan removed the remaining American troops from Lebanon, which, in the eyes of the terrorists, achieved their objective for the attack. The Beirut airport suicide bombings were followed by the bombing of the U.S. Embassy in Kuwait in December 1983 and the kidnapping and killing of the CIA station chief in Beirut the following March, again without any retaliatory response from the United States. However, in September 1984, when Hezbollah bombed the annex to the American embassy in Beirut, the United States authorized Lebanese intelligence agents to assassinate an Islamic cleric thought to be the Hezbollah leader, but instead 80 innocent persons were killed.

In December 1984, Hezbollah changed tactics by hijacking airliners and killing American passengers on the flights. The first hijacking was a Kuwaiti airliner with two Americans killed; the kidnappers escaped punishment after the plane landed in Tehran. The Reagan administration offered a $250,000 reward for information that would lead to the arrest of the kidnappers without success. The next kidnapping was TWA flight 847 in June 1985 that landed in Beirut, where it was held for more than two weeks. Although an American naval officer was shot and his body thrown onto the tarmac, the Israelis agreed to trade hundreds of jailed terrorists for release of the passengers. Once again, the kidnappers escaped but four were later captured in Germany and one was actually tried there and jailed.

Later, in October 1985, Libyan terrorists tried to hijack the cruise ship, Achille Lauro, and threw a crippled Jewish-American passenger, Leon Klinghoffer, overboard. That attack was followed by Libyan terrorists bombing airports in Rome and Vienna in December 1985, and a West Berlin discotheque frequented by American service members in April 1986. President Reagan finally signaled that the United States had enough and ordered an F-111 air attack on one of Muammar Qaddafi's Libyan residences from bases in England. Qaddafi was nearly killed which caused Libya to withdraw from terrorism until December 1988, when Libyan agents planted a bomb on Pan Am flight 103 that exploded over Lockerbie, Scotland, killing all passengers and several people on the ground, 270 in all. Two Libyan intelligence agents were subsequently tried for the crime and one was convicted in 2001. Qaddafi escaped further punishment except for sanctions imposed on his country that were subsequently lifted when Libya agreed to terminate its nuclear program in June 2003 shortly after the start of the Iraq invasion, having been sufficiently alarmed by a post 9/11 American ultimatum to either join the American effort in the war on terrorism or expect regime change in Libya, as in Iraq.

By the late 1980s, Osama bin Laden was fighting in Afghanistan against the Soviet occupation. He correctly noted that nearly all Islamist terrorist attacks against American targets and the West had successfully achieved terrorist objectives at very little cost politically, financially, or in Muslim lives. Bin Laden's successful jihad in liberating Afghanistan from the Soviet Union and establishing the Taliban as Afghanistan's government, coupled with his observations regarding the success of the Islamist terrorist attacks, elated his embryonic radical terrorist movement. Moreover, bin Laden and his Saudi benefactors had successfully gulled the infidel CIA into supplying weapons and money for his Afghan Arab warriors, and bin Laden had been able to use the cause of Muslim liberation from Western domination as a successful recruiting tool to bring thousands of young Muslims to Afghanistan for indoctrination and training in terrorist tactics. From this springboard, bin Laden then sent hundreds of young jihadists into the Balkans and Somalia in the 1990s to continue the struggle for the cause of radical, militant Islam.

Bin Laden's nihilistic jihadists were less welcome in assisting Muslims in Kosovo and Bosnia where the European Muslims found the Wahhabis simultaneously far too violent and reactionary. In typical Wahhabi fashion, they led violent attacks on nonbelievers and painted over or obliterated magnificent, centuries-old frescoes on the walls of ancient mosques and desecrated cemeteries and statues. However, bin Laden's apparent success in driving the United States from Somalia in 1993 by simply downing two Black Hawk helicopters with American land-to-air missiles left over from Afghanistan, and killing a few elite Army Rangers, caused him to develop an exaggerated view of al Qaeda's capabilities. He also underestimated American resolve and the difficulty of driving the American infidels from the Middle East. With the end of the first Persian Gulf War in 1991, bin Laden obsessively focused on removing American and other infidel forces from the holy lands of Saudi Arabia. He believed that the United States had become a soft "paper tiger" since Vietnam without the courage, determination, political will, or perseverance as a nation to succeed in prolonged and bloody military conflict. It was from this psychological orientation that bin Laden planned a series of escalating and bolder attacks on American interests in the Middle East, and ultimately on the American homeland itself.

In February 1993, a massive explosion from a truck bomb in the parking garage of the World Trade Center in New York killed six people and injured over 1,000; this was one of the few instances in which terrorists were captured and six were successfully prosecuted for the crime and received long sentences. The target, as on 9/11, was a symbol of America's global economic might. Even though CIA director James Woolsey suspected that the terrorists were a part of a larger terror network operating from the Sudan and called al Qaeda, the Clinton administration believed that justice had prevailed through criminal prosecution of the terrorists and that the bombing was a law enforcement problem rather than a military matter.

The first World Trade Center bombing was followed by the shooting of two American diplomats in Karachi, Pakistan in March 1995 and the killing of five Americans with a car bomb in Riyadh, Saudi Arabia in December 1995. On June 25, 1996 a large truck bomb destroyed the U.S. Air Force Khobar Towers dormitory in Dhahran, Saudi Arabia in the Shiite Eastern Province near the oil fields, killing 19 American airmen and wounding 240 others, including civilians of several nationalities. The goal of the attacks in Saudi Arabia was to drive the Americans out of the country. Again, the Clinton administration sought justice for these crimes against Americans through law enforcement action and the intervention of the FBI rather than military action but with very limited success due to lack of support from Saudi authorities.

Al Qaeda stepped up its anti-American campaign in 1998 with the simultaneous bombings of U.S. embassies in Kenya and Tanzania, killing over 200 people, mostly Africans. Distracted by impeachment hearings stemming from his sex scandals which had shocked the Muslim world, President Clinton at last identified bin Laden as the perpetrator and authorized the Pentagon to fire several cruise missiles at an al Qaeda training camp in Afghanistan and destroy a building in Sudan that was believed to be an al Qaeda weapons factory. The American president also launched covert CIA counterterrorist operations against bin Laden's operations but failed to make any significant progress against al Qaeda.

Bin Laden now realized that he had gained the attention of the United States, but this recognition and his success made him even more aggressive. In October 2000 he dispatched a team of suicide bombers against the U.S. Navy destroyer USS Cole, which had docked in Yemen's port of Aden for refueling. Yemen has had a long history of political instability and radical support for ultra-conservative Saudi Arabian Wahhabism. Bin Laden's father was born in Yemen and the Saudi-Yemen border has long been in dispute, making the country a safe haven for radical, Islamist terrorists. Seventeen American sailors were killed and 39 were wounded in the attack on the USS Cole.

President Clinton was involved in Israeli-Palestinian peace talks at Camp David at the time of the Cole attack and failed to condemn al Qaeda for its direct assault on U.S. military operations or take any action against bin Laden. Nor did the incoming Bush administration take any action when it took office in January 2001 and bin Laden was once again left with the perception of a resonant victory against the infidels with no retaliation coming from the American "paper tiger." A summary of important militant Islamist attacks against the U.S. and the impotent pre-9/11 American responses are shown in Table 3.3 below.

Table 3.3
Summary of Significant Militant Islamist Attacks Against America

Event	Year	Result	American Response
Iranian Shiite Revolution	1979	52 American hostages held for 444 days	Failed US rescue attempt
Bombing of U.S. Embassy & Marine Barracks in Lebanon	1983	Killed 241 Marines & 63 employees, wounded 201	US withdrew troops from Lebanon
Bombing of US Embassy in Kuwait	1983	Killed 6	No action
Bombing of US Embassy Annex in Beirut, Lebanon	1984	Killed 80	No action
Aircraft & Cruise Ship Hijackings	1984-85	Several Americans killed	No action
Loss of 2 Black Hawk helicopters in Somalia	1992	18 Americans killed	US withdrew troops from Somalia
Bombing of World Trade Center in NYC	1993	Killed 6, wounded over 1,000	Arrested & convicted Islamist ringleader & others
American diplomats shot in Karachi, Pakistan	1995	Killed 5 Americans	Investigation, no action
Bombing of US Air Force dormitory in Saudi Arabia	1996	Killed 19 American airmen & wounded 240	FBI investigation, no action
Bombings of US Embassies in Africa	1998	Killed over 200, mostly Africans	Fired several cruise missiles at bin Laden
Bombing of USS Cole in Yemen	2000	17 killed, 39 wounded	FBI investigation, no action
Attacks against American Homeland	9/11/2001	Nearly 3,000 killed, thousands wounded	US launched Global War on Terrorism (GWOT)

Al Qaeda's repeated attacks on the United States were low-cost propaganda victories for bin Laden and they resounded loudly throughout the Muslim world. Osama bin Laden soon became sufficiently encouraged to bring a devastating attack directly to the Great Satan's homeland as he did on September 11, 2001 in one of the most brazen and sophisticated terrorist operations in history. Nearly 3,000 innocent people died when al Qaeda martyrs hijacked four airliners and flew them at high speed into the Twin Towers of the World Trade Center in New York City, the Pentagon in Washington, DC, and into the ground in central Pennsylvania, apparently targeting the United States Capitol or White House. For nearly 25 years, the United States endured repeated attacks from radical, militant, Islamists but U.S. retaliatory responses were ineffective and futile, providing motivation for the attackers to raise the ante and strike once more, as they did on 9/11.

Not since Pearl Harbor, nearly 60 years before 9/11, had the United States been so shocked. In addition to hatred of infidels that is a root belief of Wahhabi-Bin Ladenism, an even more important reason for this daring attack on the world's greatest power was to advance Osama bin Laden's dream of consolidating his influence and power in the Muslim world. By appealing to the biases and hopes of millions of disaffected young Muslims, bin Laden had hoped to restore Islam to its previous glory and prominence before Islam's armies of conquest were turned away from Europe at the gates of Vienna on September 11, 1683. Despite moral qualms in much of the Muslim community about the loss of innocent life, the events of 9/11 established bin Laden and his radical Islamists as true Muslim warriors in centuries' old jihad against the infidel West. And with rhetoric especially appealing to the Arab-Muslim world, bin Laden claimed that all former Muslim lands such as Spain must be reconverted to Islam and restored to their former glory.

Following September 11, 2001, it became apparent that the American public lacked fundamental knowledge and understanding of the nature of the militant Islamist enemy and the seriousness of the Saudi-Wahhabi threat to Western civilization. It has also been easy and sometimes convenient for people to forget the cause of 9/11, but the fact remains that 15 of the 19 hijackers on September 11, 2001 were a new brand of ruthless terrorists that came from Saudi Arabia and were profoundly influenced by the teachings of the Muslim Brotherhood theorist, Sayyid Qutb, and the virulent Saudi Arabian Wahhabi Sunni Islamic sect. Osama bin Laden came from a wealthy and well-connected Saudi Arabian family with roots and established family contacts in turbulent Yemen. The Saudi government, wealthy Saudi individuals, and members of the Saudi ruling family have

supported international terrorism with cash grants through multi-layered networks of Islamic charities around the world and directly to global terrorist organizations such as al Qaeda, the Palestinian Liberation Organization (PLO), and
Hamas. It has been well documented in the international press that wealthy Saudis and members of the Saudi royal family financed al Qaeda before September
11th and that many wealthy Saudis continue to support and finance al Qaeda.

Senior members of the Saudi royal family openly praised Palestinian suicide
bombers and rewarded their families with cash grants, and the Saudi ambassador
to Britain, a member of the royal family, even published a poem eulogizing 9/11
and Palestinian suicide bombers. It has been well reported that the Saudi government and wealthy Saudi citizens continue to finance and support radical, militant
Islamist clerics around the world who spread Wahabbi-Salafism, a doctrine that
preaches intolerance and seeks to replicate the totalitarian Islamic society and
legal structure that exist in Saudi Arabia today. Speaking about Saudi Arabia during the summer of 2003, Senator Jon Kyl [2003], Republican from Arizona and
Chairman of the Senate Judiciary Subcommittee on Technology, Terrorism and
Homeland Security, stated:

> The problem we are looking at today is the state-sponsored doctrine and fund-
> ing of an extremist ideology that provides the recruiting grounds, support
> infrastructure and monetary lifeblood to today's international terrorists.

Today a monumental struggle is taking place for the heart, mind, and soul of
Islam. This struggle is being waged between Islamic forces of moderation and bin
Laden's radical, militant Islamist forces who are dedicated to reactionary Wahhabi-Salafist goals of turning back the clock to the 7th century and the early days
of Mohammed when Islam was supposedly "pure" and untainted. The struggle
for the heart and soul of Islam is between the militant Islamist forces of darkness
with their hate-filled ideology and the civilized world of Western values that
include secularism, pluralism, openness, tolerance, freedom, and democracy.
Without question, the struggle for the soul of Islam is the most significant ideological battle taking place in the world today and one that profoundly impacts the
lives of nearly everyone in the world because of the intensity of the issues and the
sheer numbers of people involved. Senator Charles Schumer, Democrat from
New York, was even more direct in condemning the Saudi government in a 2003
press release:

"This week's attacks [in Saudi Arabia] should underscore a very important point to the Saudi royal family: It's that playing both sides of the coin won't work when it comes to fighting terrorism," Schumer said. "The Saudis need to get over this Syndrome where they tell the US and the West what we want to hear but then tell the Arab street something else. If they don't get serious, there are going to be more attacks. The Administration needs to make that point forcefully to the Crown Prince. The first step in that effort is shutting down these Madrassa schools...while Islam is a peaceful religion the madrassas distort this message by preaching hate, violence and intolerance toward the Judeo-Christian world. These teachings have created a 'lost generation' in Saudi Arabia, where thousands of young Saudis are being indoctrinated with the idea that terrorism is an acceptable way to articulate their Islamic beliefs. In order for your government to be a true partner in the war on terror, it must stop funding those schools which preach extremism and to denounce their teachings."

Inscrutable Saudis—Gullible Americans

The analogy of a desert mirage has often been used to describe Saudi Arabia as a country that is ever changing and different from what it appears to be, populated with delightful, often incomprehensible, and always inscrutable desert people. The Saudis are ethnic Arabs, mostly from Bedouin origins and nomadic tribes that wandered the vast Arabian Desert for centuries, moving from oasis to oasis with caravans of goats and camels. Tribal culture, family and clan loyalty, and the incessant demands of the harsh desert heat and blowing sands have deeply marked the people of the Arabian Peninsula who proudly call themselves "Saudis" and defenders of Islam's holiest places.

Cities of Salt by the late Abdul Rahman Munif [1987] is a revealing and moving account of the people of the desert written in novel form and provides a thinly veiled description of the desert kingdom and the impact of development in the early days of oil exploration. The author was born in Jordan of a Saudi father and, though the book is unfortunately banned in Saudi Arabia, like many other publications, it tells a universal tale of the tribulations of noble desert people adapting to massive change and a turbulent new world. To Westerners who have lived in Saudi Arabia and even to some native Saudis, the kingdom remains an enigma because of deeply rooted social taboos and tight control by a royal family that rarely reveals its inner self to outsiders while having close marriage and business ties to thousands of Saudi citizens. Westerners who have lived in the desert kingdom will agree that the people of Saudi Arabia are gracious, proud, and generous and make lavish displays of hospitality to their guests. In striking contrast, fanatical Wahhabi believers and ultra-conservative Wahhabi clerics captured the country's foreign aid and missionary program in the 1980s and spawned a global resurgence of militant, reactionary Muslim fundamentalism upon the world.

The Saudi government has a long history of "double-dealing" with the West, "gulling the infidel," as it is called, beginning with the clever old king, trading oil for security and buying patronage while spreading Wahhabism with its hatred of the West and calls for death to nonbelievers, including non-Wahhabi Muslims, Christians, Jews and others. The desert kingdom still remains inscrutable and enigmatic because the inner workings among senior members of the royal family are very closely guarded. Moreover, senior Saudi princes and wealthy Saudi businessmen have made regular payments to bin Laden and the al Qaeda network since at least 1995, and it is certain that many still continue to do so today, but with greater difficulty.

From the beginning, the Saudi royal family believed that their American friends would be easy to "gull" or "manage," especially with money. A distinct pattern of deceptive Saudi behavior—"gulling the infidel"—has continued from the early days of Wahhabism in the 18th century all the way to the present as a deliberate way of deceiving the West. For years, the rulers of the inscrutable desert kingdom have played both sides in a strategic game of deception and duplicity, a process that experienced Saudi observers call the "two faces" of the sphinx-like Saudis. The Saudi ambassador to the United States, Prince Bandar bin Sultan bin Abdul Aziz, has stated publicly that the Saudis have successfully cultivated nearly every senior United States government official that could help the Saudi cause with lucrative consulting contracts after their government service was finished. It should come as no surprise that Saudi money and Saudi lobbying effectiveness have resulted in muted responses by the United States government when it comes to criticism of Saudi behavior for failing to take actions against funding for terrorism, as was the case for over two years following 9/11. As Saudi oil wealth continued to accumulate beyond the wildest dream of older generations, well-placed Saudi businessmen and members of the royal family amassed fantastic fortunes in just a few years. Illegal commissions from government contracts using complex off-shore corporate schemes were common, and still are, and lucrative franchises were granted to well-positioned Saudis to distribute American products throughout Saudi Arabia and the region. While all this was developing, an international Wahhabi terror network inspired by Egyptian and Syrian Muslim Brotherhood radicals and the philosophy of Sayyid Qutb was slowly but deliberately unleashed upon the world and funded from Saudi oil revenue. Over a 25-year period, the Saudis provided as much as $70 to $90 billion in direct government support and charitable funding for Wahhabi missionaries around the world, a practice that continues. As the state religion of Saudi Arabia, Wahhabism has been exported by Saudi oil wealth to at least 60 countries or more. Regrettably, few in the West paid attention to the emerging Saudi Wahhabi threat until the events of 9/11 forced the United States to implement a bold, new strategy for the region with the invasion and liberation of Afghanistan and Iraq and an antidote to radical, militant Islam called freedom and democracy.

In his recent book, Gerald Posner [2003] summarized the failures of the United States to prevent 9/11 and exposed alarming relationships between al Qaeda, the Pakistani government, and members of the Saudi royal family. Posner stated that when American Special Forces captured Abu Zubaydah, Osama bin Laden's operations coordinator and a key member of al Qaeda, on March 28, 2002 in western Pakistan, Zubaydah was wounded in the shootout and subsequently provided detailed information to his interrogators about bin Laden's support from members of the Saudi royal family and the Pakistani government. After the Soviets withdrew from Afghanistan and the Soviet Union collapsed, bin Laden became a hero of legendary status in Saudi Arabia. However, he quickly denounced his country for Crown Prince Abdullah's refusal to accept the use of his Afghan Arab brigade to repel Saddam Hussein's invasion of Kuwait in 1990 and for the subsequent presence of 550,000 American troops on "holy" Saudi soil during the 1991 Gulf War. Posner stated that the Saudis then made a typical deal with Osama bin Laden, using millions in Saudi oil money to bribe bin Laden into permanently leaving the kingdom. In return, the Saudis would finance bin Laden's terrorist training camps in Afghanistan and as part of the agreement, bin Laden agreed not to turn his fighters against the Saudi kingdom or the royal family. According to Posner, this account comes directly from American interrogations of Abu Zubaydah after his capture in March 2002, when he also provided names of members of the Saudi royal family who had provided funding to al Qaeda. When his American interrogators accused Zubaydah of lying, he identified a triangular relationship between Saudi Arabia, Pakistan, and bin Laden. Saudi Arabia had maintained close relationships with Muslim Pakistan for many years and Saudi-Pakistani support for al Qaeda came as no surprise to the American interrogators. According to Posner, Abu Zubaydah said the Saudi connection came through HRH Prince Turki al Faisal bin Abdul Aziz, son of King Faisal and the kingdom's longtime chief of intelligence. Zubaydah said that bin Laden personally told him of a meeting in 1991 when Prince Turki agreed to let bin Laden leave Saudi Arabia in exchange for providing secret funds if al Qaeda would not promote jihad against the kingdom and the royal family. The Pakistani contact was a high-ranking air force officer named Mushaf Ali Mir and bin Laden was able to strike a deal with him to obtain arms and supplies for al Qaeda, a deal that Zubaydah said was "blessed" by the Saudis.

The other Saudi princes identified by Abu Zubaydah were Prince Ahmed bin Salman bin Abdul Aziz (nephew of King Fahd and owner of the 2002 Kentucky Derby winner, "War Emblem"); his cousin Prince Sultan bin Faisal bin Turki al Saud; and another relative, Prince Fahd bin Turki bin Saud al Kabir. Prince Turki was removed from his intelligence post and reassigned as Saudi ambassador to Great Britain in London. He has denied Abu Zubaydah's allegations, and in late 2004 won a libel suit in London from the Hachette Filipacchi publishing house after its subsidiary printed allegations of Turki's support of al Qaeda in the book *La Guerre D'Apres* by Laurent Murawiec [BBC]. Within months of Abu Zubaydah's revelations, according to Posner, all three young Saudi princes and the Pakistani Air Marshall died mysteriously, apparently killed on the orders of the Saudi royal family.

In addition to support from the Saudi royal family and other wealthy Saudis, al Qaeda and its related Islamist terrorist groups have received generous support from international Muslim charities managed and funded by Saudi Arabia. One of the pillars of Islam is charitable giving and over the past 25 years government charities have funneled billions of dollars around the world to propagate the country's strict Wahabbi faith. In the 1990s, many of the kingdom's most militant young men were dispatched overseas to proselytize and work with government approval as Wahhabi missionaries for militant activities abroad while holding diplomatic passports. The government of Saudi Arabia and its ultraconservative Wahhabi religious leaders funded Osama bin Laden and the Taliban in Afghanistan as well as large international charities such as the Al Haramain Charitable Foundation, the Muslim World League, and the World Assembly of Muslim Youth (WAMY). Only in late 2004 did the Saudis reluctantly announce that they had reorganized the Al Haramain Charitable Foundation but even that announcement remains suspect in the face of conflicting Saudi statements and the enormity of the international web of charities that the Saudis have extravagantly deployed throughout the world. The parent organization of WAMY is the International Islamic Relief Organization (IIRO) and it is a part of the Saudi government. It has also been widely reported that Saudi funding continues to support organizations such as the Council on American-Islamic Relations (CAIR), which is the most active and militant Islamist political organization in North America with chapters in nearly 30 American cities [Levitt]. According to reliable press reports, several other Muslim organizations in the United States such as the

Islamic Society of North America and the Islamic Council of North America are led by extremists and are funded directly or indirectly by the government of Saudi Arabia [Jacoby and Brink].

Even though the Saudis have demonstrated greater cooperation with the United States in the war on terrorism, Christianity and Judaism are still banned in Saudi Arabia and non-Wahhabi Shiite minority in the Eastern Province of Saudi Arabia are persecuted and forbidden to build their own mosques. From its beginning, Wahhabi beliefs against the veneration of idols and images have resulted in the destruction of ancient Islamic monuments and cemeteries in the holy cities of Mecca and Medina that they control. Even music is banned by ultra-conservative clerics and vestiges of slavery, which was not abolished in Saudi Arabia until 1962, may still be seen in the kingdom today. Wahhabi religious police patrol the streets in every Saudi city, strictly enforcing rigid provisions of harsh Islamic law. Saudi charities pay the salaries of Islamic religious leaders around the world and promote Wahhabi terrorism as a fundamental part the Saudi government's foreign policy. This type of Saudi behavior is evidenced by the recent expulsion of a Saudi religious affairs diplomat from Germany following investigations stemming from 9/11 planning activities in Germany and is a deliberate Saudi attempt to "gull" the West, especially the United States and Europe, into believing that Saudi missionary work is simply benign proselytizing that should be tolerated under the West's freedom of religion privileges.

The Gulling of America by Saudi Arabia

The "gulling" of America, or how the United States has been consistently hoodwinked by its Saudi friends, began many years before, in the early days of the old king, Abdul Aziz ibn Saud. As President Franklin Roosevelt first learned in 1945, the Saudis are fierce anti-Zionists determined to use their strategic oil resource as a weapon against Israel and the West if necessary. King Faisal, the second son and successor to his father after his full brother King Saud was deposed by the royal family, organized the Arab oil embargo against the West in 1973-74 in retaliation for American support of Israel in the October 1973 Yom Kippur war after Egypt invaded the Sinai Peninsula and threatened Israeli defeat. Fortunately, the Saudis learned that withholding oil from the market can be an expensive tactic to employ, both for themselves and their customers. When King Faisal was assassinated in 1975 by his deranged Wahhabi nephew, several Saudis claimed that the assassination was a CIA covert operation in retaliation for the oil embargo, but no concrete linkage was ever established. The real plot in the gulling of America that unfolded in the last two decades of the 20th century was purely Saudi in its origin and execution, using money to buy influence and silence critics with their immense oil wealth.

Faisal was succeeded by King Khaled, his full brother and another of the seven sons of the old king's favorite wife, Hussa bint Sudairi. Khaled continued traditional anti-Zionist Saudi policies, even denouncing President Carter's Camp David agreement and the Egyptian-Israeli peace treaty. King Khaled died from chronic heart disease in 1982 and was succeeded by King Fahd, who agreed to the deployment of 550,000 American troops into Saudi Arabia to defend the kingdom and its oil fields from Iraq's 1990 invasion of Kuwait. Except for foreign guest workers, infidels and other foreigners are excluded from traveling to Saudi Arabia because their presence is seen as a violation of the sacred and holy land of Islam.

That violation soon served as the catalyst for Osama bin Laden's declaration of war against the House of Saud and the "Great Satan," the United States of America. Although Fahd suffered a series of strokes and has been largely incapacitated since 1995, his half brother and legal successor Crown Prince Abdullah has tried to maintain reasonably good relations with the United States since 9/11 while faced with growing internal disaffection and terrorist threats at home. In a veiled threat of a renewed oil embargo during his April 2002 meeting with President Bush in Crawford, Texas, Abdullah warned that the President should tread carefully in defending Israel. Soon after that visit, George W. Bush became the first American president to announce American support for recognizing an independent Palestine state. Abdullah has walked a careful tightrope with Wahhabi fundamentalists in the kingdom and with Saudi supporters of al Qaeda who have attacked and killed over 200 Saudis, Americans, and other foreigners, even beheading an American employee of the Lockheed Martin Corporation in 2004.

Abdullah will also face a serious succession dilemma when King Fahd dies, especially if he bypasses the aging and partially paralyzed Prince Sultan or Prince Nayef, two of the favored "Sudairi Seven," and designates a younger non-Sudairi as the new crown prince. Resolution of the succession dilemma is becoming a day of reckoning for the kingdom: will the choice of the next crown prince after Abdullah be a Western-leaning member of the royal family or an ultra-conservative, reactionary Wahhabi supporter of al Qaeda? Either alternative could lead to a fierce internal struggle or civil war, especially if a charismatic, arch-fundamentalist cleric were to emerge, similar to Iran in 1979 when the Shah was deposed, and with the world's oil reserves held in the balance. Or, if the world is fortunate, perhaps a younger, more enlightened member of the royal family will emerge from the next generation of well-educated princes who can transform the country into a modern constitutional monarchy while preserving its traditional culture and Islamic values. If there is time.

While the United States and its allies have the military capability to secure the oil fields in a crisis, the global war on militant Islamist terrorism would become much more complex and dangerous if the Saudi royal family were to fall under the control of a conservative Wahhabi cleric or member of the royal family loyal to Osama bin Laden. In analyzing present-day Saudi Arabia, it is useful to remember the events that led to the fall of the Shah of Iran in 1979 and the establishment of the revolutionary Shiite Islamist theocracy under Ayatollah Khomeini. It is also important to note Osama bin Laden's goals, stated several times to the world between 1996 and 2004:

1. Replace the House of Saud in Saudi Arabia with an even more reactionary Taliban-like Islamic state, just as Khomeini targeted the Shah's regime.

2. Drive the United States from the region and reinstate the Muslim Caliphate as leader of the Sunni Muslim polity, absent since the overthrow of the Ottoman Empire after World War I.

3. Utilize Saudi oil proceeds to establish Taliban-like regimes throughout the region, proselytize the rest of the world, gain control over the Muslim world, and launch a final attack on the West.

4. Force the United States into bankruptcy.

The Saudis created the bin Laden problem by letting radical Egyptian and Syrian members of the Muslim Brotherhood poison their universities and by their consistent behavior in buying influence to gull critics into silence with money, as they have done for many years. The process of "gulling" America started when the old king met President Roosevelt in 1945 and the duping process soon involved the major oil producers and nearly the entire oil industry, as well as the United States government and hundreds of firms desiring to do business in Saudi Arabia. For years, the only information available on Saudi Arabia in the West was provided by ARAMCO. Even the United States government (including the CIA) was dependent on ARAMCO for information and intelligence on the royal family, but ARAMCO reports rarely criticized their hosts or even commented on the emerging dangers of Wahhabism and Islamist fundamentalism or the infiltration of Saudi universities by radical, militant members of the Muslim Brotherhood from Egypt and Syria.

Moreover, American politicians, retired ambassadors, retired generals, and more recently, academicians, were placed on the Saudi payroll, selling their professional credibility as defenders of the desert kingdom in Washington and European capitals and at prestigious American and European universities. The gulling of the academic community, especially Middle East studies departments in the United States and Europe, is particularly alarming. Just as Abdul Aziz ibn Saud bribed Egyptian academicians for their support, many of the most prestigious colleges and universities in the United States and Europe have accepted tens of millions of dollars in Saudi endowment funding for international Islamic centers resulting in loss of academic freedom, objectivity, and independence. In the early 1990s, the Saudis funded a special $20 million gift in honor of President Clinton for an Islamic studies department at the University of Arkansas; $5 million for the University of California at Berkeley; $2.5 million for Harvard University; and more than $30 million to dozens of other prestigious colleges and universities willing to take foreign money and not criticize Saudi Arabia, the ruling royal family, or its form of Islam [Kaplin]. American schools were not the only recipients, as shown in the following press release from the Royal Saudi Embassy in Washington, DC, announcing a $30 million gift to Oxford University in England:

> Custodian of the Two Holy Mosques King Fahd Ibn Abdul Aziz has donated twenty million pounds sterling (over U.S. $30 million) to the Islamic Studies Center at Oxford University in England. The announcement was made in London by Prince Bandar Ibn Sultan Ibn Abdul Aziz, Saudi Arabia's Ambassador to the United States, at a reception held by Prince Charles of the United Kingdom, which was also attended by a number of Arab and Islamic diplomats, officials from Oxford University, and businessmen from the Gulf Cooperation Council (GCC) states. Prince Bandar stated that this donation comes within the framework of King Fahd's constant efforts in the service of Islam throughout the world. Prince Charles expressed appreciation for the donation, and praised the significant role being played by King Fahd. It is worth mentioning that Prince Charles recently delivered a lecture highlighting the teachings of Islam and underscoring the noble values it advocates [Royal Embassy of Saudi Arabia to the United States].

The effect of these large Saudi handouts has been to silence critics and buy the support of academicians who routinely denounce Israel and the West and refuse to criticize the Palestinians, Saudi Arabia, or other autocratic Arab states. The result is blatant violation of long-standing and venerable academic principles, with the following failures of the academy:

- No full-length, objective academic study of Osama bin Laden

- Factual, analytical errors, serious academic mistakes, and intolerance of opposing points of view

- Unwillingness to confront oppression of women and repression in the Arab world

- No objective examination of violent global Jihad and Muslim anti-Semitism

- Obvious extremism, openly expressed hostility toward the United States and Israel

Millions in direct Saudi government funding were funneled either directly or through Saudi charities for Islamic Centers at major American universities to buy academic influence. Funds from one of the world's wealthiest individuals and more enlightened members of the Saudi royal family, Prince Al Waleed ibn Talal ibn Abdul Aziz, number five on Forbes' 2004 rich list, have been provided for international centers of Islamic and American studies with typical Wahhabi strings attached. Shortly after 9/11, New York Mayor Rudy Giuliani rejected Al Waleed's $10 million donation for his bigoted statements critical of American Middle East policy and Israel that were seen as a condition of providing the gift.

The Saudis have been very adept in assembling and maintaining a large and strong team of supporters in the United States and Europe, and they have been astutely led in Washington, DC for over 20 years by Prince Bandar bin Sultan bin Abdul Aziz, Saudi ambassador to the United States since 1983, and nephew to King Fahd. Bandar spent 17 years in the Royal Saudi Air Force as a fighter pilot, graduating from the RAF's West Point, Cranwell, the U.S. Air Force Command and Staff College and The Industrial College of the Armed Forces in Washington, DC. Bandar knows his way around the power centers of the American Capital and along the way managed to complete a graduate degree in international relations from the School of Advanced International Studies at Johns Hopkins University. Bandar was promoted to the rank of Minister in 1995 but his influence in Washington, London, and Saudi Arabia seems to have slipped since 9/11 and especially since the American invasion of Iraq. Bandar's lower profile indicates a division between Bandar's father, Prince Sultan bin Abdul Aziz, who is Minister of Defense and Aviation, Minister of Interior Prince Nayef, and Crown Prince Abdullah, the acting ruler and next king. In any event, Bandar has been extremely effective as ambassador for over 20 years, gaining access to the White House under successive presidents as well as to senior levels in the Defense

Department, State Department, and key Congressional Committees. Bandar is well known in Washington for his lavish private parties, fondness for the Dallas Cowboys football team, and many well-placed contacts throughout the country.

Ominously, Bandar's ambassadorship bears a striking similarity to that of the son-in-law of the Shah of Iran, Ardeshir Zahedi, who commanded the spotlight of Washington diplomacy for many years before the Shah was overthrown by radical, militant Islamist Shiites in 1979. Like Bandar, Zahedi had nearly unlimited power in Washington and enjoyed full access to the White House, State Department, Congress, and senior levels in the private sector. Zahedi now lives in exile in Switzerland.

DETERIORATING SAUDI-AMERICAN RELATIONS

The United States paid little attention to Saudi Arabia until the Arab oil embargo following the October 1973 Arab-Israeli war, and much has happened since then to change the basic relationship between the United States and Saudi Arabia. When the Arab oil embargo led to the quadrupling of oil prices in the 1970s, the Saudis quickly received a windfall of billions of dollars in oil income, marking the start of the Saudi oil bonanza. But no sooner had the Saudis started to enjoy their new oil riches than the Shah of Iran was overthrown in 1979 and Shiite fundamentalist revolutionary leaders established a Shiite Islamic theocracy in Iran. In the same month, November 1979, Wahhabi extremists seized the Grand Mosque in Mecca and in December the Soviet Union invaded Afghanistan to counter Islamic instability along its southern borders.

These overpowering late 1979 events prompted Osama bin Laden to create his Saudi Brigade and the Saudi and American governments generated funding for Mujahadeen Afghan fighters—"holy warriors"—to counter the atheistic Soviet incursion into Afghanistan. The Iran-Iraq War broke out in 1980 and in 1981 Wahhabi-influenced Egyptian radicals assassinated President Sadat and recently radicalized Saudi Wahhabis started funding radical, militant schools (Islamist madrassas) throughout North Africa and Pakistan, preaching hatred and death to infidels, and providing inspiration for the Afghanistan Taliban regime that came to power after the Soviets withdrew from Afghanistan in 1989. The fall of the Iron Curtain that same year signaled the ultimate demise of the Soviet

Union and two years later Osama bin Laden claimed victory against Soviet communism and atheism.

Impact of the First Gulf War

When Iraq invaded Kuwait in 1990 and the United States and its allies sent nearly one million troops into Saudi Arabia and the neighboring Gulf countries, the subsequent 1991 Gulf War motivated Osama bin Laden, with the support of Saudi Wahhabi clerics, to take on the other "Great Satan," the United States. In their mind, America's sin was intruding on Islam's holy land with 550,000 crusading American infidel soldiers, undermining Islam, and threatening Muslim customs with offensive Western culture and values such as freedom and democracy. Throughout the 1990s, Saudi-backed Hamas suicide bombers stepped up attacks on Israel while Saudi-funded Wahhabi forces supported violent jihad in the Balkans.

With the September 11, 2001 attacks against the American homeland, Osama bin Laden and his Saudi hijackers became 21st century Wahhabi "martyr" heroes in the eyes of almost all the Arab world. Even today Osama bin Laden derives great appeal among many people in the Arab world and especially in Saudi Arabia. A majority of Saudis and the very Wahhabi Islamist teachers and clerics that are still part of the autocratic Saudi government have elevated bin Laden to the status of a modern Arab Robin Hood and marvel at his elusiveness in fighting American military forces and the seductive quality of his Koranic statements on Al Jazeera television and the Internet. Recent Arab opinion polls indicate that most Arab people typically receive their news from Al Jazeera or Al Arabiya and say that their idol is Osama bin Laden because he defends Islam. They also say that suicide "martyrdom" is justified in their eyes because the greatest glory is to die in the defense of Islam and that their friends agree with their opinions.

After the Iranian Shiite revolution and seizure of the Grand Mosque in Mecca by Wahhabi militants in 1979 and the subsequent Soviet invasion of Afghanistan, King Fahd directed the deployment of billions in foreign assistance through Wahhabi-controlled institutions to fund new Wahhabi schools and mosques, especially in Western Pakistan. The Saudis had opened Pandora's Box and the satanic genie of radical, militant Islamist fundamentalism was no longer contained.

Decade of the 1990s

During the decade of the 1990s following the demise of the Soviet Union and the first Gulf War, the world experienced an unprecedented period of economic growth, following a new wave of technology and rapid globalization that had started a decade earlier. American values of freedom, democracy, and privatization were validated around the world as ideal political and economic concepts. They swept around the globe as the winning alternatives to totalitarian Communism while capitalism, free markets, and free trade radiated as beacons of hope, and cumbersome state-controlled industries transferred to more efficient private ownership. The result was the most extensive and most rapid globalization process that the world economy had ever witnessed and it was further fueled by the computer-telecommunications revolution, mushrooming global Internet connectivity, and the seemingly endless American "dotcom" stock market bubble that finally burst in early 2000.

The United States looked inward in the 1990s even as war was declared several times by Osama bin Laden, with successive al Qaeda-supported terrorist attacks against U.S. facilities in Saudi Arabia, Somalia, Kenya, Tanzania, and Yemen. The result was a perception throughout the Arab-Muslim world and by bin Laden and his fellow Islamist militants that the United States and Western democracies in general were decadent, impotent, selfish, and immoral paper tigers. Bin Laden's incorrect analysis inspired a sense of renewed hatred for Western ideals of freedom and democracy which he believed undermined "pure" Wahhabi-Salafist values. In parallel, throughout the 1990s, a creeping spread of hate-filled Wahhabi-Salafism enveloped the world through expanded Saudi funding of international Islamic charities, schools, and mosques, while bin Laden issued periodic fatwas with a bleated call for reinstatement of the Sunni Muslim Caliphate and death to infidels and nonbelievers.

The loss of the Muslim Caliphate remains a serious problem for the Sunni Islamic faithful because today Islam has no central religious authority, no Pope-like leader, as Sunni Islam had experienced under successive Caliphates that ended with the fall of the Ottoman Empire at the end of the First World War. The two major groups in the world of Islam are represented by the Sunnis with about 90 percent of the world's 1.5 billion Muslims and the Shiites with 10 percent or so. Islam has had a long history of both tolerance and extremism, with great and lasting cultural and scientific achievements during its "Golden Age" while Europe was trapped in medieval superstition, oppression and economic stagnation. But the world of Islam differs from the rest of the world in that, with the exception of Turkey, it does not acknowledge or recognize compatibility with the separation of church and state as practiced in the West. In Saudi Arabia, government and religion are one and the same. Ultra-conservative Sunni Wahhabism is the state religion, commanding nearly every facet of life in the desert kingdom. As the most fundamentalist Islamist sect in the world today, Saudi Arabia's Wahhabis administer the quintessence of the most reactionary form of Islamic law.

For over 25 years, Saudi Wahhabism has been spread around the world using billions in Saudi wealth coming from its vast oil reserves along the shores of the Persian Gulf in the Eastern Province. While the world's economy has rapidly globalized over the last 25 years and trading nations have become more interdependent, Saudi Arabian Wahhabism has had free rein to use the most modern technology paid for by its oil wealth to spread its hate-filled dogma with little or no competition in the struggle for the heart and soul of Islam.

Beginning of an Arab Spring

Today the world is witnessing the onset of dramatic change in the Middle East that is long overdue, yet the world is also witnessing a nihilistic form of terrorism, dedicated to the destruction of freedom and democracy in the name of Allah through indiscriminate bombings, barbaric violence and grotesque beheadings. Good people of many persuasions around the world ask, "How could such utter barbarism occur in the 21st century?" The answer, unfortunately, comes back to haunt us in the origins of radical, militant Islam and one of America's closest allies in the Middle East, Saudi Arabia. Bernard Lewis [2003], distinguished emeritus professor from Princeton University and one of the world's foremost Middle East scholars, has written the following insightful observation on Saudi Wahhabism:

> Imagine if the Ku Klux Klan or Aryan Nation obtained total control of Texas and had at its disposal all of the oil revenues, and used this money to establish a network of well-endowed schools and colleges all over Christendom peddling their particular brand of Christianity. This is what the Saudis have done with Wahhabism. The oil money has enabled them to spread this fanatical, destructive form of Islam all over the Muslim world and among Muslims in the West. Without oil and the creation of the Saudi kingdom, Wahhabism would have remained a lunatic fringe.

Saudi Wahhabi propaganda succeeded in ways unimaginable only a few years ago, resulting in serious assaults on Western civilization and its basic values, assaults from within and without, inspired by perceived American weakness in the 1990s and manifested by vicious anti-Americanism and disturbing neo anti-Semitism, especially in Europe.

There is a pervasive lack of knowledge and general naiveté among well-meaning people in the United States and Europe regarding the origins of militant Islamism and Bin Ladenism and the Saudi Wahhabi threat. There is also a lack of familiarity with Islam in general in the West and a deplorable lack of objective attention paid to the Saudi Wahhabi problem by the international news media and academic community. With nearly unlimited financial resources and infected with reactionary clerical fanaticism, Saudi Wahhabism inspired rapidly growing militant Islamist fundamentalism throughout the Arab world. The Wahhabi ideology of hate was reinforced with old Nazi and Soviet anti-American and anti-Semitic propaganda that still resides in the Middle East, especially in student textbooks, and by a sense of hopelessness among the large and youthful Arab-Muslim population in the greater Middle East. But, in the words of Daniel Pipes [2002]:

> It's a mistake to blame Islam, a religion 14 centuries old, for the evil that should be ascribed to militant Islam, a totalitarian ideology less than a century old. Militant Islam is the problem, but moderate Islam is the solution.

The real problem is to find the voices of moderation, but some are beginning to bravely appear, as in the Spanish Muslim fatwa that was issued against bin Laden in March 2005 on the first anniversary of the Madrid bombing. To be effective, tolerance must be reciprocal, but Islam, even in its moderate variants, rarely expresses toleration for nonbelievers or apostates. American Secretary of State Condoleezza Rice accurately described the Arab-Muslim world as suffering from "a poverty of dignity," while the supercharged Arab-Israeli conflict and corrupt, autocratic regimes in the region have created an environment primed to explode even further if political and economic conditions do not rapidly change. That is why it is vital for the West to succeed in the global war on terrorism and for the United States to succeed in its humanitarian mission in Iraq to reshape the landscape of the Middle East, undo some of the wrongs of the past, and provide the basis for hope and a better future through freedom, democracy, and economic liberalization.

The dawn of an Arab spring is at hand yet the brittle domain of Islam, especially in the Arab world, remains fixed in the past and seems incapable of creating the conditions needed to accommodate the modern world and provide freedom, dignity, and prosperity for its people. The concluding section of this chapter discusses the complexities of the Saudi-American relationship and what drove America's response to the bin Laden challenge after Saudi Arabia's long-standing "gulling" of America over the years and Saudi Arabia's reliability as a partner in the war on global terror.

RHETORICAL ROYAL REMARKS

The Saudis have a long history of double-dealing and gulling their friends and neighbors, saying one thing and doing another, and we will probably never know if is polygamy or some other personality trait that promotes gulling and provides a high Saudi comfort level in duplicitous activities. Most Saudis would agree that their country has many problems and that past difficulties were often the unintended results of typical negligent Saudi oversight, doing things the "Saudi" way. Like many countries and many people the world over, Saudi Arabia has tended to deal with problems by ignoring them as long as possible, sticking their heads in the sand. But when problems became so great that they could no longer be ignored, Saudis would typically first throw money at them to silence critics, often making a public statement in English and then another version in Arabic with a different meaning. Most Saudis know that this behavior is counterproductive and damaging, especially in the post-9/11 era of the Iraq war and al Qaeda attacks on Saudi soil. The challenge for the royal family is to reform a political system that has never been inclusive and serves to empower dissidents because open discussion is forbidden. The rulers fear to loosen their grip on power and the dilemma they face is the possibility of further empowering the ultra-conservative Wahhabi clerics and failing to reestablish trust between the royal family and Saudi citizens who realize that change must be made before it is too late.

After persistent al Qaeda attacks against targets throughout the kingdom in 2003 and 2004 that killed over 200 people, it appeared that the Saudi royal family had finally started to modify its behavior and that a slow transformation might take place in Saudi Arabia. As Saudi observers know, "nothing is easy in the desert," but one sign of progress in the summer of 2004, among others, was an open letter written by a senior member of the Saudi royal family and Governor of the western Asir Region, Prince Khaled al Faisal ibn Abdul Aziz. The letter is significant because Prince Khaled is the son of the assassinated King Faisal and grandson of King Abdul Aziz ibn Saud, and also because the beautiful Asir region of southwestern Saudi Arabia was home to many of the 9/11 hijackers and some of the most arch-conservative Wahhabi clerics in the kingdom. Here is what Prince Khaled al Faisal recently said to his people in Asir:

> I have a lively sense of the honor of being a Muslim and being led by the king, and I am particularly honored to serve Asir, a region that I fell in love with at first sight. Asiris are full of fun and optimism even when they come to me at the municipality to complain or demand new projects. And always, they begin the discussion with beautiful tales about fathers and grandfathers who took part in the struggles of King Abdul Aziz to establish this (government) structure and build this state. They are proud of the past and hopeful about the future. When they ask for a new project, they ask in a spirit of optimism, not to reproach because it isn't there. They make you feel a sense of partnership in building the future, rather than pushing you away with accusations about the shortcomings of the present.
> What happened to them?
> How did their brightness leave them?
> Who made the smiles disappear from their faces and drew curtains of misery across them?
> Who scared the children away from laughter, play, and joy?
> Who scared the adults from life? Who killed happiness and spread sorrow?
> Who convinced our sons and daughters to call their fathers and mothers infidel?
> Who teaches children in orphanages that Saudi Arabia is not their home?
> That their only home is Islam?
> That their future vocation is jihad?
> That watching Saudi television or listening to music is forbidden?
> Who transformed schools and universities into military camps?
> Who transformed our summer camps into weapon training grounds?
> Who convinced Saudi youth that the surest path to Heaven is to blow themselves up and take citizens, foreign residents, and security officers with them?
> Who did this to us? I think we all know who is responsible for all this.
> A look at the books, pamphlets, and tapes that have been distributed by the thousands in the schools, universities, mosques and charities over the past 20 years, we will see their names clearly legible in black and white. The web sites reveal the rest.
> The important question now is: Who can change this new painful reality?
> Who can return to us the minds of our sons and daughters that these demagogues have stolen?
> The answer is that all of society is responsible, from the state and our seniormost scholars to every individual citizen, but above all teachers and academics, imams and khateebs (prayer and sermon leaders), and Islamic missionaries.

To all of them, in the name of every decent citizen who loves his home and religion, I say:
Please, please give back the smile, the brightness, the life to our sons and daughters, and our home.
Thank you.

The world has already learned that toleration of unmoderated Saudi Wahhabism and Bin Ladenism can only lead to collective suicide, and Prince Khaled al Faisal, speaking to the faithful in Saudi Arabia, eloquently sounded that caution. The lethal virus of ultra-orthodox fundamentalism came back to haunt the Saudis and now they and the world are paying the price. Saudi Arabia has legitimate security concerns, and its swift actions against the al Qaeda terrorists, who have attacked multiple targets in the kingdom, were significant, but many additional questions arise from Prince Khaled bin Faisal's penetrating rhetorical remarks:

Can the Saudis secure and defend their large country and their oil fields, ports, and pipelines while controlling the Muslim charities and radical clerics whose power is at risk?

Can the Saudis delegitimize bin Laden and win the ideological struggle with the archconservative Wahhabi clerics, opening up free discussion and the political process for the Saudi middle class?

Can the Saudis document the participation of Saudi citizens in support of al Qaeda—royal family included—and publish a public report?

Will the Saudi government support the organizers of a petition for a constitutional democracy and shut down radical, jihadist web sites that freely publish Wahhabi hate messages?

Will the Saudis publicly identify, arrest, and bring to justice Saudi citizens who finance al Qaeda?

Is it possible that some members of the royal family have used al Qaeda to protect itself and its Wahhabi clerics against increased demands from Saudi reformers?

Can the Saudis slow their high birthrate, cut the huge foreign workforce, be a credible member of the World Trade Organization (WTO), bring women into the workforce, and create meaningful jobs for the large number of young people entering the workforce?

Can the Saudis manage their economy without corruption, ensure that human rights are protected according to international standards, and convince its people that manageable change will create better lives for all?

Can Saudi Arabia create a climate of tolerance for other Muslims—Shiites and Sufis included—and for Jews, Christians, and all religions, and can the royal family disestablish itself from reactionary Wahhabism?

Can the royal family and its next generation of leaders successfully guide the country toward implementing peaceful and democratizing reforms?

Can the Saudis stop the gulling of America, control its foreign intelligence agents and Wahhabi missionaries, and keep the United States as a partner during the global struggle against Islamist terror—for without the United States and the West, aren't Saudi Arabia's problems truly insurmountable?

These are difficult questions and this is a very tall order for Saudi Arabia, the United States, and the West, and though the gulling may stop, the process of introducing needed reform has only just started. It is hoped that reform will evolve in a way that is compatible with Saudi culture and that Saudi citizens continue to trust the United States as a friend and ally with a long tradition of working unselfishly to create a better world for all. The United States is far from perfect and has much to do in getting its own house in order, but since the end of Second World War, the United States has led the world in creating the United Nations in 1945, and through the American Marshall Plan in 1947 completely rebuilt Germany and Japan after their unconditional surrender. And then, after defeating the Soviet Union in the Cold War, the United States and its allies reintegrated Eastern Europe and Russia back into the democratic West.

These were colossal transformations of the international order and now the world's mission, once again led by the United States and over 100 allies around the globe including Saudi Arabia, is to eradicate radical, militant, Islamist terrorism—Bin Ladenism—and build permanent structures that will lead to a transformation of the entire Middle East through implementation of the Bush Doctrine of freedom, democracy, and economic liberalization as the antidote to hate-filled Bin Ladenism. While that is happening, the United States and its partners must remember that appeasement of Bin Ladenism can only lead to collective suicide, not only for the West, but also for the world of Islam.

And the West must also begin to take coordinated action in recognizing that continued dependence on increasingly unreliable imported oil threatens American national security and the security of the Western world.

Wahhabism's ideology of intolerance is the basis for Saudi Arabia's fanatical and destructive religious faith. It comes as no surprise that Osama bin Laden and 15 of the 19 hijackers on 9/11 were not only Saudis, but were also profoundly influenced by the teachings of intolerant, hate-filled Wahhabism and the influential teachings of Sayyid Qutb and the Egyptian Muslim Brotherhood. Political and economic reform across the Arab-Muslim world is the only credible long-term remedy to counter the depredations of militant Islam and global terrorism. The United States is guiding the West in extending NATO into Eastern Europe with a new mission to combat Islamist terrorism in Afghanistan and Iraq. The United States is leading the world's effort to move the Middle East into the 21st century with meaningful and lasting political, economic, and social reform with the banners of freedom and democracy leading the way. American idealists and allies in the war on terror believe in this epic and historic mission much as abolitionists and staunch unionists during the long and bloody American Civil War deeply believed in Lincoln's unremitting efforts to wield the "terrible swift sword" and bring freedom to an enslaved people. So, too, does the United States lead the world today in its call to free the oppressed people of the Middle East and nurture seeds of freedom and democracy in the dry and arid political sands of Arab despotism, echoing a clarion call of the eternal and self-evident truths of the American Declaration of Independence.

How the United States has chosen to deal with Saudi Arabia and its problems is the subject of the next chapter on the Bush post 9/11 foreign policy and America's new hope of freedom and democracy for all of humankind as an antidote to militant Islamism.

CHAPTER THREE BIBLIOGRAPHY

Alexiev, Alex, "Wahhabism: State-Sponsored Extremism Worldwide," *Testimony before U.S. Senate Committee on Terrorism, Technology and Homeland Security*, June 26, 2003, http://www.centerforsecuritypolicy.org/index.jsp?section=static&page=alexievtestimony.

Benoit, Bertrand, "EU Body Shelves Report on Anti-Semitism," *Financial Times*, November 21, 2003.

British Broadcasting Corporation, "News: Saudi Prince Gets Libel Damages," December 6, 2004, http//www:BBC.co.uk/2/hi/uk/-news/4072219.stm.

Central Intelligence Agency, *The World Fact Book*, Washington, DC: Government Printing Office, 2004.

Clarke, Richard A., *Against All Enemies: Inside America's War on Terror,* New York: Free Press, 2004.

CNN.com, "Terrorist acts of bin Laden 'totally banned'" Friday, March 11, 2005, http://www.cnn.com/2005/WORLD/europe/03/10/spain.fatwa.osama.ap/.

CNS News, "More Mosques in France Falling Under Sway of Radicals," www.CNSNews.com, Paris, June 30, 2004.

Colson, Chuck, "Evangelizing for Evil in Our Prisons: Radical Islamists Seek to Turn Criminals into Terrorists," *Wall Street Journal,* June 24, 2002.

Ferguson, Niall, "The End of Europe?," American Enterprise Institute Bradley Lecture, March 1, 2004, http://www.aei.org/news/filter.,newsID.20045/news_detail.asp.

Hartford Seminary, Institute for Religious Research in Connecticut, "Mosque in America," a part of "Faith Communities Today," April 2001.

Jacoby, Mary and Brink, Graham, "Saudi Form of Islam Wars with Moderates," *St. Petersburg Times,* March 11, 2003.

Kaplin, Lee, "The Saudi Fifth Column on Our Nation's Campuses," *FrontPage Magazine.com,* April 5, 2004, http://www.frontpagemag.com/articles/ReadArticle.asp?ID=12833.

Khaled al Faisal bin Abdul Aziz, Prince, "Open Letter to the People of Saudi Arabia," *Ain-Al-Yaqee, Weekly Arab Political Magazine,* July 16, 2004.

Khaled bin Sultan Abdul Aziz, Prince and General, *Desert Warrior: A Personal View of the Gulf War by the Joint Forces Commander,* New York: HarperCollins, 1995.

Kyle, Senator Jon, Statement Before Senate Judiciary Subcommittee on Technology, Terrorism and Homeland Security, United States Senate, Washington, DC: July 2003.

Levitt, Matthew, "Subversion from Within: Saudi Funding of Islamic Extremist Groups Undermining U.S. Interests and the War on Terror from within the United States," *Testimony before the Senate Judiciary Subcommittee on Terrorism, Technology, and Homeland Security, Washington Institute for Near East Policy,* Washington, DC: September 10, 2003.

Lewis, Bernard, *The Crisis of Islam: Holy War and Unholy Terror,* New York: Modern Library, 2003.

McPhee, Michele, "Eastie gang linked to al Qaeda," *Boston Herald,* January 5, 2005, http://news.bostonherald.com/localRegional/view.bg?articleid=61903.

Mintz, John, and Vistica, Gregory L., "Muslim Troops' Loyalty a Delicate Question," *Washington Post,* November 2, 2003.

Munif, Abdul Rahman, *Cities of Salt,* translated from Arabic to English by Peter Theroux, New York: Cape Cod Scriveners Company, 1987.

Murawiec, Laurent, "The Wacky World of French Intellectuals," *Middle East Quarterly,* Spring 2002, www.meforum.org/article/37/.

Pipes, Daniel, "The evil isn't Islam," *New York Post,* July 30, 2002, http://danielpipes.org/article/437.

Posner, Gerald, *Why America Slept: The Failure to Prevent 9/11,* New York: Random House, 2003.

Royal Embassy of Saudi Arabia, "King Fahd Donates to U.K.'s Oxford Islamic Studies Center," Washington, DC, Embassy Press Release, *Islam News Story,* 1997.

Schumer, Senator Chuck, "Press Release," May 14, 2003. http://schumer.senate.gov/ Schumer Website/pressroom/press_releases/PR01704.html.

Schwartz, Stephen, *Two Faces of Islam: The House of Saud from Tradition to Terror,* New York: Doubleday, 2002.

___, "Interview," *Frontpagemag.com*, December 13, 2004, http://www.frontpagemag. Com/articles/ReadArticle.asp?ID=16283.

Taspinar, Omer, "Europe's Muslim Street," *Foreign Policy*, March 2003, http://www. brookings.edu/views/op-ed/fellows/taspinar20030301.html.

Wyatt, Caroline, "Liberty, Equality and the Headscarf (France)," December 20, 2003,   http://www.mabonline.net/activities/   nat events/nationalhijabprotest/humanrights.htm.

4

The Bush Doctrine:
Raising the Cost to the Terrorists
and Providing an Antidote

This chapter discusses Middle East developments in the context of the foreign policy of the United States and Western security arrangements in the post-Cold War era. Many of the early Islamist terrorist attacks in the 1970s and 1980s occurred while the United States was still preoccupied with the Soviet Union and were considered trivial in the rigid environment of the Cold War. When the Cold War ended in 1989 with the fall of the Berlin Wall, and Iraq strayed from acceptable limits by invading Kuwait in 1990, the attention of the United States was finally directed to the Middle East. The U.S. foreign policy standard for dealing with Iraq's breach of acceptable behavior was the Truman Doctrine of containment through collective security alliances developed in the aftermath of World War II.

Following the precepts of the Truman Doctrine in the first Gulf War, President George H. W. Bush organized a vast alliance to counter Iraq's invasion of Kuwait and restore the legitimate government, returning the region to status quo ante bellum as the United States had done so successfully in following the containment doctrine in its struggle with the Soviet Union. The first President Bush was so successful in pushing Saddam Hussein out of Kuwait in 1991 with his "new world order" alliance that the concept of grand alliances became standard procedure for military planning and American responses to subsequent crises in Haiti, Rwanda, Bosnia, and Kosovo.

During the 43 years the United States followed the Truman Doctrine of communist containment, moral values in diplomacy were undercut by the stark realism of the serious threat posed by the free world's intransigent communist enemy. The United States had become uncomfortably tolerant of totalitarian states, as long as those states were on the U.S. side in the Cold War. It supported all sorts of dictators as long as they were friendly to the United States in the war against communism. When the Cold War ended with the collapse of the Soviet Union, American support for these dictators also ended and, without implying causality, the number of democracies blossomed throughout the world. In the last half of the 20th century, the number of countries with democratic governance increased from 22 to 120 nations, "an astonishing 63 percent of the people on the planet" [Koh, 147]. The exception to this remarkable growth of democratic governments was the Middle East where, because of the West's dependence on oil, the United States sought stability and was reluctant to advocate democratization or regime change in the region. The price for such advocacy was thought to be too high because the disruption of oil supplies could cause too much turmoil in the West's market economies. America's tolerance for unacceptable behavior was especially true of its relations with Saudi Arabia. But tolerance for despots and America's timidity toward the Middle East would soon be a thing of the past.

FORMULATING AND INITIATING A NEW FOREIGN POLICY

The violent attack of September 11th on the Pentagon and the Twin Towers of the World Trade Center meant that the United States desperately needed to redirect its foreign policy toward a new and unconventional enemy in the post-Cold War era. For the first time since the Barbary pirates in the early 19th century, the United States was fighting an undeclared war against religious zealots who were not a part of a sovereign state. Truman's containment policy evolved over nine years after 1939 when George Kennan wrote the first of his two famous memoranda, this one from the Riga outpost in Latvia outlining the threat to the West from the revolutionary nature of the Soviet Union's communist ideology [Yergin]. In President Truman's near-final statement of the containment doctrine in an address before a joint session of Congress on March 17, 1948, the President said:

> We have reached a point at which the position of the United States should be made clear…There are times in world history when it is far wiser to act than to hesitate. There is some risk involved in action—there always is. But there is far more risk in failure to act.

The Extension of Sovereignty

In September of 2001, the United States reached another such point in its history, requiring a new and clear formulation of American foreign policy. Only eleven days after the al Qaeda attack, on September 20th, President Bush's address to another joint session of Congress began that reformulation by stating:

> Our response involves far more than instant retaliation and isolated strikes. Americans should not expect one battle, but a lengthy campaign, unlike any other we have seen. It may include dramatic strikes, visible on TV, and covert operations, secret even in success. We will starve terrorists of funding, turn them one against another, drive them from place to place, until there is no refuge or rest. *And we will pursue nations that provide aid or safe haven to terrorism. Every nation, in every region, now has a decision to make. From this day forward, any nation that continues to harbor or support terrorists will be regarded by the United States as a hostile regime...*[Emphasis added]

In one paragraph of a 41-minute speech to a joint session of Congress and the American people less than two weeks after 9/11, President Bush laid out enough new policy, one of redefining the meaning of a nation's sovereignty to encompass nongovernmental actions taken by other parties on or from its sovereign territory, to outline his administration's immediate response to al Qaeda for the remainder of 2001. He also warned Americans that the country's first response would only be the beginning of a "lengthy campaign" in a war that would be like no other that the United States had ever waged.

Although most Americans were struck by the rapidity of the Bush administration's response, the new definition of sovereignty, just like Truman's policy of containment, had a similar nine-year gestation period. The origins of the developing new Bush Doctrine had been established in 1992 late in the first President Bush's term in office by Paul Wolfowitz, who had earlier served as head of the State Department policy planning staff during the Reagan administration, the same position George Kennan had held after the Second World War when he inspired the containment policy. Wolfowitz, a University of Chicago Ph.D. in political science and a neo-conservative (the only one in the Bush administration holding a key national security policy position), in many respects had some Kennan-like characteristics. He was an intellectual who never seemed to fit at the top in a cabinet-level position, but who exerted great influence in determining policy for the new Bush administration, serving both Cheney in the Reagan administration and later Rumsfeld as the undersecretary of defense for policy. His 1992 draft Defense Planning Guidance policy paper, which was leaked to the press and withdrawn by the more cautious first President Bush, stated:

> '...that in dealing with this [the spread of weapons of mass destruction] threat, America should not rely upon the strategies of deterrence and containment that had worked against the Soviet Union but should contemplate the possibility of offensive military action. There might be a need, the draft statement said, for 'preempting an impending action with nuclear, chemical or biological weapons' [Mann, 200].

The new principle of preemption would have to gestate for a year following 9/11, but the redefinition of a nation's sovereignty was needed both to cope with al Qaeda's lack of sovereignty and the logical difficulty of incorporating such a stateless group into the framework of international jurisprudence, and the new shape of the world in which the United States was the sole superpower. Bush's answer was quite straightforward but revolutionary for the time. Wherever al Qaeda existed or received support, that community had to be a part of some sovereign state and he proposed to hold that nation responsible for "harboring and supporting" a terrorist group that was violating all reasonable sanctions of international law. Therefore, the United States would, henceforth, hold all such nations as being hostile to its legitimate interests and subject to retribution for al Qaeda's crimes against humanity. He offered all nations a choice of whether to support al Qaeda and become an enemy of the United States or join America and be an ally in the war that had been declared on the United States and the rest of Western civilization. America's defense would no longer be bound by collective security arrangements, or actions of the United Nations Security Council. The United States was now strong enough and sufficiently committed to act unilaterally and it intended to do everything possible to safeguard its national security. The term "unilateral," unthinkable in the legacy of Franklin Delano Roosevelt and Harry Truman, was now an applicable description of America's new foreign policy, as would become clearer in Bush's subsequent addresses that unfolded the Bush Doctrine.

Application in Afghanistan—A Learning Experience

Not only did President Bush quickly enunciate a major plank in his foreign policy, but the United States brought the full force of American power against those responsible for the September 11th attack by launching an invasion of the al Qaeda headquarters in Afghanistan less than one month later on October 7,

2001. The timetable was quite remarkable in light of the remoteness of Afghanistan, the lack of access treaties with the six surrounding countries (Iran, Turkmenistan, Uzbekistan, Tajikistan, Pakistan and China) and the lack of any prior military planning to establish satisfactory arrangements with these nations to deploy sufficient military personnel, supplies and equipment. After the diplomacy and planning, there was also the sheer physical difficulty of moving the manpower, munitions, and supplies far away into the rugged mountains of remote Afghanistan.

By coincidence, the head of the Pakistani Inter-Services Intelligence agency, General Mahmoud Ahmad, happened to be in Washington on 9/11. The next day Richard Armitage, the burly American undersecretary of state and close friend of Secretary Powell, called General Ahmad to his office to lay out the administration's needs with the admonition: "History starts today," followed by, "Are you with us or against us?" [Mann, 298-9]. Ahmad wired the American requirements outlined by Armitage to President Musharraf who agreed to: (1) a secret American presence on its side of the Afghan border but no U.S. troops were officially allowed to be stationed within its borders; (2) U.S. planes could use Pakistani airspace but not its air bases, except for emergencies; and (3) the Pakistani military would increase border patrols to reduce al Qaeda escape avenues into Pakistan, but with no promises to capture and turn over would-be escapees. Indeed, Musharraf went so far as to request that the United States not invade Afghanistan and instead tried to negotiate with the Taliban regime to turn over Osama bin Laden, but to whom was never made clear [Friedman,185-6]. Needless to say, Musharraf's negotiations proved fruitless, and Americans moved quickly into Afghanistan in late September 2001.

Because three of the nations adjacent to Afghanistan (Turkmenistan, Uzbekistan and Tajikistan) were former members of the Soviet Union, the first set of access negotiations had to be with Russia, which still considered these nations part of its sphere of influence. Armitage flew to Moscow the week after 9/11 to seek Russian assistance from Prime Minister Putin. By September 22nd, the Russians agreed to help the United States in exchange for an agreement by the United States to eliminate public criticism of Russian actions in Chechnya and provide assistance in stopping arms smuggling to the Chechen rebels through Georgia where the U.S. had substantial influence. Bases in Uzbekistan and Tajikistan were thus made available to American forces and, for the first time, men and materials began moving into Central Asia. Covert American agents, veterans of the Afghan-Russian war 20 years earlier, were dropped into northern Afghanistan as quickly as possible with $70 million in hundred dollar bills to buy loyalty among the anti-Taliban mujahadeen forces and an instant American-supported Afghan army was formed, paid for, and deployed.

Another set of highly sensitive negotiations began in late September with Iran. The British Foreign Minister Jack Straw traveled to Tehran to begin discussions about cooperation with the Afghan invasion. The British had been on board in the Afghan operation from the beginning [Woodward, 2003] and maintained a long history of working closely with the U.S. in the Persian Gulf region since the first Gulf War; it was American and British fliers that enforced the "no fly" provisions of the U.N. resolutions to protect the Kurds and the Shiites in Iraq. In addition, direct discussions between the United States and Iran took place secretly in Geneva under a multi-nation umbrella. Iran agreed to cooperate actively with American efforts to topple the Taliban and agreed to close its border against escaping al Qaeda members in exchange for America's guarantee of the rights of the Shiite population in Afghanistan in a new Afghan government. Despite Bush's objections to Clinton's nation-building activities in the 2000 presidential campaign, his administration was inevitably forced into the business of rebuilding Afghanistan while its initial goal had simply been to use Afghanistan as a hunting ground in its search for the al Qaeda leader and his followers.

After the United States issued an ultimatum to the Taliban government to surrender bin Laden and his fellow terrorists and to close down al Qaeda's training camps, or suffer the consequences, the U.S. initiated a softening-up bombing operation of the few known targets in Afghanistan and announced the support of Great Britain and Australia in its military campaign to overthrow the Taliban regime. The United States received other offers of military assistance from several European nations, including France, but with the type of operation the U.S. was planning to execute in Afghanistan, other forces would have been a distraction, as they had been in Bosnia with combined NATO operations.

America's experience with covert support for Afghan guerrillas in the earlier anti-Soviet campaign meant that its CIA covert agents and Special Forces personnel were well-informed about the Afghan groups that would oppose the Taliban government. The veterans of the previous operation were in Afghanistan a week before the commencement of bombing on October 7, 2001. Those few Americans served as forward air controllers—on-the-ground spotters—for America's high tech, close air support that was launched by the Air Force from Uzbekistan and Tajikistan and from Navy planes off carriers in the Indian Ocean in support of native Afghan opposition against al Qaeda and Taliban forces. The forward air controllers, in combination with the pin-point accuracy of American air-launched guided weapons, were deadly as the terrorist forces were drawn into combat in the countryside, where the Afghans had earlier defeated the Soviets. This time it was the al Qaeda-Taliban forces that were picked to pieces by precision attacks called in by American forward air controllers armed with laser designators and riding horseback in the Afghan mountains.

Curiously, it was al Qaeda that was tactically surprised. Bin Laden had hoped that the 9/11 attack against the United States homeland would lure American forces into a quagmire in Afghanistan where he believed his al Qaeda forces could rout them using the same tactics that had been so successful against the Soviets. Instead, it was the Taliban and al Qaeda forces who failed to learn from those experiences while the United States took advantage of the lessons of the earlier war. With a minimum of American troops, the U.S.-supported forces routed the Taliban government by the end of November 2001 and seized all of the major Afghan cities by December 7th, less than three months after the initial al Qaeda attack on the United States mainland. Although Osama bin Laden escaped, presumably into northwest Pakistan, retribution had been swift indeed, and the first safe haven for his terrorist organization was neutralized. The breathless pursuit of al Qaeda that President Bush had promised on September 20th had started with blitzkrieg-like success.

The United States had learned in pursuing al Qaeda that it could lean on its allies and even nations such as Iran, which initially were considered in the enemy camp, to obtain assistance as long as it was willing to listen to the concerns of other countries and was prepared to negotiate a satisfactory response. Even the world's only superpower can sometimes accomplish more following diplomatic channels than it can militarily and often resolve the issue faster. The United States also learned that it had been mistaken to assume that it could simply hunt down terrorists in a nation without assuming some responsibility for restoring order to the chaos its military operations would create in the process. Colin Powell's admonition in the run-up to the Iraq war, "if you break it, you own it and must fix it," should and did not require the destruction of a so-called enemy state for the United States to recognize its obligation. The United States had a long record of rebuilding countries, like Germany and other European countries, Japan, and Korea, even when the destruction did not come directly from U.S. actions. Furthermore, restoring order could achieve America's ancillary goal of democratizing poorly governed, autocratic Muslim nations. Indeed, the latter lesson became a fundamental objective in Bush's new American foreign policy. No more "status quo ante bellum" as a basic principle in America's new military intervention policy; future military operations would have to do much more than simply win military battles—they must win the war, which meant restoring order, rebuilding damaged infrastructure and providing the structures needed for implementing democratic reform.

The United States also learned that the United Nations, even with all of its problems from dysfunction to corruption, had an important role to play in organizing and giving credibility to a new Afghan government. The United States asked for and received U.N. assistance in organizing an interim Afghan government and elections for a permanent government. A U.N. team worked through the fall of 2001 in identifying and choosing representatives from the various Afghan ethnic and tribal groups for a December conference in Bonn, Germany to elect an interim authority until U.N. organized elections could be held in October of 2004. In Bonn, Hamid Karzai was chosen by the delegates as the interim leader. Karzai was a tribal leader of the Pashtuns, the largest ethnic group in the country, which controlled the southern and eastern portions of Afghanistan and overlapped into western Pakistan. Pashtu is spoken by about half of the Afghans, who are 99 percent Sunni Muslims. Karzai, over the objections of the Pakistani intelligence service, had effectively led a small Pashtun fighting force against the Taliban that successfully negotiated the surrender of towns around Kandahar, the last major city held by the Taliban until December 7, 2001. Karzai had demonstrated his leadership qualities and was the choice of the Americans to lead the new republic [Friedman, 182-8]. The U.N. sponsored conference legitimatized their choice and NATO organized 6,000 troops for the International Security Assistance Force initially staffed with general officers from Germany, The Netherlands, and Turkey to provide security in the capital, Kabul. The war in Afghanistan had gone extremely well, and the prospects for a successful peace process for this ancient, war-torn country were excellent.

COMPLETING THE BUSH DOCTRINE AND CONTINUING THE PURSUIT

After 9/11, President Bush's experience in the first 111 days as a "wartime" president went quite well; both the President and his constituency believed that, for a former governor with little foreign policy experience, George W. Bush had stepped into the role of commander-in-chief under wartime conditions smoothly and with few missteps. Candidate Bush had no previous foreign policy experience and surrounded himself with smart, experienced people, and studied hard to prepare himself in foreign affairs. He made it clear during the campaign that Colin Powell would be his choice for secretary of state and he employed a group of highly experienced advisors during the campaign that were called the Vulcans, as detailed by Daalder and Lindsay [22-34]. During the campaign, he answered questions about his lack of foreign policy experience with, "I'll be surrounded by good, strong, capable, smart people who understand the mission of the United States is to lead the world to peace" [Mann, 255]. Eight Vulcans consisted of three advisors who would play prominent roles in his foreign policy team:

- *Condoleezza Rice,* former provost at Stanford University, expert on Russia in the first Bush administration, became director of National Security;

- *Paul Wolfowitz,* dean of the Johns Hopkins School of Advanced International Studies, former foreign policy advisor in the Nixon, Ford, Carter, Reagan, and first Bush administrations, became undersecretary of defense for policy;

- *Richard Armitage,* assistant secretary of defense in the Reagan administration and real warrior in the Vietnam War, became Bush's senior undersecretary of state; and four others who played lesser but yet significant roles;

- *Robert Blackwell,* White House adviser on European and Soviet affairs for the first President Bush;

- *Stephen Hadley,* assistant secretary of defense for international security policy in the first Bush administration;

- *Dov Zakheim,* deputy undersecretary of defense for planning and resources, also in the Reagan administration;

- *Robert Zoellick,* undersecretary of state for economic affairs and White House deputy chief of staff during the first Bush administration; and one individual who did not serve directly in the new administration,

- *Richard Perle,* held Hadley's Defense Department position in the Reagan administration and would chair the Defense Policy Board, a voluntary advisory group, for Secretary Rumsfeld.

Of this group of eight, only Wolfowitz, now a Republican, and Perle, still a Democrat, were card-carrying neo-conservatives, but all eight advisers were generally acceptable to the informal group that claimed to represent what was called neo-conservative, a political movement that continued to claim members in both of America's political parties.

As Mann's book [251-2] indicates, both the presidential candidate and his cadre of advisers took seriously the responsibility of educating George W. Bush in the fundamentals and intricacies of American foreign policy, and these advisers contributed significantly to the development of America's new foreign policy in the first administration of George W. Bush.

Expanding the Definition of Hostile Action and U.S. Defense Efforts

With his initial success invading Afghanistan and ousting the Taliban government behind him, President Bush continued public exposition of a new foreign policy in his State of the Union address on January 29, 2002. This speech became known as his "axis-of-evil" speech for the following paragraphs:

> Our second goal is to prevent regimes that sponsor terror from threatening America or our friends and allies with weapons of mass destruction. Some of these regimes have been pretty quiet since September the 11th. But we know their true nature. North Korea is a regime arming with missiles and weapons of mass destruction, while starving its citizens.
>
> Iran aggressively pursues these weapons and exports terror, while an unelected few repress the Iranian people's hope for freedom.
>
> Iraq continues to flaunt its hostility toward America and to support terror. The Iraq regime has plotted to develop anthrax, and nerve gas, and nuclear weapons for over a decade. This is a regime that has already used poison gas to murder thousands of its own citizens—leaving bodies of mothers huddled over their dead children. This is a regime that has something to hide from the civilized world.
>
> States like these, and their terrorist allies, constitute an *axis of evil*, arming to threaten the peace of the world. By seeking weapons of mass destruction, these regimes pose a grave threat and a grave danger. They could provide these arms to terrorists, giving them the means to match their hatred. They could attack allies or attempt to blackmail the United States. In any of these cases, the price of indifference would be catastrophic.
>
> We will work closely with our coalition to deny terrorists and state sponsors the materials, technology, and expertise to make and deliver weapons of mass destruction. We will develop and deploy effective missile defense to protect America and our allies from sudden attack. *And all nations should know: America will do whatever is necessary to ensure our nation's security.* [Emphasis added]

The definition of aiding and supporting terrorists had been extended to include the provision of weapons of mass destruction to terrorist organizations. As we shall see, this speech was accompanied by some frank discussions, directly or indirectly, with these and other countries possessing weapons of mass destruction, especially nuclear weapons. The most significant change in moving from the Cold War to the war on terror was to void the fundamental defensive strategy of mutual deterrence. In the Cold War, each side believed the other was rational and would not attack, knowing that it would be destroyed in a counterattack. However, such a strategy would not work against religious zealots who believe that death in battle against infidels leads to martyrdom because Islamist militants willing and eager to die killing infidels are immune to such deterrence theory. Thus, it was necessary to warn countries possessing nuclear weapons that the new U.S. foreign policy meant that the United States would hold those nations responsible for ensuring that nuclear weapons would not fall into the hands of religious extremists. The list of enemy nations was expanded to include North Korea, as well as Muslim nations with actual or potential nuclear capabilities and who were currently accommodating Islamist militants, excluding, of course, America's special Muslim ally, Pakistan.

However, as Pakistan would learn shortly, the last line of the "axis-of-evil" speech was addressed to all nations, friend and foe alike. The United States, in the future, "will do whatever is necessary to ensure our nation's security." That passage suggests that the United States of America, the world's only superpower, would act *unilaterally* whenever its security is threatened or whenever it believes that its security is threatened. The passage only refers to one collective security organization, an ambiguous and undefined "America's coalition;" it did not refer to the United Nations, NATO, or the host of other mutual security pacts that the United States created during the many decades of the Cold War. Only the United States at the start of the 21st century had sufficient military might to make such a provocative and unilateral declaration.

Nevertheless, the world's reaction to the speech centered on the "axis-of-evil" metaphor and the implication of good versus evil morality judgments that were the operational elements of the new American foreign policy. Most of America's allies did not criticize the United States for declaring that it was prepared to act unilaterally in its own defense until later, when it did so by invading Iraq without a clear U.N. Security Council mandate. Perhaps President Bush's well-deserved reputation for being plain speaking and ineloquent gave him some cover, but those who listened carefully to his major addresses and read the written words learned that the President's plain speaking conveyed precisely what he meant.

Application to "Allied" Enemy Governments

The lesson of listening to what Bush said was made clear to two of the three nations in the world (the other being the United Arab Emirates) that had recognized the former Taliban Afghan government: Pakistan and Saudi Arabia, both presumed allies of the United States. American efforts in the war on terror throughout December of 2001 and much of 2002 were directed quietly toward these two "friendly" countries. Diplomatic pressures, bordering on extortion, were forcefully exerted on Pakistan. It had also become increasingly clear that the Saudis had funded the nuclear weapons programs of Pakistan and Iraq to the tune of about $5–$7 billion and that Pakistan had also sold its nuclear weapon technology to North Korea, Iran and Libya with further proliferation coming from North Korea. Pakistan's current arsenal of nuclear weapons is directed primarily at India but is capable of reaching virtually any target in the Middle East, and it appears that both Iran and Saudi Arabia are interested in pursuing independent nuclear capabilities, ostensibly to counter Israel as well as each other. America's most immediate concern was that Pakistan's nuclear weapons, the most mature nuclear program in the Muslim world, might fall into al Qaeda hands, especially because many Pakistanis were sympathetic to al Qaeda, including senior members of the military. Americans knew that the government of President Musharraf did not have complete control of the nation's intelligence service and Wahhabi proselytizers were active in the country, especially in remote and inaccessible areas along the Afghanistan border.

In addition, for the past three decades U.S. intelligence agents had been clandestinely following Dr. A. Q. Khan, the architect of the Pakistani nuclear weapons program, in his travels throughout the world, even reportedly protecting him from arrest by Dutch investigators [Broad and Sanger]. American agents thought that Khan was under control as a result of their surveillance, but the public is still learning about the real effects of Khan's efforts to develop an international black market in secret nuclear weapons, though Americans knew that he had started selling secrets to Iran as early as the late 1980s. What the CIA did not know until recently is that Khan had obtained a small bomb design from the Chinese in the early 1980s that became the prototype for Pakistan's bomb, which could be launched with the smaller missiles Pakistan already had in its arsenal. The May 1998 atomic testing chess match between India and Pakistan, when Pakistan exploded five separate nuclear devices in a single day, much to the dismay of the world, had taken the CIA completely by surprise.

To avoid any future surprises, according to Friedman [211-230], Pakistan, Russia, and Iran were notified that the Bush administration's new U.S. policy of preemption had a special application for nuclear weapons: in the absence of any alternative solution, the United States would in the future consider employment of nuclear weapons to destroy unsecured nuclear storage sites. Again, according to Friedman, Russia cooperated fully in making its nuclear facilities available for U.S. inspections, and Pakistan, which in early 2002 was facing a diplomatic crisis with India, now found itself confronted by two nuclear threats—India and the United States. Faced with possible catastrophe, Pakistan caved in. Musharraf permitted U.S. inspectors from the military and CIA to deploy scientists in all Pakistani nuclear facilities. The documents and records in these facilities led to the conclusion that certain Pakistani scientists, in addition to Kahn, and certain intelligence service agents had to be purged from their respective weapons programs for permitting leaks of classified nuclear secrets. After securing the Pakistan nuclear weapons program, the United States then successfully mediated the dispute between Pakistan and India.

The Saudis could not be coerced or managed in this way, but they too had to be dealt with to stop the flow of Saudi funds and other material support to al Qaeda. Saudi cooperation was virtually the only avenue available short of tracking down each al Qaeda cell throughout the world and annihilating each of the cells in the global terrorist organization. There were other problems, such as: (1) the Saudi failure to cooperate with American investigators of the al Khobar bombing; (2) the unexpected firing right after 9/11 of the seemingly cooperative head of Saudi intelligence who had been the CIA's primary source of information about the Saudis and al Qaeda's network in Saudi society; (3) the January 2002 demand to remove U.S. forces from the country; and (4) the failure to provide requested information about Saudi financial contributions to al Qaeda. The Saudi demand that U.S. forces leave the country was handled expeditiously by moving the U.S. Air Force Air Control Center at the al Kharj Prince Sultan Air Base to Central Command's new headquarters in Doha, Qatar on the Persian Gulf. In response to these "unfriendly" Saudi initiatives, U.S. Special Forces arranged to conduct training exercises in Yemen, just south of the Saudi border where al Qaeda had some training camps. The U.S. military, with naval forces in the Persian Gulf, Indian Ocean, and Red Sea and ground troops in Yemen, Oman, Qatar, Bahrain, and Kuwait and a friendly government in Jordan had virtually surrounded Saudi Arabia. The exception was Iraq.

Feeling U.S. pressure, the Saudis launched an ambitious public relations program, blaming Jewish neo-conservatives in the Defense Department for the worsening problems in the long-standing U.S.-Saudi relationship. Saudi statements threatened the cessation of all U.S. negotiations until a satisfactory peace agreement between Israel and Palestine could be reached. Even though the Saudis had never before made such an overture, Saudi Crown Prince Abdullah, through an interview with Tom Friedman of *The New York Times*, proposed an unprecedented Saudi peace plan for the Palestine-Israeli dispute. This campaign was the final straw in convincing the U.S. government that the usual Saudi gulling tactics were simply a delaying technique to avoid responding to its request for cooperation against al Qaeda. The Saudis had to be squeezed and convinced that the United States was a greater danger to the Saudi kingdom than al Qaeda. George Friedman [233] argued that:

> "The United States realized it could defeat Al Qaeda only by taking its bases of support—financial, logistical, and personnel systems. That meant the U.S. had to hit the arteries—had to deal with Saudi Arabia…Al Qaeda was, in fundamental ways, a Saudi phenomenon. Its leaders and members were Saudi, its ideology was Wahhabi, and its financing drew on Saudi citizens."

In truth, the Saudis, like bin Laden and most in the Muslim world, did not respect the military power of the United States. They had observed, as had bin Laden, the American retreat in the face of successive terrorist attacks and came to the same conclusion that the United States was unable, politically, to fight seriously in extended conflicts, especially in the Middle East. America's success in ousting the Taliban in Afghanistan was also seen as an incomplete mission; no victory would be achieved until a new independent government friendly to the United States was established.

Although the United States had troops stationed all around the Middle East, these troops could only be utilized for missions that each host country had specifically approved on a case-by-case basis. Nor did the United States have a major staging area for an invasion of a Middle Eastern country the size of Saudi Arabia. The Saudi problem would have to be accommodated in the choice of the next military target after the victory in Afghanistan and after finalizing the evolving Bush Doctrine.

Putting the New Bush Doctrine Together

On June 1, 2002, speaking at the graduation exercises at the United States Military Academy at West Point, President Bush defended the most controversial portion of his State of the Union Address, the role of moral judgments in America's foreign policy. After reiterating the many dangers and uncertainties of the war on terror, especially his concern about weapons of mass destruction, he broke new ground by saying:

> Because the war on terror will require resolve and patience, it will also require firm moral purpose. In this way our struggle is similar to the Cold War. Now, as then, our enemies are totalitarians, holding a creed of power with no place for human dignity. Now, as then, they seek to impose joyless conformity, to control everyone and all of life.
>
> America confronted imperial communism in many different ways—diplomatic, economic, and military. Yet moral clarity was essential to our victory in the Cold War. When leaders like John F. Kennedy and Ronald Reagan refused to gloss over brutality of tyrants, they gave hope to prisoners and dissidents and exiles, and rallied free nations to a great cause.
>
> Some worry that it is somehow undiplomatic or impolite to speak the language of right and wrong. I disagree. Different circumstances require different methods, but not different moralities. Moral truth is the same in every culture, in every time, and in every place. Targeting innocent civilians for murder is always and everywhere wrong. There can be no neutrality between justice and cruelty, between the innocent and the guilty. We are in a conflict between good and evil, and America will call evil by its name. By confronting evil and lawless regimes, we do not create a problem, we reveal a problem. And we will lead the world in opposing it.

President Bush's three addresses, in little more than 250 days, contained hints of all of the major principles and premises of the new Bush Doctrine. If Truman's policy was aptly called "containment," to connote America's willingness to maintain the status quo between the United States and the Soviet Union, the new Bush policy could be called "condemnation," to express America's determination to eliminate al Qaeda, Bin Ladenism and radical militant Islamist groups from the face of the earth as evildoers.

For those who still had not gotten the message, the National Security Council, with President George W. Bush's letter of transmittal, issued a clearly worded 20-page document to the world on September 17, 2002, entitled "The National Security Strategy of the United States of America," that fully summarized President Bush's new foreign policy. Bush's transmittal letter laid out the basic premises, first explaining that the United States "enjoys a position of unparalleled military strength and great economic and political influence...we do not use our strength to press for unilateral advantage." That is, the United States proclaimed that it had world hegemony, predominant influence over the entire world, which it will not utilize for national gain. Second, the United States would, however, use that power and influence to defeat:

> ...shadowy networks of individuals [that] can bring great chaos and suffering to our shores for less cost than it costs to purchase a tank...To defeat this threat we must make use of every tool in our arsenal—military power, better homeland defenses, law enforcement, intelligence, and vigorous efforts to cut off financing...We cannot defend America and our friends by hoping for the best. So we must be prepared to defeat our enemies' plans, using the best intelligence and proceeding with deliberation. History will judge harshly those who saw this danger coming but failed to act. In the new world we have entered the only path to peace and security is the path of action.

That action, the strategy went on to explain, will be taken "by constantly striv[ing] to enlist the support of the international community, [but] *we will not hesitate to **act alone**, if necessary, to exercise our right of self defense by **acting pre-emptively** against terrorists, to prevent them from doing harm against our people and country*" [emphasis added]. That is, the United States in the war on terror will act both preemptively and unilaterally. The world had not seen such a declaration in the 20th century with its configuration of multi-powers, fighting to maintain a balance of power among shifting coalitions. Only a world hegemonist in a new century and a new era could issue such a stark declaration.

Although the U.S. National Strategy used the term "preemptive war," the Bush administration's incursion into Iraq was really a preventive war, as Gaddis [2005] makes clear. He defines preemption as "taking military action against a state that was about to launch an attack"; whereas prevention means "starting a war against a state that might, at some future point, pose such risks." It is the immediacy of the adverse action that differentiates preventive war from preemption. Iraq did not represent an immediate challenge, but it certainly could have been a threat in the future as it slipped out from under the U.N.-sanctioned disarmament controls.

Both the 1992 document, when first suggested by Paul Wolfowitz, and 10 years later in 2002 when enunciated by President Bush as America's new foreign policy, seemed at first to be out of line with America's heritage. However, as John Lewis Gaddis [2004] noted, John Quincy Adams, perhaps the greatest American secretary of state, who served from 1817 to 1824, developed a foreign policy based on three principles: (1) preemption, (2) unilateralism and (3) American hegemony over the Western Hemisphere, as stated in the Monroe Doctrine. Adams' foreign policy served as the basis of America's foreign relations until President McKinley added an imperialistic dimension that gained prominence at the end of the 19th century. Bush's foreign policy in the first year of the war on terrorism argued for acceptance of American world hegemony based on American military superiority. Adams' more narrowly defined hemispheric hegemony, without military strength, was dependent solely on Great Britain's willingness to employ its navy against other European powers who periodically threatened nations in the hemisphere, especially during the Civil War. Bush's 21st century foreign policy was not so different, reflecting America's extensive growth in military, economic, and diplomatic power in the 185 years since Adams became secretary of state.

In 2002 the United States was the world's only superpower and its urgent need to aggressively fight the war on terror had made it act accordingly. The Bush Doctrine did one other thing that Adams could not have imagined in the 1820s when the United States was only one of three nations in the world that democratically elected its government. Bush's policy included the promotion of freedom and democracy as a key element in American foreign policy by promising that the United States would:

1. speak out honestly about violations of the nonnegotiable demands of human dignity using our voice and vote in international institutions to advance freedom.

2. use foreign aid to promote freedom and support those who struggle nonviolently for it, ensuring that nations moving toward democracy are rewarded (in proportion) to the steps they take.

3. make freedom and the development of democratic institutions key themes in our bilateral relations, seeking solidarity and cooperation from other democracies while we press governments that deny human rights to move toward a better future.

4. take special efforts to promote freedom of religion and conscience and defend it from encroachment by repressive governments.

None of these programs sound too bold or threatening to nondemocratic states, but when grander language was employed by the President is his Second Inaugural Address to describe these programs and efforts as "ending tyranny in our world" critics were frightened into believing that the United States would henceforth embark upon an aggressive foreign policy that would threaten all totalitarian states. Comparing the Bush Doctrine with the Truman Doctrine in which a country's attitude toward communism was central to America's diplomatic relations with that country is to suggest that now the democratic behavior of a country would be a controlling factor in U.S. relations toward it.

No other president since Woodrow Wilson, during and after the First World War, had ever proposed to employ a strategy of democratization as a central plank in America's national security policy. Franklin Delano Roosevelt worked pragmatically to create democratic institutions in the post-Second World War era, which he did not live to see, but his vision was much more guarded that the optimistic and sweeping view President Bush took as a result of the growth of democratic countries in the second half of the 20th century. Indeed, an alternative title to calling the Bush Doctrine the policy of "condemnation," is to call it the policy of "liberation," as suggested by Horowitz [3]. It certainly represented a completely different approach than the Cold War when the United States rigorously denied any appetite to liberate oppressed peoples behind the Iron Curtain and failed to support popular uprisings as in the Hungarian revolt of 1956.

Even Roosevelt's more limited support for democratization was lost during the Cold War as the United States entered into a myriad of security and economic relationships with authoritarian governments opposing the interests of the Soviet Union. Paradoxically, it was American support for the autocratic government in the Kingdom of Saudi Arabia that was one of the principal reasons that prompted Osama bin Laden to launch his terrorist attack against the United States. With the new Bush Doctrine, it appeared that bin Laden and the United States shared the goal of overthrowing or modifying the behavior of the Saudi monarchy, but differed on what type of government should replace it. The United States, in the context of the Bush Doctrine, saw the theocracy that bin Laden proposed for the Arabian Peninsula as even more tyrannical than the Saudi autocracy, which Americans optimistically hope can be persuaded to evolve into a constitutional monarchy with much greater power to the people than anything bin Laden could offer.

As we shall see later in discussing the conduct of Bush's foreign policy, how the Bush Doctrine is characterized does affect judgments that are made about America's actions. Gaddis found precedents for the principles of the new Bush Doctrine in prior American policies of Secretary of State John Quincy Adams and President Woodrow Wilson. Norman Podhoretz [2004], speaking for the neo-conservatives, described the Bush foreign policy doctrine as based on four quite different principles than American hegemony, unilateralism, preemption, and democratization.

First, Podhoretz argued that the Bush Doctrine is based on the repudiation of moral relativism by establishing the need for firm moral judgment in foreign affairs and no more automatic support for dictators friendly to America's interests, which is consistent with Bush's emphasis on democratization of the Middle East. No doubt Bush believes that morality is essential to America's conduct of foreign policy. However, when the terms "good and evil" are used, Bush doesn't appear to be advocating absolute moral standards, but rather the generally accepted values of Western culture, defining evil as targeting innocent civilians for murder or brutality against women and children. It is true that Bush and others hold that it is incumbent upon the United States to act with a more consistent level of moral behavior than the United States did during its conduct of the Cold War where pragmatism often trumped morality, even though George Kennan, the containment policy's architect, held the United States to extremely high moral standards, "a test of the overall worth of the United States as a nation among nations" (shades of manifest destiny). However, it is not clear as Podhoretz argues that a pillar of George W. Bush's foreign policy is moralism. World hegemony and America's efforts to use its prominent influence for valid international purposes, not solely for its own national gain, appears to be a better predictor of American foreign affairs actions than any theory of "moral" behavior.

Second, Podhoretz believes that Bush recognized that deadly terrorists should be regarded as irregular troops of a military alliance at war with the United States, not as criminals that can be arrested by law enforcement personnel and tried by civilian courts. Although most would agree that Bush did take this logical step in constructing the new American foreign policy, after many fruitless responses employing law enforcement in response to earlier terrorist attacks, that recognition is hardly a pillar of the new Bush Doctrine. It certainly is less predictive of U.S. foreign policy initiatives than Gaddis' principle of America's willingness to take unilateral action to defeat Islamist militants in the war on terrorism as the second pillar of the Bush Doctrine.

Both Podhoretz and Gaddis agree that the third pillar of the Bush Doctrine is America's declaration of its preemptive rights to strike the enemy terrorist forces before they can launch attacks on the United States. Podhoretz provides a sound rationale for this right: moral states, following international jurisprudence, have the right to preemptively invade outlaw or immoral states. The only difficulty with such a right is who may exercise it. The United States has carefully outlined the conditions in which it will act preemptively, but what about the rights of other states, when in their own self-interest, they attempt to preemptively take action against other states? Is there a hierarchy of nations that allows only the more powerful or most democratic to have and to employ this right? The Bush

Doctrine is silent on this issue, implying that only a world hegemonist has such a power.

Gaddis' world hegemony, unilateralism, and preemptivism are three principles that follow from Bush's determination to make America's new foreign policy pro-active, not reactive, and to exercise the rights of the world's only superpower to take all necessary actions to protect America's security. Indeed, one can argue that it is the unique and predominant position of the United States in the world that makes it the number one target of Islamist militants in their battle to gain prominence in the Islamic world. Consequently, the United States must employ all of its resources, including its pre-eminence, to defend itself and its citizens from the irrational and potentially devastating attacks of Islamist militants dedicated to destroying Western civilization. Thus, America's status as the number one target for extremists justifies its exclusive right to preemption or prevention.

Podhoretz's fourth pillar for the Bush Doctrine is that the United States should not recognize any state that refuses to repudiate terrorism. He argues that Bush was prevented from supporting an independent Palestinian state as long as Yasser Arafat, an avowed terrorist and dictator, continued as its president. Gaddis' model lists only three basic principles for Bush's policy, but here we have added democratization as the fourth factor because that is Bush's antidote to bin Laden's tyrannical terrorism. It seems clear that the National Security Strategy of the United States suggests that the Bush administration believes that Wilsonian democracy offers the only possible means of rectifying bin Laden's one legitimate complaint of injustice and autocratic rule in most of the Muslim world. Moreover the new Bush Doctrine reinforced the fundamental point that freedom and democracy are the only antidote for nihilistic Bin Ladenism. Later, in his Second Inaugural Address, President Bush made this abundantly clear when he declared to the world:

> We have seen our vulnerability—and we have seen its deepest source. For as long as whole regions of the world simmer in resentment and tyranny—prone to ideologies that feed hatred and excuse murder—violence will gather, and multiply in destructive power, and cross the most defended borders, and raise a moral threat. *There is only one force of history that can break the reign of hatred and resentment, and expose the pretensions of tyrants, and reward the hopes of the decent and tolerant, and that is the **force of human freedom**.* [Emphasis added]

In summary, Gaddis' interpretation of the Bush Doctrine, with his three principles of world hegemony, unilateralism and the right to pre-emptive action, together with the addition of freedom and democratization as the antidote to

Middle East autocracy, is a better model for explaining America's new foreign policy than Podhoretz's neo-conservative formulation. The Saudis and other critics of the Bush Doctrine are wrong to characterize and discredit the policies as the product of Jewish neo-conservatives—Wolfowitz may have been the principal architect going back to 1992, but the resulting doctrine certainly reflected broader thinking than just neo-conservatism philosophy.

Republican foreign policy had supported democratization for nearly 20 years with Reagan's 1985 support of dissident Corazon Aquino for the ouster of Ferdinand Marcos, the long-time Philippine dictator. The major role for democratization in the foreign policy of a Republican president was a complete reversal of the party's support for friendly dictators. This revolution in thinking occurred, not as a result of neo-conservatism as Halper and Clarke allege, but of a pragmatic secretary of state, George Shultz, who finally convinced Reagan that "by clinging to Marcos's dictatorship...the United States might strengthen the insurgency against his regime and thus open the way for a Communist victory in the Philippines" [Mann, 133]. Significantly, the two American emissaries to the Philippines who were involved in carrying out Shultz's new initiative were Paul Wolfowitz and Richard Armitage.

James Mann [329] concurred with two of the four Gaddis principles, omitting unilateralism (which is sometimes difficult to separate from preemption) and adding the Wilsonian ideal of employing democratization as central to America's national security. All three expressed similar terms in describing the revolutionary nature of the new policy. Mann described it as "breathtaking," while Gaddis found it "breathtakingly simple" and yet paradoxically "grand," and Podhoretz was ecstatic in praising the doctrine as an extension to a new set of dangers of the Kennan vision of the United States, "the responsibilities of moral and political leadership that history plainly intended us to bear." Despite their praise, all three agreed that the final judgment on the ultimate success of the Bush Doctrine would have to wait for the evidence to unfold in the brittle and languid domain of the Middle East where oil and democracy have rarely mixed.

IMPLEMENTATION OF THE BUSH DOCTRINE

Shortly before the release of the full statement of the Bush Doctrine on September 20, 2002, President Bush addressed the United Nations General Assembly on September 12th (a year and a day after the 9/11 attack) to appeal to the international organization to enforce its own resolutions concerning Iraq's disregard of the conditions of the 1991 Gulf War cease-fire. The President argued that:

> The conduct of the Iraqi regime is a threat to the authority of the United Nations and a threat to peace. Iraq has answered a decade of U.N. demands with a decade of defiance. All the world now faces a test, the United Nations a difficult and defining moment. Are the Security Council resolutions to be honored and enforced, or cast aside without consequence? Will the United Nations serve the purpose of its founding, or will it be irrelevant?

Even though Bush had asked Secretary Rumsfeld about American invasion plans for Iraq as early as November 21, 2001, it was not until the week after Bush's State of the Union address in January 2002 that Secretary Rumsfeld was asked formally by the President to begin preparing plans for the invasion of Iraq. Even before the full statement of the Bush Doctrine had been formalized, the United States was proceeding to develop a plan to implement the new doctrine. Because Bush had promised to vigorously pursue war against al Qaeda, it was essential that the United States not lose momentum in that struggle. The United States had to move to a second target in the war on terror after the successful liberation of Afghanistan to keep pressure on bin Laden, but more importantly, to get to the source of radical, militant Islamism in the heart of the Arab-Muslim world. Why Iraq was chosen as the next theater of operations in the war on terror is a much more complicated issue and one with politically significant and long-lasting consequences for the Bush administration.

Why Iraq?

The question might better be asked: Why not Saudi Arabia? For, as George Friedman and we have argued, al Qaeda was and is very much a Saudi phenomenon. Al Qaeda was largely managed by Saudi nationals and financed by both Saudi private and public contributions that have funded radical militant Islamist activities for years. As an ideological movement, al Qaeda was an ideological offshoot of Wahhabi-Salafism, the state religion of Saudi Arabia. It was the Saudis who had all but broken off relations with the United States when the Arab monarchy had been pressed to provide sensitive intelligence information about al Qaeda and to stop the flow of Saudi funds to the terrorist organization and the Saudi global network of Islamic charities. Certainly the links between Saudi Arabia and al Qaeda were much stronger than any case for Saddam Hussein's support of al Qaeda. Without the Saudi connection, it was hard for President Bush in the 2004 reelection campaign to answer charges that the Iraq invasion had been anything but a diversion from the war on terror. There is, however, substantial evidence to show that the invasion and liberation of Iraq were anything but a diversion and that it was in fact the main event in the war on terror.

Indeed, the United States had but two options in continuing the pursuit of al Qaeda: either invade Saudi Arabia directly or invade another major country in the region to convince the Saudis of America's determination and military strength to rid the world of al Qaeda and the source of its ideology and funding. The problems of invading Saudi Arabia would have been Herculean, making military action against the Saudis a nonstarter: (1) no case against the Saudis had been made publicly or diplomatically; (2) military and political risk were monumental; (3) the Muslim world would have been inflamed because of the holy cities of Mecca and Medina; (4) the effect on American relations with its other allies would have been disastrous by destroying faith in America's word; and, (5) if world oil production had been disrupted during an invasion of Saudi Arabia, the United States would have had to shoulder the blame for worldwide economic calamity.

The other perfect country was, of course, Iraq, which shares a long 500-mile border with Saudi Arabia and could in a relatively short-term, with investment in its decaying infrastructure, become a disruptive competitive force in the Saudi-dominated oil market. Iraq had other advantages: (1) Shiite Iran, the arch enemy of Saddam Hussein, would look favorably on deposing the militant Sunni and Baathist tyrant and could become an ally in the war against al Qaeda by supplying valuable intelligence information; (2) Syria, another Baathist-ruled autocratic government and consistent supporter of terrorist organizations, would be squeezed between pro-American Iraq, Turkey, and Israel; and (3) with a change in Saudi relations, the U.S. would no longer be concerned about using the rivalry between Iraq and Iran as a protective shield for Saudi Arabia. The winner, hands down, as the next U.S. target in the war against al Qaeda was Iraq—not necessarily an optimal target, but the one most logical and available for pursing al Qaeda and simultaneously influencing change in Saudi Arabia and the broader Middle East.

Moreover, Saddam Hussein was unquestionably evil and for years had stood as a malevolent symbol for all that was wrong in the Arab-Muslim world, making all other Arab autocrats look good by comparison. The principals in the President's war council had been very much aware of how the Saudis would view another war with Iraq, completing the job that was started in the first Gulf War by toppling Saddam Hussein and instituting a democratic republic that was likely to be dominated by the Shiite majority. When Bush's laconic vice president was defense secretary in the first Bush administration, he was asked by a defense department consultant why we did not simply finish off Saddam while we had him on the ropes, and Cheney responded, "The Saudis won't like it" [Mann, 192]. They still did not like it, as Prince Bandar, the long-time Saudi ambassador to the United States through four presidencies and who was privy to virtually all of America's state secrets about its Middle Eastern policies, made clear from first learning of U.S. intentions to invade Iraq and right up to the moment on March 19, 2003 when President Bush alerted the American public that the invasion had been launched. Bandar consistently argued that it would be much better to take out Saddam covertly, which the Saudis had been promising to help with since 1994 [Woodward, 2004, 229]. But like so many of the past Saudi promises that failed to materialize, this was simply another round of gulling the Americans again. This time, however, President Bush refused to let the United States be fooled.

A Surrogate War in Iraq

Until the decision to invade Iraq was finally made in September 2002, the Bush Doctrine and its execution in the war against terrorism were immensely popular at home and abroad. Bush's approval job rating was as high as 86 percent after 9/11 and remained at 60 percent through August 2002; most nations in the world were pleased with the dramatic and swift overthrow of the despicable Taliban regime as evidenced by NATO's willingness to join the coalition in Afghanistan in the postwar peacekeeping mission. But that was all about to change as a result of the March 2003 invasion of Iraq and Bush's approval rating dropped to 52 percent by the time of the 2004 American presidential elections. The Bush administration had done an extremely poor job of explaining the Iraq invasion as an integral part of its strategy in the war on terror, partly because it could not tell the public all the reasons for the invasion. The catch-22 of the Iraq option was the need to maintain total secrecy about one significant objective. If it went public with the Bush administration's dissatisfaction with the Saudis and the shadowy nature of the Saudi relationship with al Qaeda, it would have been impossible to obtain Saudi cooperation in fighting al Qaeda and further disruptions in the Middle East could also be expected.

Now it was the United States that was gulling the Saudis, and not vice versa. Bush resolutely stuck to his increasingly unpopular war in Iraq without revealing all of the complex reasons for the invasion and subsequently was reelected by a narrow 3 percent margin in November 2004. Part of the reason for the President's difficulties was the success of the Saudi propaganda campaign in Europe, and the United States attributing the invasion to Jewish neo-conservative attempts to eliminate Iraq, Israel's greatest enemy in the Middle East. Other critics argued that President Bush, a reckless and naïve Texas gunslinger, was simply seeking revenge for Saddam Hussein's attempted assassination of his father. Ironically, these allegations served as a cover story to conceal the real link between the Saudis and al Qaeda that had been a major reason for the invasion.

Part of the difficulty in making a good case to the American people for the Iraq invasion was the pivotal role that misleading information played in selecting Iraq as a theater of operations, but there were, however, valid reasons for choosing Iraq as the second theater in the war on terror. In light of Saddam's past crimes against his people, Iraq was certainly a suitable candidate for Bush's policy of democratization of outlaw states through regime change, which had been the official U.S. policy since October 31, 1998 when President Clinton signed the Iraq Liberation Act into law. Some Iraqi links to Islamist terrorists could be made in its harboring of al Qaeda members and paying $25,000 bounties to the families of Palestinian suicide bombers. Iraq had also achieved outlaw status by ignoring over a decade of U.N. resolutions for the elimination of its weapons of mass destruction, and, as was later learned, Iraq was guilty of bribing some Western nations through the U.N. oil-for-food program to ease weapons importation sanctions and divert cash to the regime for weapons and Saddam's personal use.

In making the public case for invading Iraq, the Bush administration's principal justification was that Iraq's presumed possession of weapons of mass destruction (WMD) that could fall into terrorists' hands made Iraq a menacing and looming threat to the United States. Intelligence agencies in Europe and the Middle East, as well as the CIA, all believed that Saddam Hussein had hidden stockpiles of biological and chemical weapons and planned to develop a nuclear device as quickly as possible after U.N. sanctions were lifted. Saddam did little to counter this belief, for why else would he throw out the U.N. inspectors in 1998? Few could realize at the time that it was megalomania or perhaps the paranoia of a tyrant who refused to recognize publicly what he considered would be humiliation and weakness in the eyes of Iraqi citizens and his Middle East rivals that prevented Saddam Hussein from openly proving to the world that no such stockpiles of WMD existed. Everyone knew that Saddam was a liar, but no one understood that the "Mother of all Lies" would lead to his downfall, for his only defense, in the final analysis, would have been the truth, but that he refused to admit. Another possibility, of course, is that Saddam did, indeed, have WMD stockpiles that were moved to secret locations in Syria with Russian assistance in the days before the American-led invasion. This is still the position of the usually reliable Israeli intelligence service and other independent observers; time and the fall of the autocratic Assad regime in Syria will tell.

U.S. Diplomacy and Multilateralism

When the United States began in the summer of 2002 to talk publicly about its plans for invading Iraq, worldwide opinion that had been so supportive of the United States after 9/11 and throughout the Afghan campaign broke solidly against President Bush and favorable opinions about the United States were soon a fading memory. Repeated antiwar protests occurred in virtually all major European capitals and in many American cities. Americans would soon learn "who was for us" and "who was against us." With such adverse public reaction, foreign leaders would normally have difficulty stepping forward to the defense of the United States, and it would take real courage for a politician to agree to join the United States in its military effort to unseat Saddam Hussein.

Many Americans asked, why are so many nations opposed to America's incursion into Iraq? Americans were, after all, accustomed to having their policies supported and popular overseas. First, it was far easier and politically rewarding for European leaders, like Gerhard Schroeder of the Federal Republic of Germany, to campaign for reelection by running against the American war in Iraq because of strong antiwar feelings among their people. Second, many nations, like France, Germany, and Russia, had economic reasons through favorable trade arrangements and arms sales for opposing the removal of Saddam Hussein, and the corrupt U.N. oil-for-food program added to those economic advantages. And third and most important, as Robert Kagan [11] has pointed out:

> For along with these natural consequences of the transatlantic disparity of power, there has also opened a broad ideological gap. Europeans, because of their unique historical experience of the past century—culminating in the creation of the European Union—have developed a set of ideals and principles regarding the utility and morality of power different from the ideals and principles of Americans, who have not shared that experience.
>
> [And furthermore on page 33] The differing threat perceptions in the United States and Europe are not just matters of psychology, however. They

are also grounded in a practical realty that is another product of the disparity
of power and the structure of the present international order.

While Europe receded under U.S. protection during the Cold War, the United
States became involved more broadly in the rest of the world, among other things
incurring the wrath of Islamist terrorists that the Europeans did not yet fully
appreciate.

The domestic political problem for President Bush was that many Americans,
remembering the Roosevelt and Truman standards of international conduct,
were more comfortable with the European model of collective behavior, and
demanded an alliance with America's traditional allies. And, after remembering
the first President Bush's great success with a grand alliance in the first Gulf War,
large American-led military coalitions became the politically expected norm for
international interventions. There was comfort in numbers but failure to bring
other nations into Bush's war with Iraq would create credibility problems with
the American public. Despite the President's expressions of willingness to go it
alone in pursuit of al Qaeda, administration officials agreed that a multinational
alliance would be politically and militarily useful. Unilateralism, with its rapidity
of action, has both advantages and limitations.

Another nagging question for Americans, one that the Saudis helped to raise,
was the question of America's role in settling the seemingly irresolvable Israeli-
Palestinian dispute. Many Americans and hundreds of Europeans asked:
Wouldn't it win more friends in the Muslim world for the United States to aid in
the resolution of that dispute than changing the regime in Iraq? This is another
issue in which the Arab public and authoritarian Arab governments differed; the
plight of the Palestinian refugees was a vital issue among Muslim people, but
their governments, aside from trying to eliminate the Jewish state through war or
through support of terrorist groups, did not seem to care about the Palestinian
people and offered very little support for the refugees. The Bush policy, in light
of Yasser Arafat's rejection of President Clinton's peace proposal in 2000, was
based on the belief that there was no hope for a realistic peace agreement until the
Palestinians straightened out their own government with free elections and reined
in its terrorist factions. After 9/11, it would have been extremely difficult for any
American government to be unsympathetic to mounting terrorist attacks on
innocent Israelis. The death of Yasser Arafat, the avowed terrorist leader of the
Palestine Liberation Organization, was one of the most hopeful events in the war
on terror in 2004. If the newly elected Palestinian leader, Mahmoud Abbas, gains
control over Hamas and other militant factions, President Bush's second term

may well be the beneficiary not only of a reengaged Israeli-Palestinian peace process and the establishment of an independent Palestinian state, but of genuine peace in the region as well.

In spite of these sources of doubt about American policies, there were, fortunately, a few real allies of the United States that chose to come to the aid of the United States in the run-up to the Iraq war. First and foremost, British Prime Minister Tony Blair, over the objections of many members in his own Labor party and at great personal political risk, eloquently and courageously supported the American cause for unseating Saddam Hussein, promising 20,000 troops for the invasion. In addition, Australian Prime Minister John Howard signed up and offered 2,000 troops. Its former Dominion compatriot and long-time ally of the United States, Canada, however, opposed the invasion from the time it was first publicly considered and remained a critic as the war progressed. Poland, Spain, Italy, Ukraine, South Korea, and even Japan became part of the "coalition of the willing," to use President Bush's term. A host of other nations also signed on, but few provided material assistance. Vital base support and access in the region were provided by Turkey, Saudi Arabia, Kuwait, Bahrain, Qatar, United Arab Republic, and Oman. One public relations disaster of the Bush administration was the claim that, by including countries like Macedonia, Micronesia, the Marshall Islands, Palau, and Tonga, the second President Bush's coalition was actually larger than his father's in the first Gulf War, an alliance that contributed materially to paying the war costs, but the fact remained that about 85 percent of the forces in the March 2003 invasion of Iraq were American.

Allies can be comforting, but they can also create obligations. Partially to repay the administration's great debt to Tony Blair, the Bush administration agreed to seek additional U.N. Security Council sanctions for Iraq and approval of the invasion. The issue divided the president's war council, but President Bush finally sided with Blair and Secretary Powell, giving the secretary the assignment of rounding up enough votes in the Security Council to support America's armed intervention in Iraq. After eight weeks of intensive diplomatic discussion and debate, the secretary achieved a major diplomatic victory. On November 8, 2002 the United Nations Security Council voted unanimously (15 to 0) to approve Resolution 1441 warning Saddam Hussein that, if he "continued to violate his disarmament obligations, he would face 'serious consequences'" [Woodward 2004, 226].

The American diplomatic victory in the United Nations, though temporary, gave the Bush administration the legitimacy needed to proceed with the invasion, for it had been preceded on October 10th and 11th with the passage, by a wider margin than in the first Gulf War, of a Congressional resolution to use the U.S. armed forces in Iraq "as he [the President] deems to be necessary and appropriate." However, the U.N. action was less of a victory than an exposure of the hypocrisy of international diplomacy as practiced in the 21ˢᵗ century. The Security Council consisted of 15 countries that were both for and against war in Iraq, and all had approved the U.N. Security Council resolution with the intent of later using it against their opponents' position. As a direct result of the resolution, Saddam Hussein permitted the U.N. inspection teams back into Iraq and issued a mangled 12,000-word report on its weapons programs "that everyone believed was full of omissions and based on old materials" [Woodward 2004, 349].

Nevertheless, the opponents of war (France, Russia, China, and Germany) did not view this action by Iraq as "a material breach" of the U.N. mandate. Instead, they asked for more inspections and more time, and the diplomatic war at the United Nations continued, right up to the time of the March 19, 2003 invasion. Powell went back to the Security Council on February 5ᵗʰ to give the Council a now discredited overview of U.S. intelligence supporting the view that Iraq still had weapons of mass destruction, but opponents of the war, led by the French, refused to budge. A second Powell effort to win another Security Council resolution, again at the behest of America's British allies, did not get off the ground for lack of supportive votes. The question of invading Iraq remained a diplomatic stalemate, requiring the United States, Great Britain, Spain, Poland, Italy, and the rest of the "coalition of the willing" to invade and liberate Iraq on the basis of Resolution 1441. Both sides claimed that legal right was on their side. In answer to the question that President Bush had used to frame the debate, it is clear that the United Nations was unable to serve the purpose of its founding and was willing to risk its relevance. In addition, the hypocritical debates at the U.N. strengthened the case for the wisdom of building America's security on the Bush Doctrine's policies of hegemony, unilateralism, and pre-emption rather than multilateralism through tangled, aging and bureaucratic international organizations designed for another era.

Immediate Benefits of Invading Iraq

Because of American efforts since World War II to cover up the sins of the Saudis, it would have been much more difficult to prove outlaw status for Saudi Arabia than it was to indict Iraq, an already convicted felon, in the court of world opinion. Nevertheless, there was a much stronger and more direct link between the 9/11 terrorists and Saudi Arabia, with its militant state religion of Wahhabi-

Salafism, as the primary source of ideology and funding for bin Laden and other Islamist extremists throughout the world. Even though, based on the merits, Saudi Arabia could have logically been the second target of America's war against militant Islamists, Iraq provided an adequate and suitable surrogate and an effective means of communicating America's great dissatisfaction with Saudi support for militant Islamist terrorism.

On the other hand, the invasion of Iraq put the United States and the global economy at some risk of a possible disruption in the supply of Middle East oil. And there were other risks. Retired Air Force Lieutenant General Brent Scowcroft [2002], National Security advisor in the first Bush administration, in his essay, "Don't Attack Iraq," warned that:

> If we were seen to be turning our backs on that bitter [Israeli-Palestine] conflict...in order to go after Iraq, there would be an explosion of outrage against us. We would be seen as ignoring a key interest of the Muslim world in order to satisfy what is seen to be a narrower American interest.

Scowcroft was correct that the reaction to the invasion on the Arab street was greeted heatedly as another example of Western colonialism, but it was hardly an "explosion of outrage." However, the reaction of Islamic governments was quite different, much more subdued and even supportive in Iran. After all, the United States was removing the greatest threat to Middle East stability by ousting the region's most ruthless dictator, who by his actions and statements everyone believed was stockpiling weapons of mass destruction that could be as easily provided to terrorist organizations or directed at other Arab states, Israel, or the West.

Even before the first bombs landed on Baghdad or coalition forces had advanced north from Kuwait, outlaw states, as well as Saudi Arabia and Pakistan, got the message of America's new intolerance for harboring terrorists and the husbanding of weapons of mass destruction. Libya was the first to fold in late June 2003, shortly after the Iraq war started, and immediately ceased its nuclear development program and welcomed international inspection teams, prompting the United States to drop long-standing sanctions against the renegade country and its unpredictable and autocratic leader. Pakistan the year before had confessed its sins of selling nuclear secrets and started to reform its intelligence service. And the Saudis became more open about their role in financing international terrorism, including al Qaeda, and began shutting down Wahhabi charities and other sources of funds, while expanding oil production to meet rising global demand,

and even declaring a women's rights convention and free democratic municipal elections for regional councils in early 2005. For a new foreign policy that only first partially emerged on September 20, 2001, progress had been substantial and swift, with the potential democratization of Iraq and the greater Middle East as a special bonus to support President Bush's view that freedom and democracy would be the ultimate catharsis for Middle Eastern totalitarianism and autocracy.

DEMOCRATIZATION OF THE ARAB-MUSLIM WORLD

For a candidate who first campaigned for president by declaring his opposition to President Clinton's nation-building efforts in Haiti, Bosnia, and Kosovo, President George W. Bush, to use a term he made famous in attacking his opponent in the 2004 presidential campaign, certainly "flip-flopped" on the issue of democratization. That remarkable change in policy perspective between the candidate for president and the elected president resulted from the education that he had received from the Vulcans and a sobering evolution in the President's thinking. Traditionally, Republican internationalists had opposed advocating regime change in countries friendly to the United States, but George Shultz and Ronald Reagan had changed all that—George Bush the candidate simply hadn't gotten the message yet. Instead, the new president brought expectations about the possibilities for nation-building to new heights by incorporating it into the bedrock of America's national security policy and made it the principal antidote to radical militant Islam that redefined American relationships with autocratic governments all over the world.

As will be seen, President Bush's idea of democratization meant much more than simply allowing elections as American foreign policy was formerly practiced. In Niall Ferguson's [2001] classic 1913 story of the American ambassador to Great Britain who suggested that the American solution to a Mexican coup was "Make 'em vote and live by their decisions...[and if they didn't get it right, we'd] continue to shoot men for that little space till they learn to vote and to rule themselves." Democracy, in Bush's mind, was much more than the mere trapping of elections with the establishment of a government acceptable to the United States. America would establish a process, preferably under the auspices of the United Nations, for a democratic constitution and free elections of a national assembly, and then take its chances on the preferences of Muslim voters. The Bush administration truly believed and it was committed to the principle that freedom and democracy could take hold and prosper in the Muslim world, even though the history of democracy in the Middle East was limited to the checkered 80-year experience of the Republic of Turkey.

Today a new way is emerging in the Arab-Muslim world. For the first time since the end of the First World War, democracy, freedom, human rights, and open markets signal the prospect for a new era of enlightenment and openness that can guide the Arab-Muslim world into a better future for everyone. Gary C. Gambill [2004] stated:

> The Bush administration's Mideast democracy promotion campaign has already borne fruit. Since details of the initiative were leaked in February (2004), Arab governments have launched their own reform initiatives and allowed pro-democracy activists more freedom to organize and express themselves, while the Arab League passed an unprecedented resolution expressing commitment to "democratic practice" and human rights.

The Afghan Experience

The first test of Bush's democratization policy was in Afghanistan, and the early stages of forming an elected government proceeded quite well. Six months after the December 2001 U.N. conference appointing the interim authority, a second conference, a grand one called the Loya Jirga, was convened in Kabul for 1,500 elected delegates from throughout the country to decide on the structure of the future government, appoint a group to prepare a draft of a new constitution for Afghanistan, arrange for general elections, and ratify the election of Hamid Karzai as the interim president. A draft constitution providing for a strong presidential system of government was approved at a meeting of the Grand Assembly with 502 delegates during the period from December 14th to January 4, 2004. Karzai signed into law the Afghan constitution on January 26, 2004. Originally, the Assembly had hoped to hold elections for the first permanent president during that summer, but they were postponed because of a slow voter registration process.

By October 9, 2004, 10.5 million Afghans had registered to vote and about 8 million exercised that right with Karzai receiving 55.4 percent of their votes. Such a high turnout ratio (76.2 percent) in the country's first presidential election was indeed quite remarkable. Even more remarkable was the fact that the recently vanquished Taliban and al Qaeda forces were unable to cause any serious mischief or security challenges during the elections. Although a higher percentage of men than women voted, it was a dramatic about-face for 40 percent of the registered female voters to vote in less than "three years after the downfall of misogynist Taliban regime" [Qayash]. Hamid Karzai was sworn in on December 7, 2004 as Afghanistan's first elected president in the country's nearly 260-year history, exactly three years to the day after the fall of the Taliban. The next step in the democratization process is the election of its new parliament in September 2005. A final goal for the completion of a strong national government was the creation of a 70,000 troop national army to wrestle control from the local tribal chieftains.

Since 9/11, everything about Afghanistan has moved at fast-forward speed. There is still much to be done to restore the country's infrastructure after more than 25 years of warfare throughout the country, to find a means of stopping the poppy crop, while finding alternative ways of earning a living in this barren mountainous region of the world, and to overcome the deep-rooted ethnic antipathy that has been so prominent in Afghanistan's history. The rapid pace of developing a democratic republic augers well for both Afghanistan and the success of President Bush's democratization policy as the antidote to Islamist militancy. In September of 2001, no one could have predicted such remarkable progress in this remote and ungovernable state, let alone the removal of the Taliban government in only two months. So far, Afghanistan has been a success story for the Bush administration, and that success played well in the battle with al Qaeda for the hearts and minds of the Muslim world.

The Iraqi Experience

The description of the war in Iraq is the subject of the next chapter, but here, in a discussion of America's foreign policy in the war on terror, the effect of democratization is addressed in settling the war between the American "occupiers" and the Baathist-Islamist militant insurgency in Iraq. Originally, the Americans had hoped to hold free elections in June 2004, but the efforts of the Iraqi insurgents made earlier elections impossible due to the lack of security in the Sunni Triangle northwest of Baghdad and the unwillingness of the United Nations to conduct early elections. As a result, the Iraq elections were postponed until January 30, 2005 and even then there were debates right up to the last moment about the advisability of holding elections in the face of vicious terrorist attacks and a possible Sunni boycott.

The Americans, through Paul Bremer, administrator of the Coalition Provisional Authority, had originally proposed that a new Iraqi government be elected by district caucuses that would choose district representatives to the 275-member

National Assembly. However, the Shiite leader Grand Ayatollah Sistanti insisted on national elections, which eventually resulted in some dozen Iraq political parties running slates of candidates and claiming seats in the assembly based on the proportional total each party received in the national elections. This approach had the advantage of each Iraqi citizen being franchised without any intermediary being selected in the caucuses. However, it had the disadvantage of disenfranchising voters in most Sunni districts where the insurgency was strong and voters were intimidated.

The elections made it clear that the Iraq insurgency was only a threat in the predominantly Sunni areas of Iraq—four of 18 provinces—because the insurgency was led by Baathist party leaders who tolerated and protected the al Qaeda-led Islamist militants from other nearby Arab states. These outside militants, especially Saudi suicide bombers imbued with fanatical Wahhabi intolerance of Shiites, would occasionally venture into Shiite territory and unleash powerful suicide bombs as a means of fostering civil war, but their murderous efforts were largely unsuccessful in a strategic sense. The agents of al Qaeda had no protectors in the Shiite parts of Iraq, and the Grand Ayatollah Ali Sistanti, the highest Shiite cleric and a wise political leader, counseled his fellow Shiites to "turn the other cheek" because he knew that the militants could not spread fear and intimidation among his followers. It was quite a different story for the moderate Sunnis, who received leaflets from the Islamist militants that warned, "To those of you who think you can vote and then run away, we will shadow you and catch you, and we will cut off your heads and the heads of your children" [Filkins, 1/26/05]. Most Sunni political leaders advocated a boycott of the election, after calling for a postponement right up to January 30th. The perverse effect of this imbalance in security was to limit the participation of Sunnis in the election process while at the same time permitting the majority Shiites to go to the polls without intimidation. Thus, the majority position of the Shiites was further enhanced in the national election results.

The elections were extremely popular with the Iraqis as a whole and the turnout, even with the threats of death to all voters, turned out to be 57.8 percent of all registered voters, with turnouts as high as 92 percent in the northern Kurdish province of Dohuk to as low as 2 percent in the western Sunni province of Anbar [Burns and Glanz]. The polls were run by 100,000 Iraqi poll workers, risking their lives to bring democracy to Iraq. The U.S. military played a very low key and almost invisible role providing security around the polling places, while Iraqi military and police personnel were highly visible in protecting the election sites. The effect of voting, combined with the visible absence of American soldiers in the voting process, filtered out the American "occupier" image for many Iraqis and other Muslims watching the news on Al Jazeera television, for Americans were now seen less as occupiers and more as enablers of a new Iraq. Prior to the election, Americans were blamed for all of Iraq's problems—the lack of electricity, gasoline, crumbling infrastructure, and security. "All that seemed to have changed last Sunday [election day], when millions of Iraqis streamed to the polls…Suddenly empowered with the vote, Iraqis no longer seemed to view America as all-powerful, or themselves as unable to affect events. A result has been a suddenly more accepting view of the United States" [Filkins, 2/6/05]. Even the U.S. troops serving in Iraq were ennobled: "Soldiers ranging from privates to senior officers described last Sunday's national election as vindication for over a year of hard service. The unexpectedly strong turnout, they said, altered their perception about the willingness of Iraqis to embrace the American mission here and helped project a rare positive image of the U.S. military following such stains as the Abu Ghraib prisoner abuse scandal last year" [Fainaru].

Although the Shiite slate created by Grand Ayatollah Ali Sistanti, the United Iraqi Alliance, won 48 percent of the total vote, it fell well short of the two-thirds vote required to organize the new government. That left the Kurdish Alliance, with 26 percent of the vote, in position to broker the structure of the new coalition government with the Shiites and Sunnis. Because the Kurds favored a secular government, the two-thirds vote requirement virtually guaranteed that the new government would be secular and not an Islamist theocracy like the Shiite government of Iran, even if the United Iraqi Alliance reneged on its secular-government campaign promises. The Iraqi List, a party put together by interim Prime Minister Ayad Allawi, gathered 14 percent of the vote, leaving 12 percent of the vote split among nine different minority parties. Even with the low Sunni voter turnout, 40 Sunnis were elected to the National Assembly (15 percent of the seats), slightly less than they would have been afforded on a proportional basis since the Sunnis represent about 20 percent of the total Iraqi population [Taheri].

Despite the low showing by the American-backed Allawi party, American interests were well served by the results of the election for the formation of a secular coalition promises to include Sunni representation in the new prime minister's cabinet. Soon after the elections, Shiite leaders made it clear to disenfranchised Sunnis that they were willing to find ways to include Sunni representation in the government through their powers to appoint members of the executive branch and to the powerful committee drafting the new Iraqi constitution. "The Association of Muslim Scholars [an important Sunni political organization]...said it would abide by the results of the ballot, even if it viewed the government as lacking legitimacy" [Shadid and Struck]. The reasons for the Shiite generosity, after centuries of domination and ruthless persecution by Sunnis, are the Grand Ayatollah's attitude of forgiveness and a pragmatic realization that ratification of the new constitution requires approval by more than 15 of the 18 Iraqi provinces; i.e., the Sunnis by virtue of their majorities in four provinces had veto rights over the new constitution according to the rules for the drafting of a new constitution adopted by the coalition and its appointed interim government. Moreover, the Kurds in the north control three provinces and thereby had a constitutional "trump card" to play in negotiating seats in the new government. Forgiveness and the old-fashioned give-and-take of pragmatic politics may provide a sound basis for establishing and maintaining the new democratic republic of Iraq.

Even more important to the eventual success of the Bush Doctrine was the reaction of other Middle East Muslim nations to the progress being made in Iraq. First, the high turnout in the elections and the great personal risks of many Iraqis exceeded all expectations, sending a message about the popularity of free democratic elections throughout the Arab-Muslim world. Second, the United States signaled a clear willingness to abide by whatever decisions the newly elected government would make, including its willingness to pull out of Iraq if the new government wishes. That willingness changed the American status in Iraq from occupiers to enablers in the minds of many Iraqis and, indeed, other Muslims, including millions of Iranians chafing against the autocratic Shiite theocracy. Third, the status of the Islamist militants changed from liberator to violent reactionary, standing in the way of progress for the people. The Americans explicitly stated that they would not be driven out of Iraq by shelling and suicide bombers; Islamist terrorist attacks were now viewed as attacks on fellow Muslims. The same bravery exhibited by Iraqis in the election would soon break down the protection of the insurgents by moderate Sunnis, who in increasing numbers were willing to step forward and provide vital intelligence information for the security forces to triumph over the Islamist terrorists.

The successful Iraqi elections served as a powerful inspiration throughout the Middle East and broader Muslim world, and they were preceded by two other elections that helped set the stage and provide momentum for the process in Iraq, for many critics on both sides of the Atlantic had held little hope for a successful election process in Iraq. A positive trend started first in December 2004 with events in Ukraine, a former Soviet republic, when free democratic elections ousted a former strong-arm autocrat. Then shortly after the New Year, the Iraqi elections received another boost from an unexpected source—the Palestinians.

On January 9th, Palestinian voters freely elected Mahmoud Abbas following the death of the Palestinian dictator Yasser Arafat, and Abbas went on to proclaim his intent to end the armed Palestinian struggle against Israel. On January 30th, 8 million Iraqi voters braved bombs and bullets to cast their ballots, and on February 10th, Saudi Arabia held its first-ever municipal elections, only for men and only for half the seats at that, but the beginning of a possible fracture in the royal family's absolute rule nevertheless. The Saudi government also hosted a government conference on terrorism and a conference on women's rights, suggesting that the Saudis had taken steps to get on board the liberalization bandwagon while at the same time fighting al Qaeda at home.

More events unfolded within 30 days of the Iraqi elections. On February 26, 2005, Egypt's president, aging military dictator Hosni Mubarak, announced that in the forthcoming presidential election his government would permit other candidates to run in addition to Mubarak. On February 28th, tens of thousands of demonstrators in Beirut forced the resignation of the pro-Syrian government, and President Bush, with support from the French government, demanded that Syria immediately remove all of its 15,000 troops and intelligence agents from Lebanon. By mid-March 2005, the Syrians had pulled back to the Bakaa valley and with further American and U.N. demands they totally pulled out of Lebanon before the Lebanese elections in May 2005, and with a hint that Lebanese independence might signal an end to the autocratic Baathist regime in Syria. On March 7, 2005, hundreds of Kuwaiti women demonstrated outside the Kuwaiti parliament, demanding political rights including the right to vote and be nominated in elections. They stated that their demands do not contradict Islamic law and Kuwait's parliament agreed to address their issues as the UAE announced reforms and the Bahrain government announced that courses in democracy will be taught in the Bahrain schools. And as Muslim Kyrgyzstan threw off vestiges of autocratic leadership from its Soviet past in March 2005, hope of an Iranian spring emerged later that month when thousands of Iranian women were seen on the streets of Tehran wearing pink scarves and pink coats in defiance of the autocratic Islamist mullahs who seized power from the Shah in 1979.

From Lebanon to Palestine, Saudi Arabia, and Egypt, dramatic events unfolded following the January 2005 elections in Iraq, holding out the possibility of a true Arab spring that might begin to bloom, all because of the events surrounding free elections in Iraq which had a snowball effect, with more democratic countries supporting the American call for freedom and democracy in the Middle East. Moreover, Libya had changed its colors and gave up its nuclear weapons as people throughout the region began to sense the possibility of change.

The rapid pace of development in the Middle East surprised many people in the U.S. and in Europe, leading even the Germans and French to publicly ask, "Could Bush have been right" when he stated in his Second Inaugural Address America's goal of "ending tyranny in our world"? Truly, the paradigm in Iraq and the Middle East had totally changed, as Tom Friedman [2005] concluded in a recent column:

> [W]hatever you thought about this war, it's not about Mr. Bush anymore. It's about the aspirations of the Iraqi majority to build an alternative to Sadd-amism. By voting the way they did, in the face of real danger, Iraqis have earned the right to ask everyone now to put aside their squabbles and focus on what is no longer just a pipe dream but a real opportunity to implement decent consensual government in the heart of the Arab Muslim world.

That many difficulties lie ahead is obvious, but seeds of progress and hope have been planted and Middle East autocrats now ponder an uncertain future. It is possible that radical Islamist ideologues could replace certain autocrats as they did in Iran in 1979 when the Shah fell. It is also possible that Islamists could win democratic elections and lead governments dominated by anti-American extremists, but that is one of the risks inherent in freedom and democracy. The Middle East has been frozen in rigid autocracy for centuries, and that is now set to change because people understand that the aspirations of the Iraqi people are ultimately the aspirations of oppressed people around the world, especially in the Middle East, where the Bush Doctrine of using democracy as an antidote to radical Islamist militarism was first tested.

CONCLUSIONS ABOUT THE BUSH DOCTRINE

Perhaps the best way to judge the effectiveness of the Bush Doctrine of freedom and democracy as the antidote to Bin Ladenism is to ask the following questions: How would the outcomes in the war on terror have differed if the United States had continued to pursue al Qaeda following its Cold War rules of engagement? What would the Middle East be like today with Saddam Hussein still in power? What would have been accomplished if the United States pursued multilateral (neither unilateral nor hegemonic), non-preemptive and non-regime-change policies that existed prior to 9/11? Could the United States have escaped additional al Qaeda attacks on its homeland solely by raising its defensive fences around its borders while the pursuit of al Qaeda proceeded more slowly than the breathtaking pace the Bush administration elected to employ? Answering these questions is, of course, highly speculative, but enough reasonable approximations can be made to demonstrate the wisdom and efficacy of the Bush Doctrine.

First, the United States would probably have been able to oust the Taliban from Afghanistan and destroy the al Qaeda training camps in the country with a United Nations sanctioned coalition of NATO, Russia, Japan, China, and many other nations, providing such a coalition could have responded quickly enough. World sympathy for the United States after sustaining such an uncivilized attack on 9/11 in which so many innocent civilian lives were taken would easily have supported a unanimous Security Council resolution asking the Taliban to surrender Osama bin Laden and to close his training camps or face an invasion to capture and destroy. Even with widespread support, however, the legalistic maneuvers at the U.N. would have taken months, not weeks, before an Afghan invasion could have been undertaken and much of the same opposition to the U.S. would have surfaced as it did during the U.N. debates leading up to the Iraq war. The United States would have had to produce much more formal evidence of bin Laden's guilt, and it is doubtful that bin Laden would have been so forthright in admitting al Qaeda's responsibility. In addition, the military operations in Afghanistan would hardly have been improved by a much greater number of countries offering to serve in the invasion. Indeed, the cooperation that the allies obtained from the anti-Taliban guerrillas might have been more difficult to organize if the Russians had been participants in the coalition because of the stigma of the hated Soviet Union and its incursion into Afghanistan in the 1980s. In any event, the operation would have been much more complex and slower; the Taliban and al Qaeda would not have been expelled from Afghanistan in less than three months after 9/11. All other developments in Afghanistan would similarly have been delayed: the U.N. conference to establish an interim government and the free elections to choose a permanent government would probably have been years later. Whether the same outcome could have been achieved is, at minimum, questionable. Furthermore, the disruption of al Qaeda would have been similarly postponed, and perhaps bin Laden could have organized additional strikes against the United States before his entire organization was uprooted and dispersed throughout Pakistan and the Middle East. At least, he would have had more time for an orderly transfer and consolidation of his forces.

On the Palestinian-Israeli front, few can criticize the Bush administration for its failure to advance the cause of peace, even if the other American wartime activities crowded the issue off its agenda, for as long as Yasser Arafat remained president of the PLO, no progress in negotiations with Israel could have been expected. With the 2005 Palestinian elections and a new cooperative spirit on both sides, there is renewed hope for a viable Palestinian state and a long-term solution to the Israeli-Palestinian conflict.

The invasion of Iraq is much more problematic and, of course, that is the issue that made the Bush Doctrine so controversial in the United States and especially in Europe. Some may believe that the United States, behaving more deferentially toward Europe, could have persuaded the Security Council to sanction the invasion of Iraq and the overthrow of Saddam Hussein with a much larger coalition force that would have provided funding support for both the military and rebuilding operations in Europe. Such an outcome is, however, extremely unlikely given the strength of the anti-war movement in Europe and the lack of independent European statesmen who would have taken on public opinion in their countries as Tony Blair was willing to do in the U.K. It is easy to forget how difficult it was for Tony Blair to challenge his own Labor Party on the Iraq issue, risking his political career on a cause for which at a minimum 75 percent of the British electorate disagreed [See Stothard]. Can anyone imagine Jacques Chirac of France or Gerhard Schroeder of Germany having the political fortitude to challenge such a majority opinion, even if it had not been in their countries' and Russia's economic interests to keep Saddam Hussein in office and to maintain the status quo in Iraq? There would not have been an invasion of Iraq without the Bush Doctrine that called for the United States to act unilaterally and preemptively—preventively—in its own interests to defend the United States and the world from Islamist militants.

And without the Iraq invasion, how much cooperation would Americans have received from the Saudis in cutting off the flow of funds to al Qaeda and radical clerics around the world? The Pakistanis and the Libyans may well have become more cooperative with a U.N. resolution and coalition in Afghanistan, but it is unlikely that Saudi behavior would have changed. In all likelihood, they would have continued to stonewall American efforts to stop their funding of al Qaeda, for Saudi Arabia is still schizophrenic about the bargain the al Sauds made over a century ago with the Wahhabis to strengthen the al Saud family's claim to the Arabian throne. Without changing Saudi behavior, the danger of further al Qaeda attacks on the United States would have been significantly greater. However, what about the increased number of jihadist recruits that came to join the

Baathist insurgents in Iraq? Most of these recruits were used as suicide bombers and most came from Saudi Arabia [Nordland et al., 29]. Although that number may have been increased, even substantially, there is merit, from the standpoint of defending the United States, in drawing these extremists into an arena away from the American homeland where they could be killed or captured without threatening innocent American lives. Perhaps there was more of a rationale for the American electorate in the 2004 presidential election choosing Bush over Kerry on the basis that Bush could better fight the war against terror, even as they had increasing doubts about the advisability of the Iraq invasion and Bush did such a poor job of explaining how the Iraq war fit into the overall strategy of defeating al Qaeda.

There can be little question that the Bush Doctrine and its aggressive implementation put Osama bin Laden back on his heels and he became the reactor, no longer the aggressor. Bush's goal of taking the offensive and putting al Qaeda on the defensive certainly had been accomplished and there had been no more attacks on the American homeland since 9/11. However, it was not until the January 30, 2005 elections in Iraq that the world and, especially the Arab-Muslim world, saw the power and wisdom of the Bush Doctrine and the proposed antidote to radical Islamist militarism fully unveiled. The Afghan experience with its earlier election had been illuminating, but the pride that so many Iraqis showed in their fearless march to the polls kindled the fires for freedom and democracy that Bush believed would lead to real reform in the Middle East. Whether democracy spreads and takes root in the Arab-Muslim world will be the essential and final test of the long-term effectiveness of the Bush Doctrine.

The next chapter examines the difficulty the allied coalition faced in creating the climate that permitted the January 2005 Iraq elections. The foreign policy of the Bush Doctrine may have been sound, but its execution, as we shall see, left much to be desired for a number of reasons.

CHAPTER FOUR BIBLIOGRAPHY

Broad, William J., and Sanger, David E., "As Nuclear Secrets Emerge, More Are Suspected," *New York Times*, December 26, 2004.

Burns, John F. and Glanz, James, "Iraqi Shiites Win, But Margin Less Than Projection," *New York Times*, February 14, 2005.

Bush, George, "Address to a Joint Session of Congress," September 20, 2001, http://www. whitehouse.gov/newsrelease/2001/09/print/20010920-8.html.

___, "President Delivers State of Union Address," January 29, 2002, http://www. whitehouse.gov/news/releases/2002/01/print/20020129-11.html.

___. "President Bush Delivers Graduation Speech at West Point," June 1, 2002, http://www.whitehouse.gov/news/releases/2002/06/print/20020601-3.html.

___, "The National Security Strategy of the United States of America," September 17, 2002, http://www.whitehouse.gov/nsc/print/nssall.html.

Daalder, Ivo H., and Lindsay, James M., *American Unbound, The Bush Revolution in Foreign Policy*, Washington, DC: Brookings Institution Press, 2003.

Fainaru, Steve, "Elation, Reflection for GIs Going Home," *Washington Post*, February 6, 2005.

Ferguson, Niall, "Clashing Civilizations or Mad Mullahs: The United States between Informal and Formal Empire," *The Age of Terror*, ed. by Strobe Talbott and Nayan Chanda, New York: Basic Books, 2001.

Filkins, Dexter, "Insurgents Vowing to Kill Iraqis Who Brave the Polls on Sunday," *New York Times*, January 26, 2005.

___, "Suddenly, It's 'America Who,'" *New York Times*, February 6, 2005.

Friedman, George, *America's Secret War, Inside the Hidden Worldwide Struggle between America and Its Enemies*, New York: Doubleday, 2004.

Friedman, Thomas L., "A Day to Remember," *New York Times*, February 2, 2005.

Gaddis, John Lewis, *Surprise, Security, and the American Experience*, Cambridge, MA: President and Fellows of Harvard College, 2004.

___, "Grand Strategy in the Second Term," *Foreign Affairs*, January/February, 2005.

Gambill, Gary C., "Title Missing," *Middle East Intelligence Bulletin*, July 2004.

Halper, Stefan, and Clarke, Jonathan, *America Alone, The Neo-Conservatives and the Global Order*, Cambridge, U.K.: Cambridge University Press, 2004.

Horowitz, David, *Unholy Alliance: Radical Islam and the American Left*, Washington, DC: Regnery Publishing, Inc., 2004.

Kagan, Robert, *Of Paradise and Power, America and Europe in the New World Order*, New York: Alfred A. Knopf, 2003.

Koh, Harold Hongju, "Preserving American Values: The Challenge at Home and Abroad," *The Age of Terror*, ed. by Strobe Talbott and Nayan Chandra, New York: Basic Books, 2001.

Mann, James, *Rise of the Vulcans, The History of Bush's War Cabinet*, New York: Penguin Group (USA), Inc., 2004.

Nordling, Rod, Masland, Tom, and Dickey, Christopher, "Unmasking the Insurgents," *Newsweek*, February 5, 2005.

Podhoretz, Norman, "World War IV: How It Started, What It Means, and Why We Have to Win," *Commentary*, September, 2004, pp. 17-54.

Qayash, Rafat, "Lessons from Afghanistan's presidential election," *Afghanistan's Development Network*, November 18, 2004,
http://www.afgha.com/?af=printnews &sid=46964.

Scowcroft, Brent, "Don't Attack Iraq," *Wall Street Journal*, August 16, 2002.
Shadid, Anthony, and Struck, Doug, "Top Shiite Welcomes Overtures by Sunnis," *Washington Post*, February 6, 2005.

Stothard, Peter, *Thirty Days: Tony Blair and the Test of History*, New York: HarperCollins Publishers, 2003.

Taheri, Amir, "Iraq on the Road to Democracy," *Arab News*, February 19, 2005.

Woodward, Bob, *Bush at War*, New York, Simon & Schuster, 2003.

___, *Plan of Attack*, New York: Simon & Schuster, 2004.

Yergin, Daniel, *Shattered Peace: The Origins of the Cold War and the National Security State*, Boston: Houghton Mifflin Company, 1977.

5

The Iraq War—Where Nothing Met Expectations

Military history often takes years to be accurately researched, understood, digested, and properly written, so this account, prepared largely from contemporary reports, must be interpreted for what it is—an initial assessment and reaction from open sources. The Bush administration's successes in rapidly developing a new and comprehensive national security policy and its quick triumph in Afghanistan unfortunately did not carry over into Iraq for a number of reasons, mainly because of incredibly poor intelligence but also because of poor planning in preparing to stabilize and govern a defeated nation.

Going into Iraq was quite different from the Afghan campaign. From the start, U.S. intelligence agencies had more valid information about Afghanistan than they did about Iraq. At the outset, the agencies were not aware of the extent of the deficiencies in their Iraqi intelligence, which was too often based on the word of Iraqi exiles, whose primary objective was convincing the United States about the ease of invasion, and a few covert agents on the ground in the friendly Kurdish portion of the north. Secretary Rumsfeld and the Joint Staff in the Pentagon accepted the "rosy" picture in large part, no doubt, because it fit preconceived notions and because the CIA had so little information and so few agents in Iraq. As a consequence of the lack of good intelligence on the ground and because of misleading intelligence, the early months of the invasion produced many surprises in what the Americans found. This subsequently led to many unanticipated difficulties as American forces were required to operate in the dark, with the exception of the sketchy outlines provided by overhead satellite pictures and other electronic intelligence sources.

The most disappointing aspect of American military performance in Iraq was the lack of an adequate postwar plan which led to indecisiveness and lack of spontaneity by commanders in responding to the actual conditions on the ground due

155

to the lack of an understanding of the enemy and lack of an adequate strategy that could adapt to changing circumstances. Americans have historically been good at this because of ingenuity and the ability to adapt to the unexpected. In the past, even though there might have been huge discrepancies between what commanders had been told they might find and what they actually found, American military tradition had always taken great pride in being flexible and inventive in encountering the unexpected. Not so in this case.

The problems of poor intelligence mushroomed into even worse tactical decision-making, as the failures to respond to actual conditions led to momentary paralysis, followed by another round of mistaken tactics. The war seemed to be fought as if it were governed by Murphy's Law: not only did everything seem to go wrong that could, but when it did, the U.S. military made the wrong corrections, magnifying the ill-effects of its previous errors. The generals in the war zone and their Defense Department managers in Doha, Tampa, and Washington were out-strategized in fighting what soon became an out-of-control war against determined insurgents consisting of remnants of the defeated Baathist Army and foreign Islamist fighters.

OFF TO AN APPARENTLY GOOD START

On March 17, 2003, President Bush issued his final ultimatum: "Saddam Hussein and his sons must leave Iraq within 48 hours. Their refusal to go will result in military conflict commenced at a time of our choosing." The war got off to what seemed to be an apparently good start on March 19, 2003 when a covert CIA agent reported that he believed he knew the whereabouts of Saddam Hussein south of Baghdad that evening. The invasion was clandestinely launched as planned that afternoon with the introduction of Special Operations Forces into the west and north of Iraq; Polish forces were to capture an oil platform in the Persian Gulf and Australian forces were to safeguard a dam. At 7:12 p.m. EST, after a conference with all of his war council members, the President departed from original plans and ordered some 40 Tomahawk cruise missiles and two bunker-busting 2,000 pound bombs from two F-117 stealth single-seat fighter jets to be dropped on the Dora Farm where Saddam was supposedly sleeping. At 9:30 p.m. reports came into Washington that air raid sirens in Baghdad had gone off, and at 9:45 the White House press secretary announced that the President would address the nation at 10:15 that night. The President's address was brief and without detail, simply saying that the early stages of the military campaign against

Saddam Hussein had started, mentioning the fact that 35 nations were giving crucial support, and suggesting that the campaign could be longer and more perilous than some predicted [Woodward, 398]. Whether or not it was true, reports from the covert agents at the Dora Farm site reported that, although Saddam had not been killed, he was at least injured and shaken up in the bombing.

Two hours later, however, Saddam Hussein, looking "pale and drawn,…appeared on television to deliver a rambling, defiant speech full of exhortations to his people to resist the attackers" [Walker, 24]. Nevertheless, the Americans had scored a victory of sorts by playing into the paranoid fears of the Iraqi dictator who looked uncomfortable and unsure of himself reading his speech with glasses that made him look old and uncommanding. Although Saddam delivered several additional speeches in the next few days, beginning first on April 4th while walking through neighborhood streets of Baghdad and continuing right up to April 9th, he had already turned over the command of the Iraqi defense force to his two sons, Uday and Qusay, and soon went into hiding for fear of being overthrown by his own army. The war had started and the coalition forces had made a good start, improvising a direct attack on the head of the Iraqi government in the grand style of the American "can-do" military tradition. The failure to continue this style of adaptive warfare would prove to be much to the disadvantage of the American forces.

The Easy Part

The next day, March 20, 2003, the invasion commenced as originally planned with Special Operations Forces partially controlling the vast western desert area to prevent Scud missile firings and the southern oil fields to prevent the burning of the oil wells as had occurred in Kuwait in the first Gulf War. The major ground invasion started at 10:00 p.m. (2200) on the 20th because the planned nine hours of "shock and awe" bombing did not begin until 1:00 p.m. (1300) on the 21st as originally planned, reversing the normally predictable schedule of softening-up bombing that normally preceded American ground attacks. The enemy had come to expect that the Americans would open their military campaign with an extended air barrage using missiles and bombers to destroy or neutralize critical targets on the ground such as the Iraqi air force, command and control centers, and communication systems, as in the first Iraq war and more recently in Afghanistan. This time the Pentagon even launched a discomforting public relations effort claiming a "shock and awe" air campaign, which in fact was much lighter than in the first Gulf War because the U.S. did not want to kill innocent civilians or destroy too much Iraqi infrastructure. Baghdad's electric power system, for example, had been taken out in the first Gulf War but was protected this time around so electricity might be readily available to the victorious allied army after the fall of Baghdad.

The American invasion plan, honed to perfection by many months of planning and incessant questioning by Secretary Rumsfeld, had been to strike quickly with a small, mobile, well-coordinated and integrated military force. General Franks' plan was for the U.S. Army's 5th Corps to quickly cross the Iraq-Kuwait border and attack Baghdad west of the Euphrates. The U.S. Marine Corps would make a swift, parallel advance and attack east of the river by heading toward Nasiriya and crossing the Euphrates at that point. The British, with support from U.S. Marines, would secure Basra, Iraq's second largest city, and Iraq's port in the south.

The leading elements of the invasion force were expected to reach the outskirts of Baghdad so quickly that enemy Iraqi forces would barely have time to organize a defense of the city. Such rapid movement of the first units meant that succeeding, reinforcement units would be expected to carry out the mopping up of enemy troops that had been ignored by the rapidly moving first line of attack. By Saturday, March 22nd, the lead column of the U.S. 3rd Infantry Division was already 150 miles deep into Iraq. While the British troops advancing on Basra in southern Iraq encountered heavier than expected resistance from unconventional Iraqi forces, the British were able to secure the Rumaylah Oil Fields after the initial U.S. Marine incursion, preventing catastrophic oil fires that had been so problematic in Kuwait in the first Gulf War. After safeguarding the oil fields, the British made progress toward Umm Qasr, the Iraqi port south of Basra on the Persian Gulf, which would be vital as a key saltwater port for bringing in humanitarian relief supplies, as well as additional military personnel and equipment.

The advance forces wore hot and heavy chemical defense equipment and gas masks in fear of Saddam's use of the chemical or biological weapons that U.S. and British intelligence believed had been stockpiled to counter the invasion forces. Over time, the American soldiers ceased to wear the hot, bulky suits and gas masks, but the troops were ordered to keep them readily available at all times. The leading American forces met very little resistance as they moved around various Iraqi cities in their path, while succeeding troops behind the front line forces faced a few pockets of Iraqi resistance willing to fight for their homeland in some of the cities. The British troops invading Basra in the south met more organized resistance and faced tougher fighting and, after the Iraqis were routed, only polite acceptance from the Shiite population, not the welcoming celebrations for the liberators that the Iraqi exiles had promised the planners in Tampa and Washington.

On the fifth day of the invasion, March 24th, U.S. forward troops met stubborn resistance along the Euphrates River near Nasiriyah, Samawa, and Najaf, and later in the holy Shiite city Karbala. Embedded reporters had become accustomed to the coalition's rapid success thus far, and these anticipated combat delays caused them to challenge the administration's war plans which had only sustained a minor setback and delay. The American solution was to bring in close air support and hammer the Iraqi troops that were dug into the cities, but that took time due to bad weather caused by a severe three-day sandstorm throughout all of southern Iraq. The press came to believe that the American invasion plan was in real trouble, and for the first time reports even started to emerge from retired generals back in the United States, saying that the coalition forces did not have enough troops on the ground in Iraq. General Tommy Franks may indeed be one of the first army officers in history since Stonewall Jackson to believe that smaller, faster forces were to be preferred to larger numbers of soldiers. In that view, he certainly differed from former JCS Chairman, General Colin Powell, who planned the first Gulf War with overwhelming force that came to be known as the "Powell Doctrine," although Powell did not raise serious objections when the president's war council approved Franks' final war plan [Woodward, 125-6]. Private contractors were used to supplement traditional military logistics support functions like supply and food management that were normally operated by the military, thus explaining some of the diminished size of the invading forces who were for the most part all combatants due to the logistics "outsourcing." The United States may well have had enough fighting troops to do the job—the history books will have to tell that story—but one thing is certain: the U.S. did not have an adequate postwar stabilization plan or enough good intelligence information to deploy its combat forces effectively after the fall of Baghdad and overthrow of Saddam Hussein. Nor did the United States understand Saddam Hussein's guerilla warfare strategy and what the coalition forces were to face in the Sunni Triangle after the fall of Baghdad.

When the sandstorms finally abated and the bad weather gave way to clear desert skies in late March, U.S. Air Force and Navy pilots started flying as many as two thousand sorties a day, comparable to the level in the first Gulf War. "Something quite strange began happening; Iraqi forces that had been plotted carefully on the maps started to disappear. Iraqi forces that were thought to be there one day simply weren't there the next" [Friedman, 298]. And so far there had been no chemical or biological attacks. It seemed that the Iraqi forces had pulled back because they apparently felt too vulnerable in the open desert. By April 5th, American troops, proceeding cautiously, had reached the southern edge of Baghdad and reconnaissance probes into the city were ordered. No significant fire was drawn from these probes and commanders still did not know how much resistance could be expected in a full-scale attack on the Iraqi capital. Still not certain on the 7th of April, American forces sent a missile into a restaurant in the Mansour district of Baghdad in a diversionary attempt to kill Saddam and disrupt Iraqi resistance. Finally, on April 9th, American forces entered Baghdad and began the formal occupation without meeting any organized resistance. On that day a large statue of Saddam was dramatically toppled by American troops and the world, watching live on television, thought the war was over, just three weeks after the American liberating forces had been launched from Kuwait. Nevertheless, the American invasion forces in Baghdad were uneasy, and they had every reason to be apprehensive, for nothing about this war had so far gone exactly as had been expected and planned.

Allied forces were aware that in October 2002 Saddam had freed nearly all criminals from his bleak and miserable Iraqi prisons, so the initial American reaction to the massive looting that occurred throughout Baghdad from the moment the city was captured was to place blame on the freed criminals. Many Iraqis, however, asserted that looting and pillaging were part of the cultural heritage of their tribes and a result of being freed from Saddam's brutality. Regardless of the cause, the systematic destruction and looting of government office buildings and facilities should have been a warning to U.S. commanders on the ground that this was not just random chaos, but might well have been pre-planned and well-orchestrated anarchy. The Baathist insurgency aided by al Qaeda-inspired foreign jihadists started immediately, but Secretary Rumsfeld dismissed these lawless activities with the explanation that "freedom is untidy," a totally mistaken and erroneous understanding of what was really happening. Even the Baghdad electrical grid and pipelines from the oil fields that the coalition had so carefully protected from bombing attacks were now victims of insurgent sabotage, leaving the defeated Iraqis literally in the dark and in the heat without fresh electricity, fresh water, or gasoline for their cars. While U.S. troops held the bridges over the Tigris River in Baghdad, looting in the city was confined to the east side of the river but as soon as the troops abandoned the bridges, looting moved across the river. If the U.S. occupation forces were ever to gain control over the looters, it is now clear that they should have held the bridges until they were ready to patrol the area west of the Tigris, but the "fog of war" at the time clouded what was really happening as Saddam's guerilla warfare plans unfolded.

Failures to Adjust to the New Realities

Despite the coalition's success in meeting or exceeding its timelines for capturing Iraq and toppling its evil and infamous dictator, Saddam Hussein, nothing about the war had gone according to the assumptions upon which the invasion plans had been built. No chemical or biological weapons had been unleashed against coalition forces, nor were any of the expected stockpiles of weapons of mass destruction (WMD) found as the coalition forces raced headlong into Baghdad. The expected barrage of Scud missiles on the coalition's reserve forces in Kuwait never fully materialized—only a dozen homemade Iraqi missiles, with just one hit, and that an empty theater building—and there were no Scud missile attacks on Israel as had been expected and as had actually occurred in the first Gulf War. Indeed, except for pockets of resistance by irregular Iraqi forces behind the front lines and the regular army defense around the holy city of Karbala, the Iraqi army didn't really engage the invading coalition forces in any significant way. Nor did they surrender in large numbers, as they had in the first Gulf War; they just seemed to disappear into nowhere as the coalition forces approached, and as they did in Baghdad where coalition forces had been prepared for brutal house-to-house urban combat. Indeed, the end of formal hostilities failed to measure up to Secretary Rumsfeld's expectations for there was no formal surrender or military coup ousting Saddam Hussein and his two sons. Hostilities simply ended, much to Rumsfeld's dismay, creating a significant vacuum that led to serious security problems for the coalition forces.

The reality of the war should have become apparent to American commanders in late March when an Iraqi civilian killed four American soldiers at a checkpoint in Najaf by blowing up his car. Other suicide bombers soon attacked and killed American soldiers during fighting around Baghdad. On April 12th a resistance group surfaced that called itself "The National Front for the Liberation of Iraq," which should have removed all doubt when the group issued a statement to a number of European governments proclaiming its intention to launch armed resistance and invite Arab volunteers from outside Iraq to join in overturning the American colonial occupation. Prior to the invasion, Saddam had started importing Arab jihadists from Saudi Arabia, Jordan, and Syria. Several journalists covering the war were aware of this development but American commanders paid little or no heed. [e.g., Anderson, 261]. It was as if no one wanted to believe American forces would be facing Islamist jihadists from adjacent Arab countries, but the signs were already there. There were other signs that Saddam's loyal Sunni Baathists had never intended a stout defense, but rather planned to melt away and then wage protracted guerrilla warfare against the occupiers, like Washington did against the British in the American Revolution, centering in the Sunni Triangle north and west of Baghdad where the Iraqis had deployed a heavy concentration of troops that had never been involved in any fighting against the invaders. General Franks believed that his diversionary tactics of keeping the Fourth Infantry Division in the Mediterranean off the coast of Turkey had forced the Iraqis to defend their northern flank until well into the invasion, but even when the invading American forces reached the outskirts of Baghdad, those Iraqi troops remained intact in the Sunni Triangle. Had the U.S. been able to simultaneously invade Iraq from the north through Turkey and from Kuwait in the south as originally planned, the Iraqi forces in the Sunni Triangle would have been forced to fight. Unfortunately, the United States had been denied basing rights by a nervous Turkish parliament and the Iraqi forces north of Baghdad lived to fight another war—a bloody and bitter Sunni insurgency, reinforced with al Qaeda-inspired, teenage Saudi jihadist suicide bombers.

The real surprise was that in defending Baghdad the Iraqis didn't fight house-to-house, where the advantage of American technical and armament superiority would have been substantially diminished. It has subsequently been learned that Saddam's war plan called for such resistance, which the Iraqis thought could delay the inevitable defeat by months, but Saddam's troops were apparently unwilling to make such a suicidal effort for what they believed was a lost cause [Nordland et al., 25]. In addition, many of the top generals in the Iraqi army, who might have led a more aggressive defense, were captured early in the fighting [Ibid]. Even without a stout defense of Baghdad, Saddam's retreating forces created enough chaos and sabotage to seriously disrupt the planned American liberation of Iraq and convert it into an arduous and bloody occupation.

In the central Sunni section of the country, the problem was wartime turmoil, confusion, and chaos, but south of Baghdad where the Shiite majority resided, the occupiers found something equally unexpected but far less troublesome—stability and order. The towns had been organized prior to the invasion by local Shiite religious leaders in charge of well-established administrative structures that were capable of governing their communities. These leaders simply went about their business without recognizing control from the occupying military authorities, and without any armed resistance. Because the CIA had so few operatives inside Iraq before the war, American intelligence had no means to detect the activities of neighboring Iranian forces that were in Iraq before the invasion, as they organized and prepared southern Iraqi communities for the anticipated American defeat of Saddam's Baathist regime. The Shiites did not revolt against the Allied invasion as the Sunnis did in the north because, as the majority religious group, they were ready and anxious to assume leadership in a permanent, post-invasion government. Ahmed Chalabi, the Defense Department's initial choice for interim Iraqi government leader, is alleged to have been an agent of the Iranian government and may have purposely misled the United States about conditions in Iraq before the invasion.

Nothing in Iraq was quite as it seemed—the United States had been "gulled" by Chalabi and his "Gucci Guerillas" from London just as the Saudis had gulled the Americans for years and clandestine Iranian forces had brazenly operated under the nose of Saddam Hussein's ineffective secret police.

THE OCCUPATION

The military victory over the Iraqis was won quickly in five or six weeks and with minimal allied casualties. From the start of the war through April 24th, when most of the mopping up operations north of Baghdad had been completed, the Americans and British lost 175 soldiers and sustained 635 wounded, while the Australians had no casualties. The Americans estimated that 2,230 Iraqi soldiers had been killed and 7,400 Iraqis had been taken prisoner, while civilian deaths were estimated between 1,930 and 2,377 [Walker, 211]. Most of the damage caused by allied bombing had been confined to Saddam Hussein's palaces and discreet military installations for it was the most accurate aerial bombardment in the history of warfare.

Except for the occasional misdirected bomb or missile due to faulty intelligence or questionable attempts to assassinate Saddam Hussein, the civilian population had been spared severe damage and casualties. Many Iraqi people may even have believed that the costs in human lives were worth the benefit of getting rid of Saddam Hussein's disliked and feared totalitarian regime. Unfortunately, fighting the war was the high point of the coalition's Iraq incursion. It was downhill from there and the occupation rapidly became a nightmare with no end in sight.

Failure to Plan

When asked why the D-Day planning process was taking so long, Eisenhower remarked to Churchill that "a plan is nothing but lack of a plan is everything." The most telling reason for the ensuing nightmare in Iraq was the lack of a good plan, which to Eisenhower was "everything," and to the Third Infantry Division in Iraq, its lack of a plan was also "everything," as noted in "...the extraordinary words in the 'after-action report'...[which] reads: 'Higher headquarters did not provide the Third Infantry Division (Mechanized) with a plan for Phase IV [the postwar phase]. As a result, Third Infantry Division transitioned into Phase IV in the absence of guidance'" [Zakaria]. Planning the occupation was the responsibility of Secretary Rumsfeld, the Joint Staff, and the commander of Central Command, General Tommy Franks, and his staff. Franks had worked extremely hard since 9/11, planning and executing the successful invasion of Afghanistan and had submitted his request for retirement from the U.S. Army in late April 2003, shortly after the coalition forces were launched into Iraq. Rumsfeld even offered him the highly prized position of Army Chief of Staff, but he declined. He was apparently exhausted and not in the frame of mind required to creatively devise occupation plans as he had done in fighting earlier campaigns, but the ultimate failure belongs to Rumsfeld and his civilian cadre in the Pentagon, not Franks. Notwithstanding the deplorable lack of good, actionable intelligence information, failure to provide American occupation forces with a well thought out plan for the occupation can only be considered gross dereliction of duty because of the lives put at risk and the conditions that developed in the Sunni sector of Iraq after active hostilities between the coalition and Iraqi forces had ended.

Secretary Rumsfeld and his key civilian advisors at the Department of Defense must accept the responsibility for failure to develop a satisfactory U.S. occupation plan while rejecting inputs from other departments and agencies such as the detailed planning document developed by the State Department. It will, however, be a task for historians to evaluate whether the State Department's plan for the occupation of Iraq would have avoided the pitfalls that the military encountered after Saddam's Baghdad statute tumbled to the ground and the city erupted in chaos and looting.

Past American postwar planning activities had also been meager, but earlier commanders had been generally luckier and more successful than the effort in Iraq. For instance, in the spring of 1945, four months before the Japanese surrender, the War Department finally got around to asking Ruth Benedict, a Columbia University cultural anthropologist, to write a report on Japan to assist U.S. military in its coming occupation. The report that later was published as *The Chrysanthemum and the Sword* became a bestseller, "but most importantly, her government work ended up becoming the 'Bible' for the American troops who undertook the occupation of Japan" [Stille]. American soldiers bringing democracy to Japan after centuries of militarism had some common understanding of the Japanese culture from Benedict's report and they were able to cope successfully. But such was not the case in Iraq in spite of the fact that the United States had hundreds of social scientists, journalists, and retired military officers with hands-on experience in Iraq and the Middle East, something Benedict did not have in Japan.

An even more relevant history for the occupation of Iraq was the experience of the British—the major U.S. partner in the coalition—in 1920 when it had occupied and created the modern state of Iraq after the First World War. Iraq had been a part of the Ottoman Empire until the Treaty of Versailles broke up the empire and placed Iraq under British mandate until 1932. The early part of the 12 years of British occupation in Iraq were marked with insurrections led by both Sunni and Shiite religious groups that "soon transcended the country's ancient ethnic and sectarian divisions" [Ferguson]. The British were only able to quell the uprising by extremely harsh military action in which thousands of innocent civilians were massacred, something the coalition was loath to repeat.

Instead of concerning themselves with Iraqi culture or its history, American forces prepared for the end of hostilities as if they were rescuing flood or earthquake victims. The Pentagon plan for the cessation of fighting called for the appointment of retired U.S. Army Lieutenant General Jay Garner to serve as Director of Reconstruction and Humanitarian Assistance for Iraq. Garner was an expert in directing disaster assistance programs and had served admirably in northern Iraq with the Kurds in the 1990s. Clearly, the Defense Department believed that the principal postwar problem in Iraq would be limited to providing food and shelter to the hungry and homeless. A priority of the battle plan had been to capture Umm Qasr in the south, the Iraqi port on the Persian Gulf, and clear the sea channels of mines so that food and humanitarian relief could reach the Iraqis as soon as possible. With this emphasis, Secretary Rumsfeld was able to address concerns raised by anti-war critics who had condemned civilian casualties and suffering but failed to provide any realistic military assessment of what the troops would actually find. Through no fault of his own, General Garner lasted exactly one month in his impossible Baghdad role, coordinating unrealistic postcombat operations directly for the Pentagon, an almost assured disaster from the start.

Failing to understand Iraq's culture or history, among other things, led the American forces to underestimate the difficulties they would encounter. Insurgency was what the Americans found, but only in the Sunni areas of Iraq, with a single exception later. The Americans should have expected rebellion and insurgency led by the defeated Baathists of Saddam Hussein's regime, supplemented by Arab jihadists from neighboring countries, but the CIA unfortunately had only four agents on the ground in Iraq before the war and they were mostly with the oil sector and had limited knowledge of Saddam's military plans. If the Iraqis actually planned a war of retreat and insurgency, the Americans should have surmised that all the support systems for a guerrilla war, as the arms caches in Iraq indicated, had been in place in the Sunni Triangle northwest of Baghdad long before the invasion was launched and plans should have been adjusted accordingly. Perhaps the Baathists were not quite the fools that the Defense Department had expected; they were not about to fight the Americans in the open where superior U.S. armaments and tactical air power would have picked them to pieces as they had in the first Gulf War. Instead of meeting the enemy head on, the Baathist strategy was to drag the Americans and its coalition partners into a protracted quagmire of insurgent warfare like Vietnam, forcing the American population to eventually tire of war and demand retreat and withdrawal of U.S. forces from Iraq. While it had been al Qaeda that refused to alter its tactics during the American invasion of Afghanistan, it was the Americans that held steadfast in Iraq to what had worked in an earlier war and who refused initially to admit that they were facing a deadly insurgency of growing intensity. Occupying Iraq would prove to be wholly different from Afghanistan and the Kuwait occupation a decade earlier.

Ironically, returning Shiite exiles like Chalabi, with no reason to rebel, were largely responsible for the occupation forces' failure to provide necessary security that might have nipped the rebellion in the bud, for they had insisted that Saddam's army and police force had to be totally dismantled immediately after hostilities ended and that all Baathists in government positions be removed from office. Although a retained Iraqi army and police force could well have contained some of the clandestine Baathist insurrectionists, which would have taken some time to root out, a military police force and American combat soldiers on the ground were necessary to provide basic security for the protection of life and property. With all the criminals on the streets and with no Iraqi police or military force, it is no surprise that chaos quickly spread and, without continued employment for any of the former security personnel and no future for Baathists in the reconstructed Iraq, the insurgency rapidly grew in numbers and strength.

The decision by Paul Bremer, the American-appointed administrator of the Coalition Provisional Authority who succeeded Jay Garner, to accept the Shiite demand and dismiss the Iraqi police and military, left the occupation forces in a catch-up mode throughout the remainder of 2003 and all of 2004. Bremer's endorsement of the Shiite demand ranks as the worst and most damaging American occupation decision. Bremer [2005] later defended his decision by arguing that "[t]he disbanding of Saddam's army signaled, to all Iraqis, the birth of a new nation," and that the army had already disbanded itself. However, had Bremer announced immediately that, after checking individual records for Baathist criminals, the coalition was prepared to reestablish the Iraqi police and army forces, an effective security force could have been in place in much less time than later proved to be necessary by retraining new applicants. Because most former police and army forces were unemployed and blameless, many became recruiting candidates and joined the Baathist insurgents.

We do not pretend to understand all of the difficulties encountered in training a new Iraqi army—shortages of Arab linguists and military trainers, the hostile environment, or lack of the best qualified and motivated trainees—but the slowness of the program was a serious hindrance to release coalition troops from duty in Iraq. And we now know that the rising strength of the insurgency made it that much more difficult to train and recruit qualified Iraqi security force candidates.

Over the succeeding months, the Baathists and Islamist jihadists fought a continuous and increasingly successful counterinsurgency from the Sunni Triangle. More recently al Qaeda jihadist forces under the command of Abu Masab al Zarqawi caused many more American and innocent Iraqi casualties than occurred during the invasion. Although the al Qaeda jihadist group was by far the smaller force in the insurgency, it made up for its lack of size by a willingness to commit the most heinous acts, kidnapping foreigners and beheading its victims, and its willingness to kill more Shiite Iraqis than the Baathist Sunni insurgents were inclined to do. However, the jihadist atrocities were indicative of weakness, not strength, because the acts were offensive to the broader Muslim community, which was al Qaeda's real target audience in Iraq. Al Qaeda's objective in Iraq was to prove that Americans are cowards who lack the will to fight a protracted and bloody guerrilla war in the Middle East. American willingness to stay and fight meant that bin Laden's primary objective in Iraq could not be realized and that eventually Iraq, like Afghanistan, would be entered into the American victory column. It also meant that, while al Qaeda had to allocate so many of its recruits to the Iraqi insurgency, the American homeland was less likely to be attacked—part of the Bush strategy of a strong offense being the best defense.

Fear and intimidation spread among moderate Sunnis inside the triangle as the insurgent forces continued to grow from both the inside—as many discouraged police and military personnel enlisted—and from the outside, as more young Arabs from other countries answered the call for jihad. Such fear made the U.S. intelligence job of identifying insurgents more difficult but gradually good actionable intelligence information became more available and reliable. One significant intelligence breakthrough was the killing of Uday and Qusay Hussein, Saddam's sons, on July 22, 2003 in Mosul by the 101st Airborne troops from information received from a paid informant.

In contrast, few insurgent attacks took place in the Shiite or Kurdish areas of Iraq where the resident population refused to conceal and protect the rebels. The only guerrilla outbreak among the Shiites came in the spring of 2004 when a rebel Shiite cleric, Muqtada al Sadr, staged an uprising and moved his Mahdi Army to Najaf, one of the holiest cities in Shiite Islam. Without al Sadr's knowledge, Grand Ayatollah Ali al Sistani, the major Shiite religious leader in Iraq, actually staged al Sadr's attacks as part of a political strategy of persuading the Allied force that Iraqi Shiites were fully capable of waging an insurgency war against the occupiers if they did not follow al Sistani's plans for national elections to provide Shiite majority control in the permanent Iraqi government. Once al Sadr was informed that Shiites would no longer assist him, surrender was inevitable and al Sadr retreated to his stronghold in the slums of Baghdad to begin a peaceful campaign as a potential candidate in the January 2005 elections. However, al Sadr was not brought to justice for his alleged murders of coalition forces and fellow Iraqis, and he remained at large with limited authority to act independently, protesting from time-to-time in 2005 in the streets of Baghdad, though gaining some seats in the National Assembly from the January elections.

Further intelligence success followed, based on a collection of actionable intelligence information derived from questioning Saddam's former bodyguards and family members. In a routine military search, Saddam Hussein was captured on December 13, 2003 in a hole in the ground in the town of ad-Duar, 15 kilometers south of Tikrit, his hometown. Saddam had weapons in his possession and about $750,000 in U.S. $100 bills. He was in such destitute and desperate condition when he climbed out of his underground hole, looking unkempt and confused, that many Iraqis could not believe from the photos that this was the feared dictator who had killed and tortured hundreds of thousands of innocent Iraqis. DNA samples and dental records were used to positively identify Hussein, who soon after being shaved and cleaned up, resumed his defiant behavior, this time in an Iraqi prison and not in one of his many ostentatious palaces. Public opinion about the occupation received a brief but unsustainable bounce in popularity both in the United States and in Iraq. The problem was that the insurgency continued and would grow in violence and intensity and the Americans would face a disgraceful setback in one of their own Iraqi prisons.

The Abu Ghraib Prison Disaster

For decades, Saddam Hussein's secret police had tortured, abused, and killed innocent Iraqi citizens at the infamous Abu Ghraib Prison 20 miles west of Baghdad. The story of the torture of Iraqi prisoners by American soldiers at Abu Ghraib was broken by CBS on April 28, 2004 during its "60 Minutes II" program after the press failed to pick up on an innocuous one-paragraph press release from the U.S. Headquarters Command in Baghdad on January 16, 2004 announcing that "An investigation has been initiated into reported incidents of abuse at a Coalition Forces detention facility" [Ricchiardi]. In January, few newspapers even ran a story on the release. More than three months later, however, when CBS television ran videos filmed by the Abu Ghraib guards of taunting naked Iraqi prisoners with dogs, leashes, and female guards, making naked prisoners form human pyramids or chaining them outside their cells, a feeding frenzy of press reports exploded around the world.

Most damaging to the American cause were the Abu Ghraib videos aired by Al Jazeera and other Arab networks throughout the Muslim world, seriously offending Muslim sensitivities and sexual mores and superficially raising a question in their minds as to who was more evil, Saddam Hussein or depraved American soldiers. Although Saddam's inhuman mistreatment of prisoners and Zarqawi's beheadings were far worse than anything the Americans did at Abu Ghraib or Guantanamo, the United States had experienced a huge setback in the battle for the hearts and minds of the Muslim world. The story of American torture of Iraqi prisoners was bin Laden's greatest propaganda victory since 9/11 and it strengthened al Qaeda's call to Sunni Arab Muslims for jihadist death strikes and suicide attacks against the American infidels.

What had gone wrong? How could American military police have behaved in such an unprofessional and depraved manner? Two factors explain the disgraceful breach of behavior: (1) the deepening series of major intelligence failures that continued to plague U.S. forces and (2) an even more serious problem, the deplorable lack of military training and discipline in some of the Army's poorly-led reserve units. The disgrace of Abu Ghraib is really a microcosm of a far greater problem in the organization of American military forces and its "all-volunteer" Army consisting of active duty Army units, the Army National Guard, and the Army Reserve. In time, U.S. Army reserve forces in Iraq would reach nearly 40 percent of the total U.S. forces deployed there. As a backlash from the Vietnam war, the politically unpopular draft was ended under President Nixon and mandated service in the U.S. military stopped in 1973. The era of volunteer service had started and the active and reserve components of the U.S. military were sold to the public by the Nixon and subsequent administrations as complementary elements in the new "totally integrated" all volunteer force, a concept untested in sustained combat. With some exceptions among the better trained Army National Guard units, experience in Iraq has shown that many of the Army's reserve units were poorly trained and even more poorly led. This was especially true of the Army Reserve units at Abu Ghraib Prison where the commander, Brigadier General Janis Karpinski, a reservist called to active duty from her civilian job for service in Iraq, was suspended, demoted, and reprimanded for failure to properly train and prepare her troops in the 800th Military Police Brigade she commanded. The Army charged that General Karpinski was responsible for prisoner abuses that were carried out by soldiers under her command and occurred when she commanded 16 prisons in Iraq. Poor intelligence was bad enough, but at least it was improving, but the dilemma that the Army faced with untrained, ill-disciplined, and poorly-led reserve forces continued to deteriorate. Neither the politicians in Washington nor the military leadership in the Pentagon desired to discuss the problem because the alternative is the politically unpopular draft, but the fact remains that the Army's so-called "total force" system is badly broken and requires immediate fixing. In addition to the appalling situation at Abu Ghraib with the Army's reserve forces under General Karpinski's disgraceful leadership, poor Army intelligence and undue pressure on the CIA to obtain solid intelligence information also contributed to the conditions surrounding the Abu Graib prisoner abuse problem.

With the worsening insurgency, U.S. military intelligence forces were becoming increasingly desperate to ferret out information and captured Iraqi insurgents became the best prospects. Desperation led intelligence officers to abandon sound interrogation techniques that call for careful and repeated questioning while looking for inconsistencies in the prisoners' stories. Professional interrogators have known for years that torture, aside from being totally un-American, doesn't work and is not an effective interrogation approach. Without condoning specific behavior, intelligence personnel had clearly encouraged the military police to "soften up" the prisoners so that they would make better subjects for interrogation, even though the intelligence officers had little reason to hope that the softening up process would improve the results. The poorly-led and ill-disciplined American guards at Abu Ghraib, operating without adequate supervision or directives, followed their worst instincts, and the lowest common denominator among their ranks, a sadistic army specialist named Charles Graner, was sentenced to 10 years in prison for his unpardonable actions. Six other guards received lesser sentences and all were courts-martialed and discharged from the United States Army. The Pentagon investigation headed by former Secretary of Defense James Schlesinger found no others guilty of any crimes, including General Karpinski. However, General Karpinski was relieved from command and the official Army investigation stated that she "understaffed the prison, exercised poor oversight and failed to remind her soldiers of the Geneva Conventions' protections for detainees" [Copeland], implying culpability on her part for the lack of appropriate supervision of the guards.

So far, none of the other military investigations has found any wrongdoing that may have extended beyond the military police personnel directly involved in the abuse, nor found the military intelligence officers culpable in the case. Although Secretary Rumsfeld twice offered his resignation because of the scandal, President Bush refused to accept it both times. From the standpoint of the war on terror, acceptance of Rumsfeld's resignation offer, for both the Abu Ghraib disaster and the deplorable lack of planning for postwar operations, would have clearly demonstrated to the entire world that such conduct is totally unacceptable by American ethical standards. But at that time in 2004 President Bush was in the midst of a hard-hitting presidential reelection campaign in which his strategy was to tough-out the bad news coming from the Iraq war without admitting any errors made by his administration and force his Democratic opponent, John Kerry, to explain to the electorate what changes the Democrat would make in fighting the war that would improve the outcome. Senator Kerry did not raise the prisoner abuse scandal during the presidential campaign and a majority of the electorate didn't accept Kerry's proposals as very convincing solutions to the Iraq war problem. However, after the election, President Bush could have replaced Donald Rumsfeld for the Abu Ghraib scandal and the other strategic and tactical planning errors that had been made in fighting the Iraq war after its initial success in deposing Saddam Hussein. President Bush, who professed to be the chief executive officer for the nation, proved to be a better "policy-smith" than a CEO, as the resulting planning and ethical disasters in the Iraq occupation proved. Never admitting to a mistake may have been a sound domestic political strategy for the President, but it produced a less than optimal military operation in Iraq. Personnel changes in the management of the occupation should have been made because a loud and clear American statement was needed denouncing the horrors of the Abu Ghraib disaster. In fighting the American Civil War, President Lincoln was at first cautious about changing military leaders, but he eventually realized that ultimate success required changing leaders until he found the right generals who were able to capitalize upon the Union's strategic advantages and lead their forces to victory as Grant and his generals finally were able to do.

Another issue raised by the Abu Ghraib scandal was an ethical dilemma of how to treat terrorist prisoners in an unconventional war in which the enemy combatants, fanatical religious fanatics willing to die for their cause, did not subscribe to traditional Western standards for fighting a war under the terms of the Geneva Convention. As a consequence, the President sent mixed signals to the military security forces in establishing U.S. policy for the treatment of prisoners:

> As a matter policy, the United States Armed Forces shall continue to treat detainees humanely and, *to the extent appropriate and consistent with military necessity*, in a manner consistent with the principles of Geneva (Sullivan's italics) [Sullivan].

Secretary Rumsfeld created further confusion among the ranks by issuing in December 2002 and then, six weeks later, rescinding an order that approved the expansion of interrogation techniques for questioning the prisoners of the Afghan war who were interned at the American detention center for terrorists at the U.S. Naval Base in Guantanamo Bay, Cuba. During the six weeks, only two prisoners were abused through the use of dogs and nudity to intimidate them, but ambiguity about prisoner-treatment standards had been raised and an atmosphere of "winks and nods" at prisoner abuses had been established through the transfer of intelligence interrogators from Cuba to Iraq. British interrogators were similarly found guilty of prisoner abuses in Iraq but America, because of its global preeminence and virtuous intentions, had bitterly tripped on the slippery slope of moral ambivalence, creating a huge bin Laden propaganda victory that severely detracted from America's ability to win the war on terror. Despite the barbaric treatment coalition prisoners of war received at the hands of Islamist militants, the United States is always best served by observing and remaining true to American values. It is also important to remember that winning the war on terrorism depends on more than just capturing or killing enemy forces; the real battle is a war of ideology for the heart and soul of the more than one billion moderate Muslims around the world. Because the Abu Ghraib prisoner abuse scandal was such a monumental disaster for America's war efforts, Rumsfeld's offers to resign should have been accepted or, failing that, the senior general officers in command should have been fired and forced to resign from the Army. Anything less gave the appearance of a nation less honorable and less virtuous than its noble charters purport it to be.

A Loss of Momentum and Confidence

From the moment U.S. troops cautiously entered Baghdad in early April of 2003, the American high command and its soldiers seemed to lose confidence due to lack of leadership and lack of a comprehensive post-combat plan. Instead of proceeding to take charge of the captured capital city, the American military seemed to stand back and watch as looters decimated government buildings and facilities. Only the Oil Ministry building was protected, leading to the impression among Iraqis that the sole asset the Americans cared about was oil. Western journalists in the city had to recruit some soldiers to safeguard one last hospital that hadn't been looted, but otherwise chaos reigned supreme [Engel]. The organized sabotage of the electrical and water systems may have been difficult to stop. However, looters could have been driven off or captured and order could have been restored through the imposition of martial law. Instead, the American troops appeared to be concerned only about their own safety, not the safety of innocent Iraqis or their property. It took nearly 21 months, until the Iraqi national elections at the end of January 2005, to recover from the appalling first impression created by the total break-down in security.

The second major failure of what had become the occupation of Iraq was the immediate lack of recognition that the Iraqi army had in fact not surrendered, but was instead planning to wage a protracted insurgency or guerilla war against the coalition forces. The evidence in Baghdad was all around: (1) extensive use of dedicated irregulars and martyrs as suicide bombers, rearguard forces in attacking the invaders, and disappearing armies in the field as the coalition forces approached them; (2) hidden caches of arms throughout the countryside and the city, which even the experienced military strategist, Anthony H. Cordesman [2003], misread as stockpiles for civilians to utilize in the battle for Baghdad instead of recognizing them as supplies for an insurgent army; (3) lack of any formal surrender by the army leaders and (4) the most obvious evidence—the public releases in Europe as early as April 12, 2003 announcing the insurgency and the call to arms for a global Muslim jihad against the American infidels and their partners. All of these indicators should have immediately alerted the Pentagon and the generals commanding in Iraq to the kind of war in which the coalition forces were now engaged. But instead of aggressively launching search-and-destroy missions against the insurgents, the Americans in Baghdad hunkered down and assumed defensive positions, allowing the insurgents to organize, assume the offensive against them, and disrupt allied efforts to create a stable environment for a new Iraqi government.

One brief attempt in the first year of occupation was made to break out of this defensive posture, but it quickly floundered on the rocks of indecision and lack of American political will during an election campaign. In April 2004 after four American security contractors were ambushed, burned, and their bodies dishonored in Fallujah, a city in the Sunni Triangle about 40 miles west of Baghdad, the U.S. Marines:

> mounted an assault on the city, a punitive mission that outraged many Iraqis and was called to a halt before it achieved any of its goals. A compromise deal was cut in which former Baathists agreed to provide security. In fact, the town quickly became a haven for insurgents and terrorists [Nordland et al.].

In the Muslim world and indeed in the streets of Fallujah, this was hailed as a major victory for the insurgents and a defeat for the Americans. To turn over control of Fallujah to Baathist insurgents in the Sunni stronghold defies understanding. Indeed, after a year of fighting the growing insurgency, U.S. forces didn't even know who the enemy was. It also suggests that during the 2004 presidential election campaign, no one from the Democratic Party was following the war closely enough to raise this issue, for Bush had been ripe for the picking on problems with the Iraq war, but he was never seriously challenged by Kerry, who seemed afraid to bring up Iraq. Most U.S. commanders apparently thought they were fighting foreign jihadist terrorists, al Qaeda, when in fact the real organizer of the overall insurgency and the principal supplier of insurgents were 12-15,000 members of Saddam's former Baathist party who had enlisted support from outside Arab jihadists, primarily young Saudi suicide bombers, even before the outbreak of hostilities. In fact, the insurgency was well-planned but for whatever reason, after this happy outcome for the Baathists, who until this time had been operating in the open went underground and became deadlier and more difficult to fight and reign in.

Following an innovative and imaginative initial battle plan, an almost complete American void in planning and adapting to postwar conditions is baffling to outside observers. The only plausible explanation for the failure to react to evolving conditions is that Pentagon civilian planners, believing what they wanted to hear from Iraqi exiles, had been totally surprised by the Baathist insurgency and failed to have a proper contingency plan in place. Even the most naïve in the Pentagon and Central Command must have realized that the more time the coalition gave the insurgency to organize and recruit, the stronger the insurgency would become as the intimidation among the moderate Sunni neighborhoods spread and new jihadist recruits joined the battlefield against the American infidels. That is exactly what happened, as the number of insurgency incidents grew and the types of targets changed.

The immediate targets in the early days of the Iraq insurgency were the coalition troops—the occupiers—and the message was: "Get out, you'll never successfully occupy Iraq." The United States had a reputation in the Muslim world of an impressive high-tech military force but with little political staying power—a true paper tiger. The Baathists thought that if they could convince the American public that they were facing another Vietnam quagmire that could not be won, the fickle American public would quickly lose heart and force a pullout as the U.S. did in Somalia in 1993 and Vietnam before that.

This was Saddam's plan from the beginning. A slightly more sophisticated Iraqi tactic on that same theme was to isolate the occupiers by attacking the other organized entities that were indirectly supporting the coalition by providing humanitarian assistance to Iraqis and thus lending credibility and legitimacy to the occupation. In July and August 2003, the Jordanian embassy and the United Nations headquarters buildings were destroyed by suicide bombers and prominent international aid workers were kidnapped and assassinated as part of this expanded campaign to isolate the occupiers. The U.N. and many aid groups promptly pulled out after being attacked, blaming the Americans for failing to provide security, and providing the insurgents with another easy victory.

Before the insurgents increased the intensity and broadened the scope of their attacks, the U.S. military was literally shooting itself in the foot by canceling on April 17, 2003 its order for body armor for its soldiers and vehicle armor for its Humvee vehicles [Moss]. When the insurgency started to look more serious by May 15th, the U.S. Army was unable to simply reopen the supply chain. The body armor supplier was unable to mass produce a stock of vests, leaving many soldiers unprotected for months and 10,000 armor plates for the Humvees were lost and arrived late. Coalition forces and private individuals, unconstrained by Pentagon purchasing procedures, were able to purchase body armor on the open market for their own protection. By January 2004, the 10,000 armor plates still hadn't been located, but all Humvees operating in the Iraqi theater were at last protected. It seems that, "The bulletproof vests had been labeled high priority, but in the ensuing chaos [of military procurement for the war], everything got treated as high priority, which meant that in fact nothing was" [Moss].

The scene in Iraq was going from bad to worse for the American forces, and even though many Iraqi citizens were pleased with the toppling of the despised dictator, Saddam Hussein's ultimate capture in late 2003 did not deflect the downward trend in morale, for many Iraqis were still without electricity, gaso-line, or personal security. The only thing that the Iraqis never seemed to be short of was food, the one contingency the invading American force had been fully pre-pared to provide. U.S. soldiers who had bravely fought the Iraqi army were also getting demoralized, especially some of the untrained, ill-disciplined, and poorly-led Army Reserve units, as it appeared their government couldn't protect them from snipers, roadside bombs, and suicide bombers and wouldn't rotate them in and out of Kuwait for R&R where other reservists were assigned full-time duty without the around-the-clock anxieties of daunting counterinsurgency duties in Iraq.

AN INTERIM GOVERNMENT

In desperation, the new coalition administrator, Paul Bremer, swore into office the new Iraqi interim government two days before its scheduled initiation date of June 30, 2004 in order to confuse the insurgents and not allow them to disrupt ceremony. He had hoped that turning over authority to Iraqis would slow down the insurgency by giving Iraqis ownership in the new government, and it also per-mitted Mr. Bremer to get out of Iraq two days earlier. The Americans were now, in theory at least, supposed to be in Iraq at the request and direction of the new sovereign government. Most Iraqis simply didn't buy this, however, because they viewed the new interim government as American stooges or puppets and they were mostly returning exiles, many of whom had been or still were in the employ of the United States Central Intelligence Agency—the London-based "Gucci Guerillas." The various religious sects and ethnic groups were all represented; they were all Iraqi citizens, but they had been chosen by the Americans, not by the Iraqi people. That difference would remain critical as the American forces worked their way through what had become for them an unintelligible and con-fusing Iraqi maze.

Inability to Bring Factions Together

Ayad Allawi, the interim prime minister and a secular Shiite, accepted as his first responsibility the task of reaching out to the Sunni moderates to engage them in the new government. He appointed Hazem Shaalan, a former Baathist, as his defense minister. Allawi, from the first moment he assumed leadership in the government, was concerned that efforts to create a unified Iraq would be shattered by those seeking revenge and retribution for past injustices. He was, how-ever, unsuccessful in coming to any understanding with the Sunnis, the newly constituted minority group, partly because of American insistence that anyone who had waged a successful attack on the Americans or government forces, as well as any high-ranking, former Baathists, was automatically excluded from par-ticipation in the political process. This excluded most politically active Sunnis and the imposed conditions on the negotiations made Allawi's job virtually impossible. But Allawi's efforts certainly put the Sunnis on notice that there was willingness among some Shiites who were interested in compromise to create a new federal government for all Iraqis that included Sunnis, Kurds, and Shiites.

With the best chance for compromise behind them, the Sunni insurgency continued to grow in size and intensity and the number of innocent Iraqi and American deaths continued to rise. Meanwhile, also joining the broader insur-gency were newly radicalized Sunni Iraqis, many of them Wahhabis from the Sunni Triangle and cousins of northern Saudi Wahhabis, and Iraqi nationalists who hated the occupying force and were disenchanted by the economic turmoil and destruction caused by the endless fighting. Instead of compromising with the interim government, the Baathist insurgents established a closer working rela-tionship with the foreign Arab jihadists led by Abu Musab al Zarqawi, a Jorda-nian Takfir Wal Hijra, the fierce Wahhabi-Salafist offshoot that is violently opposed to Shiites and the West. Zarqawi sent a letter to Osama bin Laden in January 2004 offering to serve as al Qaeda's representative in Iraq in the war against the infidel Americans and this closer working relationship between Zar-qawi and the Iraqi Baathist insurgents formally brought al Qaeda into the picture as the enemy. Prior to this improved working relationship, the jihadists and the Baathists had bickered on numerous issues and started to go their separate ways; this new entente brought them closer together and heightened the effectiveness and brutality of the insurgency through better coordination, closer cooperation, and even more violent attacks against the Americans.

As a result, the number of suicide bombings increased markedly in the fall of 2004, rising from an average of about 1.5 bombings per week to more than that per day, as the al Qaeda forces combined their ability to recruit jihadists through the Baathist Party intelligence and financial network in Syria and other countries. Cars loaded with explosives and driven by jihadist martyrs were almost as accu-rate as America's precision bombing attacks, but were far more effective in spreading terror. The Baathist intelligence network, with allies in the Iraqi police and army either through political allegiance or intimidation, was vastly superior to the coalition's intelligence capabilities. In addition, Saddam Hussein had provided abundantly with the funds needed to finance an extended insurgency and it has now become increasingly clear that Syrian Baathists also provided extensive assistance to the Iraqi insurgents. With money, manpower, and intelligence, the Baathist-led insurgency was winning the battle of the occupation in late 2004, and, even worse, the foreign Arab jihadists seemed to be gaining greater control of the insurgency. The allies needed a miracle to turn the war of insurgency around and in their favor.

Fallujah—Round II

Recalling how the British had quelled the 1920 rebellion against the colonialists [Ferguson], the coalition forces decided, in desperation, to get tougher and more aggressive in their war against the insurgents. Meanwhile the American presidential election was coming to an end. In late October 2004 just weeks before the American election, U.S. forces announced their intention to end the terrorist safe haven in Fallujah, a city with a population of 300,000 and an area of about 350 square miles, by bringing in 6,000 American troops—four marine battalions and two army battalions—together with 2,000 Iraqi troops as the assault element in an attack to clear the rebellious city of all insurgent forces. A nearly equal number of troops totally surrounded Fallujah to prevent insurgents from escaping during the attack. It was unfortunately necessary to give public notice of the impending assault so innocent civilians could remove themselves from harm's way before the attack, and many insurgents also fled the city. In addition, Baathist forces feigned interest in calling a truce to try to reach a compromise, buying time to stall the second attack. With all elements of surprise eliminated, the combined attack finally began on November 8th, less than a week after the presidential elections in the United States and before the end of Ramadan, the high Muslim fasting holiday of prayer and charity.

As was to be expected when American forces bring formable air and artillery power against an enemy, the outcome was never in doubt. However, house-to-house urban combat, which lasted for nearly 12 days, is a high casualty operation and the coalition forces sustained 51 Americans killed and 425 seriously wounded while 8 Iraqi soldiers were killed and 43 were wounded. Although historically light for urban warfare, the American forces sustained an 8 percent casualty rate, "a low but not insignificant loss for less than two weeks' combat" [Keiler]. If that rate were to be sustained week in and week out, it is doubtful that the American public would be willing to continue support of the war effort. An estimated 2,000 to 3,000 insurgents were killed or captured, but probably an equal number, including virtually all its leadership including Zarqawi, escaped with the civilian population before hostilities began.

Historically, Fallujah has had a large Wahhabi population with Bedouin origins and was known as the "City of Mosques," which the insurgents fully utilized as operational defense centers. A U.S. Army report on the Fallujah fighting indicated that one out of every two mosques in Fallujah was used to hide fighters or weapons during the American offensive. One such mosque, the Muhammadia Mosque where fighting was especially heavy, took 16 hours of house-to-house urban combat to capture. The American soldiers tried not to enter the mosques first and employed Iraqi soldiers for the inside fighting. "Despite predictable claims that Fallujah was devastated, photos revealed superficial damage to most buildings and an occasional structure demolished" [Keiler]. Because of prior notice of the impending attack, almost all civilians had evacuated their homes and avoided injury. Disruption and chaos were high prices for so large a civilian population to pay to rid their city of the insurgents, especially when so many Iraqi Wahhabi Sunnis were sympathetic to the Baathist cause.

However, the Baathists and Sunnis were less sympathetic to the foreign Arab jihadists who had commandeered much of the private property in the city and left behind substantial evidence of atrocities. Although the second battle of Fallujah was, at a minimum, a significant tactical victory for the coalition, it was not the miracle that was needed to turn the tide against the insurgency. That would have to wait, but an opportunity to turn the tide was already underway.

Election Preparations

Because of the insistence of Grand Ayatollah Ali al Sistani that Iraqis would choose their first permanent legislative assembly from national slates determined by Iraqi political parties in free elections, the original plans of Paul Bremer to select legislators through regional caucuses held throughout the nation were revised. Fortunately, it was one of the few decisions in which the resolute President Bush, a vigorous advocate of free elections, was willing to change his mind, at least on how the legislators should be selected. Further, Sistani, the powerful advocate of Iraq's movement toward democracy, also insisted that free elections should come sooner rather later, finally agreeing on January 30, 2005, the earliest date the U.N. election advisors would accept.

The deposing of Saddam Hussein converted Grand Ayatollah Ali al Sistani from a devout, monastic, scholarly, and apolitical Shiite cleric into a wise and just politician who remained remote and above the fray, while from behind the scenes put together the national Shiite political slate. His goal was clearly to ensure that the Shiite majority, after decades of Baathist-Sunni domination, received its opportunity to lead Iraq. He understood that the formula for political success and stability in the divided state of Iraq required a secular democracy with power shared among the various ethnic and religious sects. Sistani, Iranian by birth and education, remained opposed to the Shiite theocracy in Iran because he believed that worldly political authority in the hands of religious clerics was totally inappropriate. Sistani and his Shiite followers, his aides assassinated and fellow Shiites massacred in their mosques, suffered deeply at the hands of the insurgents, but "[i]n the face of incessant provocation he has marginalized men of violence" [Ignatieff] by refusing to tolerate revenge tactics by his followers.

Through the constant and reassuring power of Sistani's faith and the enthusiastic support of the Kurds in the north, who could almost taste the semi-autonomy and riches that the elections were likely to provide them after years of deprivation and massacre under Saddam Hussein, the Iraqis moved resolutely toward the January 30th election date. Both the Shiites and the Kurds endured the painful increase in suicide bombings as the insurgents changed the focus of their attacks from the American occupiers to the likely Shiite victors in the coming elections. By revising the targets of their attacks, the insurgents made it clear to the Iraqi population and the greater Muslim world that the goal of the Iraqi insurgency was not to repel infidels from sacred Islamic lands, but rather to create chaos and misery among fellow Muslims as a means of obtaining political power for their own ends and their own goals, whether it be the return of Baathist control or a global Islamic caliphate with acceptance of their own ultra-reactionary views of Islam. The attacks on the Shiites by the Islamist jihadists proved to everyone in Iraq and in the Arab world that the jihadists were not interested in anything other than achieving their own goals of installing an authoritarian Taliban-like regime of complete terror that would equal or exceed the depravity of Saddam Hussein's torture chambers.

As 100,000 Iraqis volunteered to set up and conduct the elections, it became increasingly apparent that the elections would be held on schedule, and the cry from many quarters, both within and without Iraq, changed to claims that fair and free democratic elections could not be held until the whole country was secure and it was safe for all citizens to vote. These protestors ignored the fact that postponement would only reward the insurgents for their violence and encourage their continued efforts at further disruption. Further, it ignored the success story of other emerging democracies, like El Salvador, where violence was equally horrendous and it took several elections to finally succeed in quelling the violence

[Brooks]. Fortunately, on the issue of elections the American coalition remained resolute and they were held successfully on January 30, 2005, with a cleansing political effect and hopeful outcome. In this chapter's next section, the effect of holding free and fair elections will be discussed in terms of the change in the war's momentum, for the election was truly the miracle that the coalition needed to turn around the war effort in the favor of the coalition.

CONCLUSIONS AND PROGNOSTICATIONS ABOUT THE WAR

The Iraq War was not the finest hour of the U.S. military despite the brave efforts of so many fine combat soldiers and a sound invasion plan that was well executed in the early combat phases. But from the moment Saddam Hussein was toppled and his statue fell, the lack of a plan and good actionable intelligence assessments, coupled with serious misunderstandings regarding the nature of the enemy, lead to a downward spiral in coalition fortunes. Whether this confusion reflected over-confidence of military leadership, once the initial goal of the invasion was so easily realized, or the lack of a good plan and sound intelligence about what the troops were likely to encounter, the U.S. military did not recover its equilibrium until a political solution was forced on the Americans by a wise Shiite cleric. Table 5.1 summarizes selected Iraq War statistics and shows the impact of the war on the coalition forces and Iraqi civilians as well as changes that occurred in Iraq and in the lives of Iraqis during the occupation.

Table 5.1
Selected Statistics on the Effect of the Iraq War

Indicator	Prewar	July 2003	Jan. 2004	July 2004	Jan. 2005
Coalition War Deaths Per 6-Months *	-	249	329	401	505
Civilian War Deaths Per Week	-	35	125	400	450
Barrels of Oil Production (Mil)	2.3**	.9	2.4	2.2	2.1
Electricity Prod. (Gigawatts)	4.4	3.2	3.8	4.6	3.3
Telephone Subscribers (Mil)	.8	.5	.6	1.3	2.4
% Unemployed	NA***	60.0	40.0	35.0	34.0
Relative Auto Traffic	1.0	1.0	2.0	3.0	5.0
Length of Gas Lines (Miles)	NA***	.1	.5	1.0	1.0
Children In Primary School (Mil)	3.6	3.6	4.0	4.0	4.3

Sources: De Albuquerque, Adriana Lins, O'Hanlon, Michael, and Unikewicz, Amy, *New York Times*, February 21, 2005.
* "Iraq Coalition Casualty Count," http://icasualties.org/oif/.
**Encyclopedia Britannica, 2003 Book of the Year*, Chicago: Encyclopedia, Inc., 2003, page 634.
*** Not Available.

The result of the American military planning failures was endured by the ranks of the coalition forces and the citizens of Iraq. Obviously, the most significant cost in human suffering during the period was the rising number of coalition deaths and civilian casualties from insurgent attacks, the latter increasing from 35 in July of 2003 to more than ten times that number in January 2005 just before the election. Indeed, if the increases in casualties weren't bad enough, the number of mass murders through suicide bombings actually increased immediately after the election as the militant Islamists became increasingly desperate. While the prospects for a stable democratic government in Iraq grew, the militants began to target the Shiite population more frequently in the hopes of creating civil conflict to nullify the positive political effects of the election. The number of coalition military casualties during the post-election period actually declined, but increasingly brutal slayings of Iraqi military personnel offset this gain.

Improvements in security for Iraqi citizens were dependent upon the ability of the new Iraqi government to work out a compromise with the Sunni Baathist insurgents as part of the price the insurgents would have to pay to become active participants in drafting the new constitution. Although it would involve substantial personal risk for the former Baathist insurgents, the government's goals were to capture or obtain the surrender of the worst Baathist offenders and to end the Sunni protection of jihad insurgents. This could only be done by providing accurate information to the combined coalition-Iraq security forces for the identity and location of the insurgents so their operations could be disrupted and neutralized. Evidence began to appear that the Baathist insurgency had withdrawn from its active role in attacks and lost confidence in the likelihood of political success in its current partnership with the Arab jihadists as they began to see more clearly the great divergence in goals between Baathist interests and that of the jihadists. There was also evidence that the Saudis, with American assistance, had partially closed their long 500-mile desert border with Iraq, making it more difficult for potential Saudi suicide bombers to move freely into Iraq, and that the Saudis had slowed the flow of its homegrown jihadists from the kingdom. Nevertheless, ending the Baathist-jihadist partnership required a type of courage few Sunnis had evidenced, like the March 23, 2005 tip from Iraqi villagers near an insurgent training camp northwest of Baghdad that resulted in killing about 80 insurgents and confiscating valuable weapons, training manuals, and intelligence information [Wong]. Now, the immediate future of Iraq is at stake in negotiations between the new government and the former Baathist insurgents.

By comparison, the other indicators of life in Iraq are far less consequential, but they do tell a story about what it's like to be an Iraqi citizen in 2005 and they are not all bad. The number of children attending primary school, for example, increased throughout the occupation, going from 3.6 million before the invasion to 4.3 million in January of 2005. The number of Iraqi telephone users tripled since the invasion, growing from 800,000 to 2.4 million. Unemployment, although still too high, fell from 60 percent to just over one-third of the work force, a significant drop. On the other hand, the insurgents' sabotage has been effective in disrupting electrical and oil production, despite infrastructure improvements that the coalition forces have made, but today Iraq is pumping nearly 2.4 million barrels of oil per day, which is back to prewar levels. At present this represents nearly $50 billion in annual income for the new government. Iraqis are driving more and as a consequence are finding longer lines at the gas pumps. Overall, there are enough encouraging statistics about life in Iraq to suggest that, as the insurgency is curtailed, life for the Iraqis should significantly improve in the relatively near future. In addition to the physical improvements in life, a democratic government with the freedom and personal security to pursue happiness promises a vastly superior life to the one lived during the Saddam Hussein regime or one envisioned by the al Qaeda-inspired Islamist militants.

In the most optimistic appraisal, the Iraq War could soon be over and the majority of coalition troops may be able to leave the country by the end of 2005 or early 2006. American troop levels had drawn down from 151,000 in January 2005 to about 138,000 in April with additional reductions planned for 2006. The determination of the exact date that hostilities will end is now in the hands of a new Iraqi government to work out with their old nemesis, the Baathists. The coalition must be willing to accept the terms that are agreed to by Sistani and the new government. There are significant incentives in place for all parties to agree on a peaceful and prosperous future for a war-torn nation that has been fighting, externally or internally, for the past quarter century while living in fear of their own leader.

The prospects for a stable Islamic democracy in the midst of the formerly totalitarian Arab Middle East are promising, although ancient rivalries and ethnic enmity still run deep. The despised and ruthless dictator, Saddam Hussein, has been overthrown and faces Iraqi judgment and punishment for crimes against humanity. Even if these positive results were to be limited to Iraq, the Middle East would be a much better place than before the invasion and liberation began. In addition, there are signs that these accomplishments may prompt further movement throughout the region for the spread of democratic institutions, which could mean substantial improvements for all people of the Middle East. The achievement of these benefits has not been without great cost, however. By the time the coalition forces leave Iraq, nearly 2,000 American and other coalition young men and women will have given their lives to the cause of freedom and greater security for the world. About 40,000 Iraqi citizens, most of them killed by insurgents, will have died in the creation of a democratic government for Iraq. In addition, billions of U.S. aid funds have been spent in rebuilding crumbling infrastructure in Iraq. These costs, while significant, were minute in comparison to America's Vietnam War where more than 58,000 Americans and 5 million Vietnamese died with no immediate benefits from the fighting. Despite the best efforts of bin Laden and Saddam's Baathists, the Iraq War was a far cry from becoming another Vietnam as bin Laden had so hoped and many critics had so decried.

The next and concluding chapter summarizes major findings about the causes of the war on terror and how that war has been fought. It presents a scorecard for the war as of September 11, 2005, the fourth anniversary of the al Qaeda attack, and what is needed over the next generation to complete the West's victory over militant Islamists.

CHAPTER FIVE BIBLIOGRAPHY

Anderson, John Lee, *The Fall of Baghdad*, New York: Penguin Press, 2004.

Bremer, L. Paul III, "The Right Call," *Wall Street Journal*, January 12, 2005.

Brooks, David, "The Insurgency Buster," *New York Times*, February 28, 2005.

Buruma, Ian, "An Islamic Democracy for Iraq?" *New York Times*, December 5, 2004.

Copeland, Libby, "Prison Revolt" *Washington Post*, Page C01, May 10, 2004.

Cordesman, Anthony H., *The Iraq War: Strategy, Tactics, and Military Lessons*, Washington, DC: Center for Strategic and International Studies, 2003.

___, "The Best Defense Is a Good Offense," *New York Times*, December 27, 2004.

De Albuquence, Adriana Lins, O'Hanlon, Michael, and Unikewicz, Amy, "The State of Iraq: An Update," *New York Times*, February 21, 2005.

Engel, Richard, *A Fist in the Hornet's Nest: On the Ground in Baghdad before, during and after the War*, New York: Hyperion, 2004.

Franks, Tommy, *American Soldier*, New York: HarperCollins Publishers, 2004.

Ferguson, Niall, "The Last Iraqi Insurgency," *New York Times*, April 18, 2004.

Friedman, George, *America's Secret War: Inside the Hidden Worldwide Struggle Between America and its Enemies*, Doubleday, 2004.

Ignatieff, Michael, "The Uncommitted," *New York Times*, January 30, 2005.

Keiler, Jonathan F., "Who Won the Battle of Fallujah?" *The Naval Institute: Proceedings*, January 2005, http://www.military.com/Content/ MoreContent1?file=NI_0105_Fallu-jah-P1.

Moss, Michael, "Many Actions Tied to Delay in Armor for Troops in Iraq," *New York Times*, March 7, 2005.

Nordland, Rod, Masland, Tom, and Dickey, Christopher, "Unmasking the Insurgents," *Newsweek*, February 7, 2005.

Ricchiardi, Sherry, "Missed Signals," *American Journalism Review*, August/September, 2004, http://www.ajr.org/article_printable.asp?id=3716.

Stille, Alexander, "Experts Can Help Rebuild A Country," *New York Times*, July 19, 2003.

Sullivan, Andrew, "Atrocities in Plain Sight, Book Review of *The Abu Ghraib Investigations* and *Torture and Truth*," *New York Times*, January 23, 2005.

Walker, Martin (editor), *The Iraq War, As Witnessed by the Correspondents and Photographers of United Press International*, Washington, DC: Brassey's, Inc., 2004.

Wong, Edward, "Backed by U.S., Iraqis Raid Camp and Report Killing 80 Insurgents," *New York Times*, March 24, 2005.

Woodward, Bob, *Plan of Attack*, New York: Simon & Schuster, 2004.

Zakaria, Fareed, "High Hopes Hard Facts," *Newsweek*, January 31, 2005.

6

The War on Terror: Recapitulation, Prognosis, and an Unfinished Agenda

This concluding chapter seeks to answer, in turn, four questions: (1) What and who caused the war on terror? (2) Where does the war stand on 9/11/05, four years after bin Laden's 9/11 commencement of hostilities? (3) What does the United States and its coalition need to do to hold onto to its lead over al Qaeda and make the world more secure against future terrorist attacks? (4) What more will be needed over the next generation to complete the West's victory over Bin Ladenism and radical, militant Islam?

THE EXPLOSIVE MIXTURE OF POLITICS AND RELIGION

The answer to the question of what and who caused the war on terror requires a short summary of the events that created modern Saudi Arabia and paved the way for 9/11. Since the inception of Abdul Aziz ibn Saud's efforts to create an Islamic state in the Arabian Peninsula, an explosive mixture of politics and religion has marked the desert kingdom. The radical religious beliefs of Ibn Abdul Wahhab (1703-1791), brought into the al Saud clan through marriage ties, were central in bringing together the various Bedouin tribes that formed the Kingdom of Saudi Arabia. Abdul Aziz Ibn Saud first experienced the backbite of militant Islamist radicalism in the late 1920s when reactionary Wahhabi clerics accused him of heathenistic modernization and he was forced to ruthlessly suppress the leaders of his Ikhwan army, the religious zealots he had used to capture the holy cities and suppress the tribes of the Arabian Desert. Even so, in 1932 when Abdul Aziz ibn

Saud crowned himself king of Saudi Arabia to legitimatize the al Saud claim to the throne, he established an Islamic state in which Wahhabism was the state religion, Arabic the national language, and the Holy Koran its constitution. That religious tie, plus control of Mecca and Medina and the discovery of oil soon after his coronation, gave the al Saud family all the resources and legitimacy necessary to maintain absolute control over the kingdom, subject only to periodic confirmation of the family's rulings by the Ulama, senior Wahhabi clerics who function as the supreme interpreters of the most rigid form of Islamic law on earth.

Abdul Aziz ibn Saud and his successor sons found that Wahhabi-Salafism could be an effective political lever in regional disputes concerning the leadership of the Arab Muslim world. When Gamal Abdel Nasser of Egypt threatened Saudi regional leadership with socialistic pan-Arabism in the 1950s and 1960s, the Saudis encouraged the Muslim Brotherhood to lead a fundamentalist revolt against the Egyptian government, culminating in the 1981 assassination of Nasser's successor, Anwar Sadat by religious extremists. The Saudi relationship with the Muslim Brotherhood had earlier led to the founding of the Islamic University in Medina in 1961 and the subsequent Brotherhood indoctrination of Saudi universities and the broader educational system in Saudi Arabia. The migration of radical Muslim Brotherhood ideology into Saudi Arabia served as a magnet for leading Egyptian and Syrian Islamist fundamentalists and theoreticians who ultimately became leading professors at Wahhabi universities in Jeddah, Mecca and Medina, Islam's holiest cities. One of their students was Osama bin Laden, son of a very wealthy family in the construction business, who was a favorite of the royal family. He graduated from King Abdul-Aziz University in Jeddah in 1981, studying there during the turbulent years following the Iranian Revolution and the militant takeover of the Grand Mosque in Mecca. Like other Saudi schools, King Abdul-Aziz University had come under the influence of violent Egyptian Brotherhood ideology that had earlier infected Saudi Arabian Wahhabism, once a cloistered and seemingly harmless fundamentalist fringe movement with a radical religious zealotry that justified violent terrorism and jihad against all enemies of their brand of Islam.

The question of who held the political upper hand in Saudi Arabia, the al Saud family or the intolerant and extremist group within the Wahhabis, has been a recurring struggle in Saudi Arabia. It was an issue for Abdul Aziz ibn Saud in the 1920s and it became a real concern 50 years later in 1979 when Iranian Shiites overthrew the Shah of Iran and, almost simultaneously, several hundred Wahhabi extremists influenced by the Muslim Brotherhood seized control of the

Kaaba, Islam's most sacred site, in the Grand Mosque of Mecca. The ghosts of Abdul Aziz ibn Saud's Ikhwan army had arisen to confront his royal successors, who were shaking in their boots from this double catastrophe and imminent threat to their monarchy. King Khaled, the reigning Saudi monarch at the time, could only gain sufficient authority to send troops into the Grand Mosque to capture or kill the radical insurgents by enlisting the support of the Ulama. The ringleaders were publicly beheaded but the price that the royal family had to pay for Ulama support and for many years of royal family indiscretions in a decadent life style was to open the royal purse strings to support worldwide charities sympathetic to the spread of Wahhabi-Salafism. Some of these funds found their way into the financing of al Qaeda.

Desperate to defuse the radical Wahhabi movement within the kingdom, the royal family seized upon the Soviet Union's invasion of Afghanistan in 1979 as an Islamic rallying cause and encouraged its Wahhabi clerics and youthful radicals to migrate there as Islamist jihadists in a holy war against godless communism. The diversion worked for a while, but only at a very high future cost to the kingdom, for the jihadists came back a decade later better trained in terrorist tactics and brimming over with confidence and zealotry from having defeated at the time one of the world's two formidable superpowers.

When the Iraqis invaded Kuwait and threatened to invade Saudi Arabia in 1990, Osama bin Laden offered his "Afghan Arabs" into the service of his country to defeat the Iraqi imperialists and claim Kuwait for the Saudis. Instead King Fahd, Khaled's successor, sought help from the United States and soon nearly one million foreign troops including 550,000 American infidels descended upon the holy land of Islam, infuriating bin Laden and leading him into direct conflict with the Saudi monarchy and the Great Satan, the United States of America. His goal of ridding the holy land and all of the Middle East of the infidel Americans and overthrowing the Saudi monarch was a product of the first Gulf War.

Osama bin Laden, whose primary long-term goals relate to capturing the Muslim world for an extreme form of Islam and establishing a reactionary Wahhabi-Salafist Caliphate to lead the Sunni Muslim polity, sought to overthrow the corrupt and decadent Saudi monarchy and force the Americans to respect Islam by withdrawing their troops from the Middle East. His experience in Afghanistan and the relative ease with which his jihadists defeated the Soviets, as well as his observations of the puny American responses to previous terrorist attacks, led him to put the American goal ahead of the Saudi one. He believed that the United States was a "paper tiger" that he could easily defeat and thus gain a broad reputation throughout the Muslim world as one of Islam's great warriors in defense of the faith. He had already routed the Americans out of Somalia. His new plan began in 1993 with the first bombing of the World Trade Center, which the United States treated as a law enforcement matter without recognizing its serious global terrorist implications. In 1996 American servicemen were attacked and killed in Dhahran, Saudi Arabia with the truck bombing of the U.S. Air Force al Khobar Towers dormitory complex; the Americans again treated the attack as a law enforcement matter but the FBI received little or no cooperation from the Saudi government. When in 1998 al Qaeda simultaneously bombed the U.S. embassies in Kenya and Tanzania, bin Laden finally got the attention of the U.S. government, but America's response was limited to launching a few cruise missiles at an al Qaeda training camp in Afghanistan and a mistakenly identified weapons factory in Sudan. In 2000 al Qaeda's suicide bombing attack on the USS Cole, docked in Yemen, killed 17 U.S. sailors and wounded 39 others, but again drew no direct American response. His next attack on the United States on September 11, 2001, one of the most devastating attacks on the United States in its history, did, however, draw a considerable response and finally a declaration of war.

THE SCORE AFTER FOUR: GOOD GUYS 9, BAD GUYS 3

So, where did the United States stand in its global war on terror as of 9/11/05, the fourth anniversary of the 9/11 attack? Using a baseball metaphor—for what could be more American—the Yanks were way ahead after four innings of a one-sided match (it was not a game, for war is certainly not a game). What follows is a scorecard chronology of the four years since 9/11/01 in America's war to defend innocent Western lives and engage in an ideological battle for the support of moderates in the Muslim world.

Little Offense for al Qaeda

Capturing the advantage by beginning the war with a sophisticated and highly complex terrorist attack on thousands of innocent civilians, or infidels as al Qaeda viewed them, working in two buildings that were symbols of the United States—the Twin Towers of the World Trade Center in New York City and the Pentagon in Washington, DC—al Qaeda certainly came on with "shock and awe." In baseball there is some advantage to scoring first, especially with a leadoff homerun and, in playing by its own rules, al Qaeda certainly achieved that advantage, but its 1-0 lead didn't last long.

Al Qaeda even got the response it sought from the United States when the West's hastily assembled military coalition intentionally drove into al Qaeda's deliberately set trap in Afghanistan. But it turned out to be a trap for the Islamists, because in Afghanistan the British and American coalition was able to utilize its high-tech weaponry, with little Western manpower and an army of paid Afghans, to rout al Qaeda and its affiliated Taliban government in less than two months. Osama bin Laden, al Qaeda's leader, and his second in command, Ayman Al Zawahiri, the radical Muslim Brotherhood theorist, were able to narrowly escape to the more remote mountains of northwest Pakistan at great cost to themselves and their movement. The Americans, who were new at fighting terrorist organizations, instinctively launched the right offense, destroying al Qaeda's command and control center and disrupting internal communications—its eyes and ears. Thus, the United States scored at least three runs—the ouster of the Taliban, the destruction of al Qaeda headquarters and training camps and the isolation of bin Laden—in the bottom of the first inning, to go ahead by a score of 3-1 and take a lead that it has not relinquished since.

The big problem for al Qaeda in its new headquarters in the Vale of Peshawar in Northwest Frontier Province of Pakistan was its isolation and the very rugged living conditions and limited communications in the area. Bin Laden's Afghanistan headquarters had been quite comfortable, with an extensive group of cohorts and their wives and children living and ruling "over mini-emirates of their own" [Taheri]. More important to the terrorist movement, in Afghanistan they were accessible to al Qaeda members, with relatively easy access to the headquarters for training and instructions. In their banishment to this remote area, these communications were drastically reduced in number and the speed so important to directing a military operation. For example, as Amir Taheri reported:

> "Abu-Mussab Al Zarqawi, the leader of the Al-Qaeda group in Iraq, tried to obtain a fatwa [edict] from them authorizing the mass murder of Iraqi Shiite women and children[, i]t took Al Zarqawi nearly six weeks to obtain the green light he wanted from Al Zawahiri" [Taheri].

The United States could easily argue that it had bin Laden exactly where it wanted him—out of sight and sound. Although he and his number two henchman managed to get out a total of eight messages through Al Jazeera, the Arab satellite television network, since their Pakistani confinement these messages have been costly and difficult to release in a timely fashion. An example is bin Laden's ill-timed and ineffective video attempting to influence the 2004 American presidential election. In addition, the number of written communications, books, and pamphlets has dropped drastically, from 83 in 2001 to only one since 9/11.

It now seems right for the U.S. government to agree with the suggestion of Tom Friedman in a recent *New York Times* [2005] column that the United States should withdraw its $25 million reward for killing or capturing Osama bin Laden because he is no longer worth it. The reward could be widely publicized with an announcement that it would be withdrawn at some future date to put pressure on top members to cash in and give up the movement as its defeat and the loss of their lives become ever more inevitable. Enhanced incentives may not produce the desired traitor, but it surely would raise doubts within al Qaeda about the trustworthiness of many of its members and force bin Laden into even further reclusion.

As a result of bin Laden's isolation, al Qaeda has no longer been able to function as a well-structured network carrying out the orders of its commanding general and central planning staff. It has been reduced to a hodge-podge of isolated terrorist cells, operating virtually independently, a mixed blessing for the West. On the positive side, highly sophisticated, complex terrorist attacks, like 9/11, are less likely to occur from such a disconnected network. In addition, various parts of the network have been forced to operate with competing objectives; Zarqawi in Iraq has called for the faithful to concentrate on fighting a Middle East jihad, while bin Laden has urged al Qaeda members to create another 9/11-type attack in the United States to show the world the power of the global Islamist movement. On the other hand, the West's intelligence agencies now have to work harder, or at least differently, because the al Qaeda planners are more diverse and, consequently, less predictable but still just as deadly, yet their freedom to move and operate in Europe has not been weakened. Unless the terrorist cause and its ideology are defeated, the danger in the West of a large number of innocent victims being killed or injured remains high and the cost of maintaining heightened and costly security systems must be continued. Moreover, failure of the terrorist insurgency in Iraq may make the global al Qaeda network more desperate and cause it to concentrate on launching suicide strikes on the American homeland.

But since its defeat in Afghanistan, the al Qaeda movement has mounted little offense. Significantly, there have been no attacks on the American homeland since 9/11. Besides rallying its forces to the cause of insurgency in Iraq, al Qaeda's only major hit-and-run score was on March 11, 2004 in the simultaneous bombing of four rush-hour commuter trains in Madrid that killed 191 people and injured more than 1,500. The immediate effect of the tragedy in Spain was to change the outcome of the Spanish election, bringing into power a socialist government that immediately removed the Spanish forces from the Iraq coalition and a resounding victory for the terrorists by showing Western capitulation as the direct result of their violent and deadly attacks. The timing and complexity of the assaults in Spain had the earmarks of a centrally planned bin Laden operation, but the arrests of some 75 suspects, mostly Moroccan nationals, did not produce clear answers to the questions of how and by whom the attack was organized. It could have been either a bin Laden initiative or the fortuitous timing of an independent Spanish cell with ties to North Africa. If it was the latter, together with the demonstrated incompetence of overlapping European intelligence agencies in solving the case, Europe may well be in more danger than the United States for future terrorist attacks because of the larger number of highly active Islamist cells in Europe than in the United States and because of Europe's large, discontented Muslim population, its open borders, and a liberal EU-wide immigration policy.

One other factor that has dampened the ability of al Qaeda to mount a vigorous offense against the United States and its Western allies has been the success of coordinated international efforts to cut off the flow of funds, especially Saudi funds, for financing terrorist operations. Bin Laden erroneously believed that it was the success of his "Afghan Arabs" that had bankrupted the Soviet Union, but the U.S.-led campaign to force the Saudis and its Muslim charities to withhold their support of radical Islamist causes has restricted the resources now available to the terrorists. Part of the reason so many Islamist terrorists flocked into Iraq to join the insurgency was that the funds Saddam Hussein stole from the people of Iraq were among the few remaining sources of cash available for financing al Qaeda operations. The decline in the rate of new Islamist recruits for Iraq may reflect the drying up of Saddam's money or a lessening of interest in the Iraqi cause by the militants. As the United States applies greater pressure on Syria, which is also home to millions in Saddam's stolen funds, the insurgents in Iraq face increasing problems funding their operations and recruiting teenage jihadist suicide bombers. If the new Iraqi government is successful in splitting the Baathist and jihadist insurgencies, even that limited source of funds will no longer be available for al Qaeda. Its only remaining assets will be its knowledge and understanding of terrorist strategy and tactics and the radical religious fervor and zeal of its members.

The Islamist threat, as we have seen, has derived from Saudi Arabian Wahhabism that the Muslim Brotherhood had radicalized after the death of Nasser and that the Saudis then exported around the world as an ideology of hate using their billions in oil wealth amassed over the last 30 years. In the aftermath of 9/11, American policy makers viewed al Qaeda as a totalitarian ideology every bit as pernicious as the fascist and communist ideologies that threatened freedom and democracy in the 20th century. Al Qaeda had violently burst forth upon the world scene for a number of reasons, but primary among these were the extent and persistence of autocracy and the deficit of freedom that has existed in the Middle East since modern states and boundaries were established there following the First World War. In the eyes of the Bush administration, the strategic antidote to Middle East autocracy and tyranny was freedom and democracy. To achieve the goal of freedom and democracy after 9/11, the United States pursued an offensive strategy, taking the fight to the enemy first in Afghanistan and then into the heart of the Arab-Muslim world, in Iraq.

America on the Offense

For the past four years, the United States has been on the offense, breathlessly pursuing al Qaeda with three powerful thrusts: (1) first in Afghanistan; (2) then moving against the policies and programs of its allies, such as the Russians, Pakistanis, and Saudis, that it viewed as supporting or insufficiently opposing Islamic terrorist organizations; and (3) invading Iraq and toppling Saddam Hussein who, in addition, to horrendous cruelty to his own people over many years, was in fact a terrorist himself and gave aid and comfort to terrorist organizations, which could possibly have included weapons of mass destruction such as chemical and biological weapons. The attacks against the American homeland on 9/11 forced policy makers to reassess the entire gamut of America's national security requirements since the onset of the Cold War. It also forced policy makers to understand the origins and extent of the ideology and threat from radical, militant Islamism, and to determine what Western civilization must do to counter the threat posed by al Qaeda and its banner, the "World Islamic Front for Jihad against Crusaders and Jews."

As the United States mobilized its resources in responding to the 9/11 attacks, all instruments of national policy and strategy were examined—ideological, political, economic, diplomatic, and military—and the President declared to the world that Western civilization, led by the United States, would embark upon a great and sobering generational war against a totalitarian ideology that preaches hate and intolerance. American policy makers recognized that they were dealing with a nihilistic form of barbarism set to destroy all advocates of freedom and democracy and that the enemy was ruthlessly intent upon controlling the Middle East and its oil wealth—nearly two-thirds of the earth's oil reserves—with a reactionary pan-Islamic Caliphate that would try to eventually control Europe and the entire world. Policy makers agreed that the enemy—radical, militant Islamists symbolized by Bin Ladenism—despised Western values and fought to replace those values with an extreme and barbaric Islamic code similar to what the Taliban forced upon the people of Afghanistan. The administration's policy makers concluded that the only effective antidote to such an ideology of intolerance and hate would be an ideology of hope represented by what the militant Islamists despise most about the West—freedom and democracy as advocated by decadent America.

The Afghan invasion was by far the most popular of America's post 9/11 initiatives and the most visible and dramatic victory, especially in light of the Soviet Union's debacle there in the 1980s, and the U.S. military scored the most runs for the good guys in the shortest amount of time. It was America's flashiest and swiftest offensive show in the war on terror. However, the profound damage that this military action did to al Qaeda's organization escaped popular notice because the elusive Osama bin Laden had not been captured, keeping alive his legend in the Muslim world as a great Islamic warrior defiant of the West and his reputation in the West as a shrewd, scheming, and evil mass murderer.

Even if bin Laden had been killed or captured in Afghanistan, militant Islamists would have continued their ideological struggle against the infidels in the United States and the West. Like bin Laden, militant Islamists would have sought to install pro-Wahhabi, Taliban-like regimes throughout the Middle East, drive the United States and all Westerners out of the region to establish a Wahhabi-inspired Muslim Caliphate, and then utilize the vast regional oil resources to proselytize their radical religion throughout the rest of the world. Had bin Laden been killed, the militant Islamists might have gone further underground until the West became less alert to terrorist risks, but they would have reemerged, better-organized, bitter in defeat, and seeking revenge, an even more dangerous threat to peace-loving people in both the Muslim and Western worlds.

Indeed, the West may well be better off that bin Laden survived the first thrust because it is easier to visualize evil and malevolence when those abstractions are personified in a villainous face that can be seen around the world making prophetic statements that assure his own doom. If coalition forces had killed or captured bin Laden in Afghanistan, it would have been politically difficult for the United States not to have declared victory, claimed justice for the innocent victims of 9/11, and returned to the old American policies of ignoring tyranny and injustice in the Middle East for the sake of stability and freely flowing oil. As a consequence, the two remaining thrusts of America's war on terror would have been political nonstarters. What would the West and, for that matter, the Muslim world have lost?

America's second thrust in the war on terror was its least visible and most unglamorous—two diplomatic incursions into (1) relations with Pakistan, Iran, Libya, and Russia to ensure that their weapons of mass destruction programs were under strict security controls and that WMD were not available to terrorists and, (2) a series of forceful U.S. diplomatic moves with Saudi Arabia to stop the Saudis from funding al Qaeda and proselytizing for their Wahhabi-Salafist state religion all over the world. Other Saudi reforms were also highlighted, but America's first priority was to stop the spread of the ideology of Wahhabi-Salafism and the evil step-child it inspired, al Qaeda.

The first diplomatic initiative successfully safeguarded the nuclear programs of Russia and Pakistan, forced Libya to totally abandon its nuclear weapons program, and placed Iran on notice of the consequences of any transfer of knowledge or weapons to terrorist organizations. Three runs scored by the good guys in the second inning can be verified from the change in behavior of all three nations, but the effect on Iran's nuclear efforts is still difficult to discern and requires continued careful monitoring to prevent the launch of a future bases-loaded homerun in the bottom of the ninth by Iran.

America's diplomacy during this entire episode was strengthened because of the new urgency with which the United States pursued its efforts. Having had three thousand innocent Americans killed using the country's own hijacked airliners made the Bush administration realize just how many more American victims could be murdered by nuclear or biological weapons in the hands of terrorists such as bin Laden. As a consequence, these separate bilateral negotiations took place with a far different and sterner tone than any prior American diplomatic discussions. The capture of bin Laden would have reduced the legitimacy for such strong and urgent talk from American diplomats, for when American diplomats spoke to these nations the threat of bin Laden still hung heavily over the negotiations.

However, the success of the first set of forceful American diplomatic negotiations with Russia, Pakistan, and Libya did not carry over to the Saudis. Despite the same challenging and provocative tone in American discussions with members of the Saudi royal family, Saudi Arabia persistently refused to acknowledge culpability for the 9/11 attacks and continued to deny knowledge of Saudi involvement in the financing of al Qaeda, even as some wealthy Saudis and members of the royal family continued their support for bin Laden. Instead of responding positively to the American inquiries, the Saudi government terminated its previous understanding with the United States by asking it to remove all of its troops from Saudi soil and even hinted at severing diplomatic relations unless the United States resolved the long-standing impasse in the Israeli-Palestinian dispute. The Saudis, so accustomed to gulling Americans, failed to understand that their inaction and recalcitrant behavior were almost a full admission of guilt for an unsavory relationship with al Qaeda and the massive funding that had been supplied to expand the Wahhabi-Salafist faith through their foreign embassies under the cover of Saudi foreign aid.

It was this Saudi behavior that played a crucial part in formulating President Bush's decision to undertake the third thrust in the war on terror, a massive American-led allied invasion force into the heart of the Arab-Muslim world, an invasion of Iraq to depose Saddam Hussein and declare the Bush Doctrine of freedom and democracy as the antidote to "Bin Ladenism." The Saudis did not believe the American president had the resolve—the "Chutzbah"—to take such action but they were wrong again in their misjudgments of the second President Bush. As soon as the Saudis realized the seriousness of Bush's determination to leave no stone unturned in America's pursuit of al Qaeda, they slowly acquiesced, providing the United States with sensitive information it had requested, and beginning to stop the flow of Saudi funds to al Qaeda. Saudi Arabia's demands for a resolution of the Israeli-Palestinian impasse were also tabled, but it did not cease urging the United States to reconsider its Iraq decision right up to the moment of the invasion in March 2003. Prince Bandar bin Sultan, after 25 years of highly visible service in representing Saudi interests in Washington, was the first Saudi 9/11 casualty of Crown Prince Abdullah's ire after his ascendance to power in the post-Fahd era. The Saudis had gambled and for the first time in decades had lost in its diplomatic poker game with the United States. And the United States scored another big run in its war on terror with al Qaeda, making the score 7-1 in favor of the good guys at the end of the second inning as a result of its dealings with Saudi Arabia.

The strategic thrust into Iraq, the third and fourth innings, allowed the United States to pick up a couple of runs through the expeditious invasion and toppling of Saddam, but the United States gave up one run to al Qaeda and the terrorists with the way it handled the postwar occupation, and especially the Abu Ghraib prison scandal. So the score was 8-3 by the end of the third inning and the radical militant Islamists had not succeeded, yet many opponents of the Iraq War still failed to accept the gravity of totalitarian militant Islamism and its ideological source, Saudi Arabian Wahhabism. The one-sided score at the end of three innings reflected the fact that since 9/11, the U.S. and its coalition partners overthrew two brutal regimes, liberating over 50 million people in the process. There were no mass uprisings in the Muslim world, as predicted before the Iraq war, and no Muslim government fell or shifted support to al Qaeda. Moreover, the world witnessed positive change among countries in the region, from Libya to Lebanon and Saudi Arabia to the Gulf States. Iraqi sovereignty transferred on June 30, 2004 and free national elections were held in Iraq on January 30, 2005.

Security responsibilities transitioned to the new Iraqi government and U.S. forces in Iraq planned reductions from 138,000 troops in the spring of 2005 to as few as 50,000 by 2006 and with the potential for a NATO command structure similar to Afghanistan. A homerun that could eventually seal the match for the good guys might come from Turkey's example as a long-standing Muslim member of NATO, permitting NATO to extend its collective security guarantees to traditional enemies like Iraq and Iran and eventually to the Persian Gulf states through the creation of "Southeast NATO," or "SENATO," consisting of selected NATO Muslim member countries. A long-term U.S.-led NATO force in the region could have a broader mission to protect the Persian Gulf oil fields while providing regional security that could also extend to the Israeli-Palestinian settlement as a respected international buffer under a formal U.N. charter.

The U.S quickly recovered from its disastrous occupation and the Abu Ghraib prison disaster and scored a resounding bases empty homerun with the January 30, 2005 elections, making the score 9-3 in early 2005. Indeed, the primary difficulty in scoring the war in Iraq is that the significant benefits of the Iraq invasion rested more its externalities, rather than its direct immediate effects inside Iraq. By externalities we mean the way the United States was seen in a new light in the Arab-Muslim world as a result of the following:

- Determination of the Bush administration to track down and prosecute bin Laden, as evidenced by American diplomacy with Saudi Arabia, Libya, Pakistan, Syria, and others;

- Reelection by the American people of its wartime president on a platform of the Bush Doctrine, as evidence of America's firm commitment to those policies;

- Willingness of the Bush administration to stay and fight even when things weren't going well, in stark contrast with America's previous reputation in the Middle East as a "paper tiger" without strong political will; and,

- Commitment to freedom and democracy, as evidenced by the Iraqi reaction to America's willingness to cede total power to the freely elected government and abide by its decision on the duration of the American troop presence in the country.

The last attribute is the most significant because freedom and democracy are America's ultimate antidote to Wahhabi-Bin Ladenism and the definitive proof of the American commitment to democracy is in its willingness to abide by the decisions of the Iraqi people in determining their future.

At the same time that America's image in the Muslim world was undergoing substantial improvement, al Qaeda and the militant Islamists were also being seen in a different way. They were no longer viewed as defenders of the faith against the infidels from the West, but rather as terrorists who would kill anyone—infidels or fellow Muslims—to advance their distorted view of Islam. America's victory in the war against terrorism was won by its fourth anniversary of that war and it was won because of American values. Americans changed the subject of the war: the war was no longer seen as East versus West or Muslims versus Infidels, but instead it was seen as free peoples—"Societies of Freedom"—versus people enslaved by fanatical religious doctrines or totalitarian governments—"Societies of Fear"—[Sharansky]. The war was won by a firm commitment to American values and it is those eternal values that have triumphed.

HOLDING ON TO THE LEAD

Achieving victory over a relatively small radical religious terrorist group is not an unexpected feat for the world's only superpower. Felled by his own hubris and megalomania, the biggest strategic error bin Laden made was to believe that the shortest and best route to conquering the Muslim world was to take on the infidel West and its leader, America, the "paper tiger." That bin Laden lost, and lost big, in this misjudgment is not surprising. However, what is surprising is the way the United States responded to being challenged by a fanatical religious organization, al Qaeda. The United States responded in kind by generally staying true to its basic values and whenever it strayed from those values, as it did in the disastrous Abu Ghraib prison scandal, it paid a high price. When the United States was not true to its values, it suffered loss of respect and diminished progress in spreading freedom. Moreover, America's unfortunate failures also jeopardized making its citizens more secure, the overriding objective of American foreign policy in the first four years of the Bush administration's global war on terror.

But America's fundamental resilience gave it new knowledge and determination from its encounter with evil and persistent terrorism. It learned that American citizens cannot be safe in the modern world, even with its technologies for mass destruction, unless those types of weapons of mass destruction are finally brought under absolute and total control by the world community. These weapons almost created parity between big nations, even superpowers, and small groups of zealots who are fearless in their determination to defeat superpowers, regardless of the consequences to their members or to other people anywhere on the globe.

The world after 9/11 had changed dramatically, and the United States decided to begin its new mission by resolutely pursuing and eliminating the terrorist organization that had killed so many of its innocent citizens and sent shock waves throughout its land and the entire world. With the initial part of its mission virtually accomplished at the end of four innings in what could be a long, extra-inning match, America's next priority is to lead the world in overhauling and reinvigorating world institutions such as the United Nations so they can effectively manage the new world order of the 21st century and ensure lasting security, freedom, and opportunity for all people, everywhere.

Back to Multilateralism

The Bush policies of unilateralism and preemption/prevention were adopted in the immediacy and demanding aftermath of the 9/11 moment. The United States believed that al Qaeda could strike again quickly after 9/11 and that the United States had to mount a rapid offense to keep the militant Islamists on the defensive, so al Qaeda could not strike again until better homeland security arrangements were in place and working. The strategy proved to be effective, but its pushy unilateralism could perhaps have been more diplomatic. The United States government also might not have understood how much of a deterrent its Afghan offensive had been in disrupting al Qaeda's operations. In addition, the diplomatic difficulties the United States encountered in persuading the Saudis to cut off the flow of funds to al Qaeda magnified American concerns about another imminent attack. Because the threat from al Qaeda seemed so severe in the immediate aftermath of 9/11, the American president's war council advisors continued to believe that offensive speed was of the essence for an effective defense of American and Western security. Under such circumstances, U.S. policy makers realized that multilateral action through either the United Nations or NATO against the terrorists could not possibly be undertaken quickly enough to meet the speedy schedule that the Bush administration had outlined for an effective offense.

Because of its assumptions, the Bush administration never really gave multilateralism a chance and, in many respects, it fomented international opposition to the invasion of Iraq by its early declaration of America's willingness to go alone, if necessary, and take unilateral military action to protect its citizens from further attacks. The Bush administration simply did not believe that it had sufficient time, like the first President Bush had in the 1990-91 first Gulf War, to bargain diplomatically with its European allies, many of whom had self-serving interests in keeping Saddam Hussein in power. Under a more patient timetable, the United States could have behaved with much more diplomatic charm and offered customary inducements to join its cause in unseating the sadistic Iraqi dictator, Saddam Hussein. Here is a case in which the picture Democrats had painted in the 2000 presidential campaign of George W. Bush as an arrogant, undiplomatic, Texas gunslinger came back to harm the American cause in 2002 and 2003. Bush's sense of urgency in defending his country was mistaken by many at home and abroad as stereotypical behavior that was expected of him. In any event, by the time Secretary Powell took the American case for invading Iraq to the U.N. Security Council, the result was foredoomed because of recalcitrant French meddling, the economic interests of Germany and Russia, and the lack of political fortitude by many European leaders.

The important conclusion from this review of the Bush post-9/11 policy is that it was the special circumstance of the moment, together with the heightened concern about American security, which led to the unilateral defense approach of the first Bush term. Those times are now past and the immediate dangers of another imminent al Qaeda attack are diminished, which of course doesn't mean that another attack still couldn't happen, but the probability of such an attack has been lowered. In addition, the United States now has a different set of near-term objectives: (1) bringing all WMD under absolute control to prevent al Qaeda or any other terrorist groups from killing innocent persons or extorting nations for concessions or tribute; (2) the Bush policy initiative of bringing freedom and democracy to the remaining third of world that is still enslaved in tyranny and autocracy, especially the Middle East; and (3) overhauling and reinvigorating institutions such as the United Nations and NATO to improve their effectiveness in the new post-9/11 world. These goals are essentially multilateral by nature and can be much better accomplished by broad multilateral efforts through existing

channels than the previous, urgent, and time-specific Bush policy of acting unilaterally outside the well-established multilateral framework.

A new style of foreign policy, as well as a new secretary of state, Condoleezza
Rice, emerged early in 2005 in the second Bush term. Although many observers
credited their criticism of President Bush's "abrupt and arrogant" actions for the
administration's change in style, the real reason was a change in circumstances.
There was no longer an urgent and tight time frame for reducing imminent security risks and a different set of goals were being sought that could only be
achieved through multilateral cooperation. In his second term, President Bush
now has the luxury to use diplomatic charm and America's traditional set of trading inducements to bargain with other nations to gain broad acceptance of America's national security policy objectives. The objectives of this new and friendlier
diplomatic and multilateral initiative are:

1.   Achievement of a permanent peace treaty between Israel and the new
      sovereign and independent state of Palestine, Secretary Rice's number
      one priority;

2.   Creation of a permanent and iron-clad system of controlling nuclear,
      biological, and chemical weapons to prevent terrorist organizations and
      sovereign states from extorting other nations, which is conceptually the
      most difficult and complex objective, but is superior to the former ad hoc
      approach of negotiating separately with each nation that raises a WMD
      threat.

3.   Reform the United Nations to make it more representative of the 21st
      century balance of world power and a more effective instrument for
      peace, human rights, and the relief of human suffering.

4.   Work with the Europeans to reinvigorate NATO and its southern flank
      as a newly structured security organization prepared to face the 21st cen-
      tury threat of radical, militant Islam along the Mediterranean Basin,
      Middle East, and Central Asia.

5.   Initiate a reopening of the Kyoto Treaty so that the United States could
      indicate a willingness to participate in a worldwide effort to reduce
      dependence on fossil fuels and combat global warming.

Except for the first goal, the Israeli-Palestine peace treaty, which is difficult but
becoming more solvable, accomplishment of the other goals may likely take
longer than the remaining time President Bush has in office. However, each of
these long-term goals can be broken down into concrete steps that can be taken

during the second Bush term in office to advance progress toward their eventual accomplishment. Establishing such a set of American foreign policy goals clearly differentiates the unilateral and preemptive stage of the administration's global war on terror and the subsequent phases that require broad and well-coordinated multilateral efforts. In addition, all of the goals, in one sense or another, are related to fighting terrorism and improving political conditions, primarily in the Arab-Muslim world. Undertaking such an agenda would represent a diplomatic way of calling an end to the unilateral and preemptive phase of the global war on terror, without fully renouncing a sovereign right to that approach should the United States ever again be faced with an imminent national security risk that, in its view, requires independent and unilateral action.

Lessons Learned about Using Military Options

The most controversial aspect of American actions in the past four years has been its willingness to employ military force to obtain its strategic objectives. The American use of massive military force in 1990-1991 and again after 9/11 has represented a seismic policy shift in the post-Vietnam era. Although the United States used military force in Somalia, the Balkans, and as peacekeeping troops in Haiti and other trouble spots around the world in the 1990s, these engagements were lower-risk operations of limited duration. In Afghanistan and Iraq, American troops were employed in fighting that was often more intense than Vietnam, but this time without the unfortunate high casualty rates even though the risks were equally great, especially with the severity and intensity of the Iraqi Baathist-Islamist insurgency. Several lessons were learned.

First, the vast majority of the American people supported the President's aggressive use of military force in the global war on terror against the enemy, al Qaeda. In its initial attack on innocent Americans, al Qaeda had invited retribution, and the causes of justice and national security required the type of search-and-destroy operations that only the deployment of strong and well-trained military forces could accomplish. America's political will for fighting a war against radical, militant Islamists was as strong as it had been in the nearly 50-year Cold War struggle against the Soviet Union and communism before the tragic and unfortunate Vietnam experience sapped American willpower. America's rapid victory in Afghanistan buoyed support for U.S. military intervention and made it possible for President Bush to continue the pursuit of its policies into Iraq, even though the administration unfortunately failed to present a cogent case for the linkage of the Iraq war to the overall goals of the global war on terror.

Second, American support of military action has very definite limits, as President Bush learned after a quick victory in conquering Iraq and deposing Saddam Hussein. The slippery slide into a growing war of fierce insurgency and undetermined duration raised all sorts of issues, some reminiscent of Vietnam. In the run-up to the 2004 American presidential election, the more the evidence suggested that the American occupation might slip into a Vietnam-type quagmire, the stronger the war opponents' case for withdrawal became. However, even during the bitter 2004 presidential election, a majority of Americans seemed to understand that the United States could not abandon Iraq without conceding a major victory to Osama bin Laden and his militant Islamists. Even amidst all the criticism of the administration, both at home and abroad, Americans understood the stakes involved in the war. And despite their disappointment with the results on the ground in Iraq and the lack of a clear-cut victory, the American public reelected President Bush in November 2004, indicating that a majority had retained a sufficiently strong political will to continue the fight, ostensibly for as long as it takes to win.

Third, advocates of the use of military force should heed an important lesson. Never commit too few American troops to an aggressive military action that the United States can't win with minimum military casualties in a reasonable period of time. Americans have reached a plateau of understanding that means they will no longer be quitters in their battles with radical, militant Islamists, but neither do they have the patience of Job in decisions involving the continued use of military force with no end in sight. It is for that reason that war advocates must be prepared to fight smarter wars if they need to commit American forces to military action in the future.

Fourth, Americans also received a rudimentary education in what it will take to fight a better and smarter war. Although improvements can be made in having a larger supply of qualified soldiers available before entering an engagement, which probably means paying better salaries to obtain larger enrollments in the voluntary army, the principal deficits in the Iraq war were in contingency planning, the quality of intelligence information about the enemy, and the poor training, lack of leadership, and limited capabilities in U.S. Army Reserve units. The planning, leadership, and training deficiencies are more easily remedied because the training of professional military officers teaches them how to plan for battlefield contingencies and Americans have generally been good at that aspect of training, planning, and adapting to the uncertainties of fighting. The fundamental planning lesson that was learned in Iraq is that the Pentagon civilian leadership and the military hierarchy must require the field commanders (i.e., Central

Command in the case of Iraq) to develop broad contingency plans for post-combat operations that are continually updated during the battle phase and allow enough time for such detailed and comprehensive planning to occur. Moreover, implementation of the post-combat plan should rest solely with the military commander until the administration's objectives are achieved.

The intelligence deficiency plagued the American military establishment from 9/11 throughout the entire period of the global war on terror and is the most serious systemic problem that exists today. The failures are many and well-documented: (1) poor intelligence led to the lack of advance warning of the 9/11 attack; (2) major failures in assessing the WMD threat in Iraq; (3) lack of knowledge of Iran's pre-war clandestine organizing Iraqi Shiites; (4) inability to alert the American military of the impending Baathist-Islamist insurgency; and (5) lack of understanding the nature and origin of the Iraqi insurgency operations during the occupation phase. Although Friedman's [2004] skepticism about how much can ever be learned and predicted from any intelligence apparatus is understandable, the United States must improve its intelligence gathering and analysis functions as comprehensively and as quickly as possible. It has to do far better, and the recently mandated reorganization of intelligence assets is a necessary first step in repairing America's overlapping and dysfunctional intelligence apparatus (15 different agencies) and calling for a high priority in implementing the best of the commissions' recommendations and periodically reassessing the progress of the reforms with periodic corrections as needed.

Regardless of how long it takes to repair U.S. intelligence capabilities, America's global war on terror has led to placing the military option back on the table as one of the tools that policy makers can again employ in the conduct of American foreign policy and the defense of U.S. national security interests. Americans and the rest of the world are aware that this significant change in American policy resulted from bin Laden's mocking his American infidel enemy as a "paper tiger." Bin Laden's derision backfired and the ultimate availability of America's military option is once again an effective foreign policy tool, as President Theodore Roosevelt recommended at the start of the 20th century: "Speak softly and carry a big stick." For if conditions necessitate, such as radical, militant Islamists creating civil war and chaos in Saudi Arabia, the United States will be prepared to defend its vital interests in the region with all of its resources, including military intervention.

The Carrot of Freedom and Democracy

Fortunately, the primary antidote that the Bush Doctrine has wisely proposed for defeating radical, militant Islamism is freedom and democratization, and it should not normally require the use of military force. The preferred American approach to the promotion of democracy has been to play a supporting role as the United States did with Corazon Aquino when Ferdinand Marcos was eased out of the Philippines. Political freedom has its own energy for conquering fear and oppression, and as more Muslims and other enslaved peoples around the world become aware that they too can independently obtain their own human rights and freedom, the likelihood of the need for American military intervention will substantially diminish. Saddam Hussein's insidious strength as an ironclad ruler and ruthless dictator made both him and his regime an exception to the general rule that despots cannot contain the instinctive human desire for freedom. Perhaps even in Iraq, Saddam's days would eventually have been numbered if tyranny's circle could have been effectively broken elsewhere in the Middle East. But that was not possible, and by starting with the toughest case and the people with the most to gain from being liberated, the American-led intervention in Iraq has made the dream of freedom and democracy more accessible and more attainable than it has ever been in the history of the Middle East. Smaller wonder that the seed of democracy has spread so quickly throughout the region since the Afghanistan elections in October 2004 and the elections in Palestine and Iraq in January 2005.

By the spring of 2005 Arabs were shouting "kifaya" in the streets of Cairo and Beirut, meaning "enough" in Arabic. Charles Krauthammer wrote in *The Washington Post* that the ice is breaking, the region is changing—remarkable, unexpected, hugely significant progress, with hope of an Arab spring. "We are at the dawn of a glorious, delicate, revolutionary moment in the Middle East" [Krauthammer]. A snowball effect developed after momentum began to build with elections in Afghanistan, Ukraine, Palestinian Authority, and Iraq between October 2004 and late January 2005. Democracies around the world started to get on the bandwagon, working with the United States, as the French did with Lebanon and Syria, rather than working against American interests. The Bush policy has not been the sole factor in creating the movement toward democracy, but by putting democracy into Iraq and in the heart of the Arab-Muslim world, and by turning power over to the people with a free election, the region is now riding the worldwide trend toward democracy. For as the President said in Brussels in February 2005, "...the United States is <u>the</u> beacon of liberty in the world…and we have a solemn responsibility to promote freedom…for we owe it to these people to help them be set free" [emphasis added].

America's foreign policy may not need to aggressively promote democracy for this is one political movement that has proved to be self-promotional, as the rapid spread of freedom and democracy throughout Eastern Europe demonstrated after the fall of the Iron Curtain. American foreign policy, and for that matter, the foreign policies of all major democracies in the developed world, now need to nurture the forces of freedom and democracy by providing technical and economic assistance to these emerging governments and by being patient with the development of the fragile and complex process of bringing power to the people. Human mistakes will be made as a natural part of development and learning, but the Western world should be reluctant to intervene unless cruel and inhuman treatment becomes a real prospect for a very large number of people as it was in Iraq. Having an effective international organization to manage this process will be of tremendous benefit to put pressure on autocrats and assist in the process of giving birth to freedom, which is a strong reason for giving reform of the United Nations highest priority.

The United States is in a position to make the tragedy of 9/11 a profound stepping stone for the betterment of all humankind. Continuing its resolute response and emphasizing American values as the antidote to terrorism could well provide the most appropriate memorial to the innocent victims of 9/11 and their families. The paradox of the United States is that it has always started its global struggles by overestimating the strength of its enemies, and it has concluded its struggles by accomplishing far more than could reasonably have been expected or imagined at the outset. After four years, the war against al Qaeda and radical, militant Islamists has not proven to be an exception to this American paradox, but the West's 9-3 lead over al Qaeda can easily be sustained and strengthened by following a more popular and cooperative multilateral plan, as long as the United States continues to be vigilant and prepared to use all available options—ideological, political, diplomatic, economic, and military—as the need should arise.

SEEDS OF HOPE—ROOTS OF CHANGE

In the longer-term, how will the United States continue to build its lead in the global war on terror and ultimately triumph over al Qaeda and other extremist terrorist organizations over the next generation? Osama bin Laden and his al Qaeda cronies may well be dead and buried by the end of President Bush's term in office, but that does not mean that total victory over the militant Islamists will have been achieved.

Reform of Islam Needed

The history of Islam reveals periodic movements of radicalism dating back to the 13th and 14th centuries when Ibn Taymiyah (1263-1328) reacted to the Mongol victory over the Arabs by blaming negative developments in the faith since the era of the Prophet. Ibn Taymiyah, like Ibn Abdul Wahhab, called for a return "to the fundamentals of the Quran" and "the habits and religious practice of the Prophet Muhammad, which were recorded for posterity by his companions and family and are regarded as the ideal Islamic norm" [Armstrong, 104 and 202]. Ibn Abdul Wahhab made much the same suggestion in the 18th century, but his radical view was kept alive by Abdul Aziz ibn Saud's official endorsement of Wahhabism in establishing the Saudi monarchy in the 20th century.

Both Ibn Taymiyah and Ibn Abdul Wahhab looked to the past when the condition of the Arabs looked bleak and they were radical reactionaries in the fullest sense. This backward view of battling the challenges of modernity is the root of contemporary radical, militant Islamism. Tom Friedman observed soon after 9/11: "Christianity and Judaism struggled with this issue [of modernity] for centuries, but a similar internal struggle within Islam to reexamine its texts and articulate a path for how one can accept pluralism and modernity and still be a passionate, devout Muslim has not surfaced in any serious way." The reformation of Christianity, fueled by the latest 16th century technology of the printing press, forever changed the way Western nations viewed the relationship between church and state and redefined the political rights of humankind, but there has been no similar reformation of Islam.

Most mainstream Muslims around the world were intimidated into silence due to the events of 9/11 and its aftermath, but signs of a Muslim reformation began to emerge. The Bush Doctrine was predicated upon the belief that the genie of freedom had been released to the world, especially with satellite television and the Internet providing the means for people to communicate their thoughts and ideas and break down the walls of rigid, autocratic regimes. The movement toward freedom and democratization is certainly the way to provide an environment for the destruction of radical, militant Islamism in a multi-generational war of ideology, but it can only go so far. The movement must also bring about a reformation in Islam, but reform and modernization of Islam can only come from within the faith itself, not by preaching infidels, and it will likely require several generations.

There are some hopeful signs. Gamal Banna, the 84-year-old brother of Hassan Banna who founded the Muslim Brotherhood in 1928, "has created a stir in Egypt recently" by arguing that "Islam allows for freedom of thought and evolution. Reform requires an open mind...Change is the greatest priority" [Williams]. In the article, Banna also challenges the commentary attributed to the prophet Mohammed, much of which Banna believes "was invented and even falsified in the earliest centuries of Islam by self-styled jurists." Just as the Protestant Reformation called into question the authority of the Roman Catholic Church, mainstream Muslims must learn to challenge the monopoly that Sunni and Shiite clerics have had on interpretations of the Koran. However, that challenge must be made by mainstream Muslims as a by-product of the democratic political freedom that the United States is trying to bring to the Middle East. Support of autocratic governments in the region by Islamic clerics has been largely based on their concern that political freedom will lead to exactly this sort of challenge to clerical authority. Freedom is always opposed by special interests that have something to lose in the process of spreading freedom into the political arena and other aspects of life.

Even though the West cannot participate directly in the religious issues surrounding the battle for the soul of Islam, the West's penetrating ideology of freedom and democracy represents strong and compelling ideas that the West needs to strongly promote in its war of words and ideas. America's "Voice of America" needs a stronger and more compelling call, for Al Jazeera, Al Arabiya, and hundreds of Islamist web sites on the Internet have outpaced U.S. information efforts, and mainstream Islam has been largely silent on the root cause of today's radical, militant Islamist terrorism that has been derived and nurtured from the dominant Wahhabi-Salafist religious creed practiced in Saudi Arabia.

A Generation of Peace

Beyond that, American leaders must inspire young people into U.S. government service and use all of the instruments of American national security policy—ideological, political, diplomatic, economic, and military—to implement comprehensive solutions to one of the world's long-neglected regions, the Middle East, and build the framework for a generation of peace so that today's suicide bombers can outgrow their militancy through hope for a better future and jobs to support their families. To do this, the United States must partner with Arab-Muslim forces of moderation and implement long-term policies and strategies that will create a generation of peace and put in place the economic and political framework needed as a cornerstone for open and pluralistic societies. The goal of the United States is now to democratize the Middle East and experience has shown that democracy will accelerate there because the demise of one dictator tends to send shock waves throughout the region and into neighboring countries.

Historically, American foreign policy almost never looks good in the short term, for there are always critics and naysayers, and it is often difficult to grasp the historical perspective of unfolding events that frequently conflict. But when considered in the longer perspective of history and over many years, the United States has done a far better job implementing its foreign policy than other countries and it has had resounding success in the process, restoring Western Europe and rebuilding Japan after World War II, and now the Middle East. It is well to remember that the press, pundits, and even historians tend to focus on problems and mistakes of the moment, yet memories tend to be short. Even today the long struggle of the Cold War seems like ancient history to many, as America's critics become more vocal in their often biased censure of the only remaining superpower. But a simple fact remains: The United States is the principle exponent of decency and equality in the world today and its goals are to give to all people the same opportunity for life, liberty, and the pursuit of happiness that is inscribed in the "self evident truths" of its own Declaration of Independence.

But how does the world secure peace and justice in the 21st century and how does the United States convince the world that its major goal is truly to enhance human dignity for people of all faiths? In the twelve months following 9/11, the Bush administration formulated a new national security strategy and sold it to the American people and to the world. That strategy is now unfolding in the Middle East as al Qaeda and the Islamists are on the run and scattered, with funding drying up, recruiting down, and the number and effectiveness of its attacks declining. In modern times, the world has witnessed several expressions of America's idealism starting with Wilson's 14 Points following the First World War, then Carter's "moral component" of national security policy as a counter to Kissinger's "realpolitik," and now Bush's bold and daring initiative to promote freedom and democracy in the Middle East.

Where are we today? To start, it is clear that Christians, Jews, and Muslims are children of the same God and the same father, Abraham—brothers and sisters—with the same "...eyes, hands, organs, dimensions, affectations, passions..." [Shakespeare]. Together, they make up over half the people on the planet. But some might say that organized religion is the problem and not the solution and that Christians, Jews, and Muslims have abdicated moral responsibility and have failed to find solutions to the world's vexing problems of autocracy, poverty, and war. Some say that Christianity has abdicated responsibility in containing the excesses of freedom, ceding its moral compass to others, like Muslim Brotherhood theoretician Sayyid Qutb, who said that the modern world had lost its way and can only be brought back to its moorings through rigid Islamic law that condemns modernization and nonbelievers.

Where are the echoing voices of Paul Tillich (1886-1965) and Reinhold Niebuhr (1892-1971) today? Tillich witnessed in NAZI Germany the acquiescence of established churches to National Socialism and it was Niebuhr who wrote during the dark days of World War II, "For democracy is a method of finding proximate solutions for insoluble problems" [Niebuhr].

Perhaps new middle ground that predates both Christianity and Islam could support a shift in global ethics involving a recovery of Plato and Aristotle as described by Stanley Hauerwas at the Duke University School of Divinity: Ethics based on character and virtue on the model of Aristotle [Hauerwas and Pinches]. Plato and Aristotle viewed virtue as being fundamentally heroic, especially in the actions required to defend a democratic Greek city-state by force of arms. Aristotle addressed what is "best," in the broadest sense, for human beings and noted that ethical inquiry seeks to resolve disagreements that arise over the fundamental human goal of determining what is "best" for humankind. Aristotle's search was for the "highest good" and as Plato argued in the *Republic*, the best type of "good" is one that is desirable both in and of itself and also for the sake of what it achieves.

Bin Laden argues, quite implausibly, that to achieve the ultimate good that he envisions, he must destroy the enemies of true Islam and kill all nonbelievers. Because the struggle bin Laden has embarked upon is fundamentally ideological in nature, and because bin Laden's message echoes widely throughout the Muslim world, especially the Arab-Muslim world, the West must prepare itself and its future leaders, not only with practical knowledge, but also with the tools of ancient virtue and ethics and an appreciation for the long-term nature of the struggle and the very hard work that lies ahead.

Light Some Candles

The United States and the West must prepare future leaders and find trained graduates for critical positions in the West's multi-generational struggle against radical, militant Islamism. The U.S. Army and CIA are trying to recruit Arabic linguists but few qualified candidates are available. The American government needs people who speak Arabic and are students of Middle East history and culture but few are available. The country needs American students to challenge themselves with Fulbright scholarships in places like Syria, Jordan, Saudi Arabia, Kuwait, Iraq, and elsewhere in the Middle East, and the U.S. needs to bring more people from the Arab-Muslim world to study in the United States. Disgracefully, few are available, while public diplomacy scholarships in the United States are down from 15,000 at the peak of the Cold War to fewer that 1,000 today. These serious national deficiencies need to be addressed by America's colleges and universities and the U.S. government should provide incentives to students to take up the challenge to study Islam, Arabic, and Middle East history.

Finally, the United States needs help through all of its voices in lighting candles of knowledge and hope to shine into the darkness of the demonic forces that have been released upon the world, to enlighten the darkness of terrorism, the darkness of Islamic fundamentalism, and the darkness of radical, militant Islamism. The momentum that has been built since 9/11/2001 reveals that ideologies of hate will ultimately disappear and that true peace will come to regions of the world like the Middle East only when autocracy ends, justice prevails, economic opportunities are provided, and national security issues are resolved by planting and nourishing seeds of hope and roots of change in those ancient lands.

CHAPTER SIX BIBLIOGRAPHY

Armstrong, Karen, *Islam, A Short History*, New York: Random House, Inc., Modern Library Edition, 2000.

Bush, George W., "President Discusses American and European Alliance in Belgium," the White House, Office of the Press Secretary, Concert Noble, Brussels, Belgium, February 21, 2005.

Friedman, George, *America's Secret War, Inside the Hidden Worldwide Struggle between America and its Enemies*, New York: Doubleday, 2004.

Friedman, Thomas L. "Lets mark Osama bin Laden down to a penny," *New York Times*, February 6, 2005.

___, "The Real War," *New York Times*, November 27, 2001.

Gaddis, John Lewis, "Grand Strategy in the Second Term," *Foreign Affairs*, January/February 2005, http://www.foreign affairs.org/20050101/john-lewis-gaddis/grand-strategy-in-the-second-term.html.

Hauerwas, Stanley and Pinches, Charles, *Christians Among the Virtues. Theological Conversations with Ancient and Modern Ethics*, South Bend: University of Notre Dame Press, 1998.

Krauthammer, Charles, "The Road to Damascus," *Washington Post*, March 4, 2005,   http://www.washingtonpost.com/wp-dyn/articles/A5695-2005Mar3.html.

Niebuhr, Reinhold, *The Children of Light and the Children of Darkness*, New York: Charles Scribner's Sons, 1944.

Sharansky, Natan with Dermer, Ron, *The Case For Democracy: The Power of Freedom To Overcome Tyranny and Fear*, New York: Public Affairs, 2004.

Taheri, Amir, "Losing Battle for Islamists," *Arab News*, March 26, 2005, http://arabnews.com/services/print/print.asp?artid=61079&d=26&m+3&y=2005&hl=Losi....

Williams, Daniel, "Aging Egyptian Says 'Religion Allows Freedom of Thought,'" *Washington Post*, March 7, 2005, http//:www.washingtonpost.com/wp-dyn/articles/ A12340-2005Mar6.html.

APPENDICES

APPENDIX A:

CHRONOLOGY OF KEY EVENTS IN THE HISTORY OF SAUDI ARABIA

610—Prophet Mohammed's Divine Revelations started

632—Death of Prophet Mohammed

1187—Saladin (Iraqi Kurd) defeated Crusaders and recaptured Jerusalem

1453—Beginning of Ottoman Empire

1683—Islam's conquest of Europe halted at gates of Vienna (September 11th)

1703—Birth of Ibn Abdul Wahhab, founder of Wahhabi-Salafist movement

1744—Wahhab-al Saud agreement and marriage pact (approximate date)

1792—Death of Ibn Abdul Wahhab

1798—France (Napoleon) invaded Egypt, occupied Palestine

1801—Wahhabis destroy holy Shiite shrines in Iraq (Karbala and Najaf)

1871—Ottomans took control of al Hasa province in eastern Arabian Peninsula

1891—Al Saud family exiled to Kuwait by Rashidi family

1902—Abdul Aziz ibn Saud took control of Riyadh, brought Al Saud family back into Saudi Arabia

1912—Ikhwan founded, grew quickly based on Wahhabism, provided support to Abdul Aziz ibn Saud

1913—Al Hasa Province taken from the Ottomans by Abdul Aziz

1921—End of Ottoman Caliphate; Abdul Aziz ibn Saud assumed title "Sultan of Najd"

1924—Mecca recaptured by Abdul Aziz ibn Saud

1925—Medina recaptured by Abdul Aziz ibn Saud, Ikhwan revolt began

1926—Abdul Aziz ibn Saud proclaimed "King of the Hijaz" in the Grand Mosque of Mecca

1928-30—Ikhwan revolt defeated by Abdul Aziz ibn Saud, leaders beheaded in public

1932—Abdul Aziz ibn Saud proclaimed King, country unified under the name Kingdom of Saudi Arabia

1933—Saud, eldest son of King Abdul-Aziz ibn Saud, named Crown Prince
Oil concession granted to Standard Oil of California (SOCAL)

1938—Oil discovered, production started under ARAMCO (Arabian American Oil Company)

1953—King Abdul Aziz ibn Saud died, succeeded by son Saud; son Faisal named Crown Prince

1957—Birth of Osama bin Laden

1960—Saudi Arabia founding member of OPEC (Organization of Petroleum Exporting Countries)

1964—King Saud deposed by his brother Prince Faisal

1967—Third Arab-Israeli War ("Six-Day War")

1972—Saudi Arabia received 20 percent of ARAMCO from American oil companies

1973—Fourth Arab-Israeli War ("Yom Kippur War"), Saudi Arabia led oil boycott, oil prices quadrupled

1975—King Faisal assassinated by nephew, succeeded by brother Khaled

1979—Saudi Arabia severed diplomatic relations with Egypt after Egypt made peace with Israel
Wahhabi/Muslim Brotherhood extremists seized Grand Mosque in Mecca
Saudi government regained control, publicly executed 60 extremists
Shah of Iran overthrown by Shiite cleric Ayatollah Khomeini
Soviet Union launched invasion of Afghanistan

1980—Saudi Arabia received full control of ARAMCO

1981—Saudi Arabia founding member of Gulf Cooperation Council (GCC)
Osama bin Laden completed university in Jeddah

1982—King Khaled died of heart attack; succeeded by brother, Crown Prince Fahd

1986—King Fahd assumed the title "Custodian of the Two Holy Mosques"

1987—Saudi Arabia resumed diplomatic relations with Egypt, severed since 1979

1990—Iraq invaded Kuwait
Saudi Arabia condemned Iraqi invasion of Kuwait
Nearly one million foreign troops in Saudi Arabia including 550,000 Americans
U.N. imposed trade sanctions Iraq

1991—U.S. & coalition forces launched air war against Iraq in January, rapidly liberated Kuwait
Cease-fire announced in February
U.N. Security Council specified conditions for lifting sanctions and destruction of Iraq's WMD

1992—King Fahd proclaimed new "Basic Law," responsibilities of the ruler, Consultative Council

1993—King Fahd divided Saudi Arabia into 13 administrative regions

1993—Saudi Consultative Council inaugurated with chairman and 60 members chosen by the King
Iraq refused to remove missiles in defiance of cease-fire agreement and U.N. sanctions
Allied warplanes and warships attacked Iraqi missile sites and nuclear facility near Baghdad
U.S. fired 24 cruise missiles at Iraq headquarters for assassination attempt on first President Bush

1994—Osama Bin Laden stripped of Saudi nationality, King Fahd ill
Iraqi troops moved toward Kuwait, pulled back when U.S. dispatched carrier group, 54,000 troops and warplanes

1995—King Fahd had stroke(s); day-to-day operation of country transferred to Crown Prince Abdullah

1996—U.N. allowed Iraq to make limited oil sales under corrupt oil for food program

1996—Bomb exploded at American al Khobar military complex near Dhahran killing 19, wounding 300

1997—King Fahd increased number of Consultative Council from 60 to 90
Iraq refused to disclose details of banned weapons programs
U.N. imposed new restrictions for inspections
U.S. & British military buildup in the Persian Gulf

U.N. Security Council condemned Iraq's actions as "flagrant violation" of U.N. resolutions

U.S. & British planes bombed Iraq for Saddam Hussein's defiance of U.N. weapons inspectors

Air strikes halted after four days; Iraq cut off all cooperation with U.N. weapons inspectors

1998—Iraq Liberation Act of 1998, H.R. 4655, signed into law by President Clinton

1999—Twenty Saudi women attended a session of the Consultative Council for the first time

2000—Amnesty International described Saudi Arabia's treatment of women as "untenable"

Hans Blix assumed post of executive chairman of U.N. weapons inspectors for Iraq

U.S. stock market crashed—Internet dot com bubble burst

2001—British workers arrested in Riyadh after series of bomb attacks, British & American national killed

Saudi Arabia, Iran signed agreement to combat terrorism, drug-trafficking, organized crime

September 11th—15 of 19 hijackers in attacks on New York and Washington, DC were Saudis

Bin Laden taunted "infidel" Bush over Sept. 11 attacks

U.S. pressured Saudi Arabia to reform, cut off funding for terrorism; Saudis uneasy over U.S. ties

King Fahd stated terrorism prohibited by Islam

Saudi government issued identity cards to women

Taliban overthrown in Afghanistan; bin Laden escaped into Pakistan

2002—New Saudi criminal justice system banned torture and provided right to legal representation

Bin Laden said on al Jazeera, "battle has moved inside the United States"

Saudi investors withdrew billions from U.S. in protest of lawsuit filed by relatives of 9/11

Saudi border crossing with Iraq reopened for first time since Iraq 1990 invasion of Kuwait

Saudi foreign minister said U.S. cannot use Saudi facilities to attack Iraq, even if approved by U.N.

U.N. Security Council modified U.N. sanctions against Iraq to speed delivery of food and medicine

President Bush stated world leaders must enforce U.N. resolutions against Iraq or U.S. acts alone

U.N. Security Council voted 15-0 for a resolution to disarm Iraq

Stated goal of U.S. government was regime change in Iraq

Iraq released a 12,000-page document on its weapons programs

2003—U.S. and coalition partners invade Iraq

U.S. agreed to withdraw troops from Saudi Arabia, ending military presence since 1991 Gulf War

Suicide bombers killed 35 people at housing compounds for Westerners in Riyadh

More than 300 Saudi intellectuals, women and men, signed petition for political reform

Government said elections for municipal councils would be held within a year, first elections ever

Police broke up rally in Riyadh calling for political reform, 270 people arrested

Suicide attack by al-Qaeda militants on residential compound in Riyadh, 17 dead, many injured

King granted powers to Consultative Council to propose legislation without king's permission

2004—Saudi Arabia stated it would negotiate substantial reduction of Iraq's debt

Stampede at Hajj pilgrimage, 251 dead

Attacks near Riyadh, car bomb at security HQ killed four, wounded 148, group linked to al-Qaeda

Attack at Yanbu petrochemical site killed five; attack and hostage-taking in al Khobar, 22 killed

Bin Laden offered truce to Europeans for withdrawing troops from Muslim nations

Three gun attacks in Riyadh in one week, two Americans, one BBC cameraman dead

American engineer abducted and beheaded, security forces killed local al-Qaeda leader

Amnesty offered for Saudi militants with limited effect

Attack on U.S. consulate in Jeddah, five staff members and four attackers killed

Two car bombs exploded in central Riyadh; security forces killed seven suspects in raid

2005—Palestinian and Iraqi elections (January)

Saudi municipal elections for half the seats, king appointed other half, women could not vote

Saudi Consultative Council increased to 120 members

Saudi Arabia confirmed killing 15 Islamist extremists including al Qaeda leader for Saudi Arabia

Syrian forces completed withdrawal from Lebanon

New democratically elected Iraqi government formed

Crown Prince Abdullah and President Bush met in Crawford, Texas

Oil peaked at all-time high, exceeded $60 per barrel

APPENDIX B:

ABOUT THE AUTHORS

B. Wayne Quist, Colonel, United States Air Force, Retired

B. Wayne Quist is the author of several publications and articles in the field of radical, militant Islam, national security policy, and American history. He has been featured as a popular speaker on the ideology of al Qaeda and recently lectured at the Nobel Peace Prize Forum. Colonel Quist has a B.A. degree from St. Olaf College plus advanced degrees from the University of Southern California and The National War College in Washington, D.C., specializing in the Middle East. Colonel Quist's accomplishments have been recognized by the U.S. government and several schools and international industrial associations, and he currently serves on the Board of Directors of the Kierkegaard House Foundation in support of the Kierkegaard Library at St. Olaf College in Northfield, Minnesota. Colonel Quist was commissioned a second lieutenant in the United States Air Force through the Air Force Reserve Office Training Corps (ROTC). He retired from the Air Force in the rank of full colonel (O-6) and with 3,500 flying hours as a navigator and AWACS mission commander. While serving in Washington, DC, he worked in the Pentagon, later directed the Air Force AWACS program, and led the first deployment of AWACS into Saudi Arabia in 1979 following the Iranian revolution. After leaving the Air Force, Colonel Quist and his wife, Pam, lived in Brussels, Belgium for several years where he headed a Fortune 500 company's Europe and Middle East operations. Colonel Quist is currently a partner with an investment banking firm where he specializes in the sale and recapitalization of privately held companies in the United States, Europe, and the Middle East. The Quists have one son, Peter, and one grandson, Christian.

David F. Drake, Ph.D.

David F. Drake has written and spoken extensively on health economics, finance, and regulation. He has authored several articles on health economics and national health insurance topics and *Reforming the Health Care Market: An Interpretative Economic History* was published by Georgetown University Press in 1994. For the past 13 years Mr. Drake has researched and written about such diverse topics as health economics, political economics, foreign affairs, and the detective stories of Georges Simenon and Agatha Christie. Mr. Drake is completing a manuscript on political economy, *Staying the Course: America's Formula for Economic Success*, and has completed *The World's Greatest Detective: Hercule Poirot or Jules Maigret*. Mr. Drake received his doctorate in business administration from the University of Chicago Graduate School of Business, where he earlier received an MBA. His bachelor's degree in economics, with minors in history and political science, was awarded by Carleton College in Northfield, Minnesota, his birthplace. He taught in the Graduate School of Business at the University of Chicago from 1962 to 1982 and served as a lecturer in community medicine at Northwestern University School of Medicine from 1970 to 1995. Mr. Drake retired as Senior Vice President and Secretary-Treasurer of the American Hospital Association in 1992 after 25 years with the Association. His last 10 years with the AHA were spent as corporate secretary, chief financial officer, and senior executive in charge of internal administration of a $125 million a year hospital trade association. Mr. Drake and his wife Joyce have two sons, Winston and Andrew, and two grandchildren, Ethan and Abby.

Index

A

Abbas, President Mahmoud 137, 147, 151

Abdul Azziz ibn Saud xix, 4, 5, 7-13, 19, 21, 23, 27, 30-1, 43, 63, 93, 96, 104, 205-6, 208, 215-6

Abdullah bin Abdul Aziz ibn Saud, Crown Prince 23-6, 36, 51, 61, 91, 94, 97, 124, 197, 218, 220

Abu Ghraib Prison xx, 145, 169-72, 185, 197-9

Adams, Secretary and President John Quincy 126, 128

    Monroe Doctrine 126

Afghanistan xiv, xix, 8, 10, 17, 29, 38, 42, 47, 52, 66, 80-1, 84-5, 91-2, 98-9, 107, 114-8, 120, 122, 124, 132, 134, 142-3, 149-50, 153, 155, 157, 164, 166-7, 189-90, 191-2, 194-5, 198, 203, 206, 217-8

    Soviet Union invasion, 1979 80, 99

    Coalition invasion, 2001 114-18

    Elections of 2004 142-3

Afghan Arabs 1, 38, 42-3, 189, 193

Ahmad, General Mahmoud 115

Ahmed bin Salman bin Abdul Aziz, Prince 92

Akbar, Sergeant Hasan 71

Al Arabiya 58, 99, 209

Al Jazeera 58, 75, 99, 145, 169, 191, 209, 218

Al Qaeda [see also Qaeda] xiii, xv, xvi, xvii, xix, xx, 1, 4, 10, 24, 26-7, 34-5, 38, 41-2, 46-8, 50, 52-3, 63, 67-70, 73, 75-9, 81-2, 84-88, 90-2, 94, 100, 103, 105, 109, 113-7, 122-5, 132-5, 137, 140, 142-4, 147-51, 160, 162, 166-7, 169, 174, 177, 183-4,187, 189-201, 203, 207, 210, 219, 221

Allawi, Prime Minister Ayad 145, 176, 177

Al Waleed ibn Talal ibn Abdul Aziz, Prince 97

American Muslim Council 68

Anderson, John Lee 161, 184

Anti-Semitism 40, 75, 76, 82, 97, 102, 107

Aquino, President Corazon 131, 206

Arab American Oil Company [ARAMCO] 11, 21-2, 95, 216-7

Arab-Israeli War 12, 22, 45, 98, 216

    Six Days War, 1967 45, 216

    Yom Kippur War, 1973 17, 46, 93, 216

Arab League 15, 54, 56, 61, 142

Arab Oil Embargo 12, 13, 17, 19, 22, 46, 93, 98

Arafat, President Yasser 130, 137, 147, 150

Aristotle 211

Armitage, Undersecretary Richard 115, 119, 131

Armstrong, Karen 190, 212

Assad, President Hafez al 55, 136

Atta, Mohammed 48

Attaturk, Kemal 79

Australia 116

Ayyiri, Yusuf al 53

Azzam, Abdullah 45, 47

B

Baathist Party 53, 144, 174, 177

Baghdad, Iraq 25, 36, 39-40, 72, 140, 143, 156-66, 168, 169, 173, 174, 182, 184-5, 217

Bandar bin Sultan bin Abdul Aziz al Saud, Prince 25, 90, 96-8, 134, 197

Bahrain 10-11, 21, 62, 123, 138, 147

Balkans 73, 84, 99, 203

Banna, Gamal 209

Banna, Hassan al 41, 43, 209

Basra, Iraq 158

Bedouin 2-4, 8-9, 20, 24, 28, 30, 52, 61, 89, 179, 187

Beirut, Lebanon 83, 147, 206

Benedict, Ruth 164

Benoit, Bertrand 107

Bergen, Peter 26, 36

Berlin, Germany 72, 82-3, 111

Berman, Paul 63

Bin Laden, Osama [see also Osama bin Laden] xiii, xiv, xix, 1, 10, 26, 33, 41-7, 77, 79-80, 82, 84, 87, 91-2, 94-5, 98-100, 106, 115, 117, 128, 149, 151, 177, 188-9, 191-2, 195, 204, 207, 212, 216-7

Bin Ladenism xiv, xv, xviii, xix, 1, 9, 33, 35, 48, 49, 50, 62, 78, 79, 87, 102, 105-6, 125, 130, 148, 187, 195, 197, 199

Blackwell, Robert 119

Blair, Prime Minister Tony 138, 150, 154

Bonn, Germany 74, 118

Bosnia 84, 111, 116, 141

Bremer, Paul 143, 166, 176, 179

Bremmer, Ian 19, 36

British 10-12, 21-2, 28, 40, 54, 58, 73, 75, 107, 116, 138, 139, 150, 158, 162-3, 165, 172, 178, 191, 218

Broad, William J. 122, 151

Brooks, David 181, 184

Burns, John F. 144, 152

Buruma, Ian 184

Bush, President George H. W. 113, 119, 137, 201

    Grand Alliance 111, 137

    New World Order xvii, 111, 153, 200

Bush, President George W. 138, 197

    Addresses: 9/20/01, Declaration of War on Terror 113

        1/29/02, "Axis-of-Evil" Speech 120-1
        6/1/02, West Point Graduation 124-5
        9/12/02 U.N. General Assembly 131-2
    Bush Doctrine xix, 51, 78, 106, 111, 113-4, 118, 124-5, 127, 128-32, 134, 139, 146, 148, 149-51, 197-8, 206, 208

Democratization 112, 128, 129, 130-1, 135, 141-3, 206, 208

Job Ratings 134-5

National Security Strategy of United States of America 125-7

C

Cairo, Egypt 46, 54, 206

Caliphate 27, 40-2, 54, 78, 95, 100, 180, 189, 195, 216

Canada 17, 138

Carter, President Jimmy 12, 17, 80, 83, 94

    Carter Doctrine 94

    Camp David Agreement 12, 17, 18

Central Intelligence Agency 5, 13, 51, 57-60, 73, 78, 83-5, 93, 95, 116, 122-3, 135, 155-6, 162, 166, 170, 211

Chalabi, Ahmed 163, 166

Chechnya 72, 75, 115

Cheney, Vice President Richard 113, 134

China 3, 16, 19, 27-8, 30, 61, 115, 139, 149

Chirac, President Jacques 150

Churchill, Prime Minister Winston 40, 163

Clarke, Jonathan 131, 153

Clarke, Richard A. 69, 70, 108

Clinton, President Bill 82, 85-6, 96, 135, 137, 141, 218

Cohen, Richard 28, 36

Coalition xvii, 18, 47, 56, 77, 120-1, 134, 138-9, 140, 143, 145, 146, 149-151, 157, 159-61, 163-9, 172-9, 181-4, 187, 191, 193, 195, 198, 217, 219

Cold War xv, xvii, xviii, 14, 18, 21, 46, 55, 106, 111-2, 121, 125, 128-9, 137, 148, 154, 194, 203, 210, 212

Colson, Chuck 68, 108

Copeland, Libby 171, 184

Cordesman, Anthony H 173, 184.

Council on American-Islamic Relations [CAIR] 92

Crusades 42, 74

D

Daalder, Ivo H. 119, 152

Damascus, Syria 40, 213

De Albuquence, Adriana Lins 181, 185

Delong-Bas, Natana J. 33, 36

Dermer, Ron 213

Dhahran, Saudi Arabia 85, 190

Dickey, Christopher 153, 185

Doha, Qatar 123

E

Egypt 8, 9, 12, 43-7, 49, 53, 55-7, 72, 93, 95,
    147, 188, 209, 215, 217

Eisenhower, President Dwight D. 12, 163-4

Elections of 2004 118, 142

Engel, Richard 173, 185

European Union 53, 72, 79, 136

Even, Shmuel 56, 64

F

Fahd bin Abdul Aziz ibn Saud, King 13, 21,
    23-4, 26, 50, 74, 81, 92, 94, 95, 99, 109,
    189, 197, 217-8

Fahd bin Turki bin Saud al Kabir, Prince 92

Fainaru, Steve 145, 152

Faisal bin Abdul Aziz ibn Saud, King 13, 21,
    23, 46, 91, 93-4, 104, 216

Fallujah, Iraq 174, 178-9, 185
    April 2004 Assault 174,
    Round II, November 2004 178-9

Fandy, Mamoun 46, 63

Farah, Douglas 43, 64

Ferguson, Niall 73, 108, 141, 152, 178, 185

Filkens, Dexter 144-5, 170

First World War 4, 8, 11, 40-1, 54, 79, 100,
    128, 142, 165, 194, 210

Frank, General Tommy 159, 164

Friedman, George 115, 118, 123-4, 132, 152,
    159, 185, 205, 212

Friedman, Thomas L. 25, 124, 148, 152, 192,
    208, 212

G

Gaddis, John Lewis 126, 128-31, 153, 213

Gambill, Gary C. 142, 153

Garner, General Jay 165

Geneva Convention 171-2

Germany 40, 72-8, 83, 93, 106, 117-8, 136,
    139, 150, 201, 211

Giuliani, Mayor Rudolf 97

Glanz, James 144, 152

Gold, Dore 40, 43, 63

Grand Mosque 14, 80, 81, 98-9, 188-9, 216-7

Graner, Specialist Charles 170

Great Britain 9, 73, 92, 116, 127, 139, 141

Greece 76

Guantanamo Bay, Cuba 10, 172

Gulf War 13, 36, 50, 56, 64, 68-70, 82, 85, 91,
    99-100, 108, 111, 116, 132, 134, 137-9,
    157-9, 161, 166, 189, 201, 219

Gulling 4, 20, 51, 78, 90, 93, 95-6, 103, 106,
    124, 134-5, 197

H

Hadley, Stephen 119

Haiti 111, 141, 203

Hajj 3, 11, 55, 70, 219

Halper, Stefan 131, 153

Hamas 50, 52, 88, 99, 137

Hauerwas, Stanley 211, 213

Hawes, Crispin 19, 36

Hezbollah 83

Hizazi, Raed 67

Horowitz, David 128, 153

Howard, Prime Minister John 138

Hussein, Qusay 157, 168

Hussein, Saddam 13-4, 18, 28, 47, 51, 53, 55-
    6, 82, 91, 111, 133-6, 138-9, 148, 150, 156-
    69, 174-5, 178-81, 183-4, 193-4, 197-8,
    201, 204, 206, 218

Hussein, Uday 157, 168

Husseini, Hajj Amin al 55

I

Ignatieff, Michael 180, 185

Ikhwan army 4, 8, 9, 33, 187, 189

India 16, 19, 39, 72, 122-3

Indonesia 14, 17

International Energy Agency [IEA] 16, 36

International Islamic Relief Organization [IIRO] 92

Iran 1, 10, 15-8, 22, 26, 28, 39, 52, 54, 72, 80-2, 94-5, 98, 115-7, 120, 122-3, 133, 140, 145, 148, 180, 188, 196, 198, 205, 217-8

   Iranian Shiite Revolution, 1979 21, 80, 99

   Iran-Iraq war, 1980 18, 81-2, 98

Iranian Shiite Ayatollahs 55

Iraq xix, xxi, 1, 8, 10, 12, 14, 17-9, 24, 27-8, 39, 47, 52-3, 55, 66, 69, 71-2, 74-8, 80-2, 84, 91, 94, 97-9, 102-3, 107, 111, 116-7, 120-3, 132-41, 143-51, 153-9, 161--77, 179-85, 191-4, 197-8, 201, 203-7, 212, 215, 217-9

   Casualties during 2003-2005 181-2, 184

   Kuwait invasion, 1990 82

   Elections of 2005 143-6, 151, 179-81, 198-9, 206, 219

Iraq Liberation Act of 1998 218

Islam xv-xx, xxi, 1-5, 7-9, 11, 13-4, 20, 26-9, 31-3, 36, 38-46, 49-50, 52-4, 57, 59, 63-66, 68-73, 75, 77-8, 80-1, 84, 87-9, 91-2, 94, 96, 99-104, 106-9, 141, 153, 168, 180, 187-9, 199, 202, 208-9, 211-2, 215, 218, 221

Islamic Council of North America 93

Islamist jihad [jihad, jihadist] xiii-xvii, 1, 9, 33, 36, 39, 41-2, 44-5, 47, 49-50, 52-3, 57, 66, 68 75, 84, 87, 91, 97, 99, 104-5, 150, 160-2, 166-7, 169, 173-5, 177-80, 182, 188-9, 192-4

Islamic law or shariah xiv, xvii, 3, 4, 7, 26, 28,-9, 31-5, 41-2, 44, 48, 52, 55, 65, 78, 93, 101, 147, 188, 211

Islamic Society of North America 93

Islamists xiii, xiv, xv, xiv, xviii, xx, 41, 48, 52, 65, 67-8, 75, 77, 82, 87, 108, 140, 182, 184, 191, 195, 197, 199-200, 203, 204, 205, 207, 208, 210, 213

Israel 15, 40, 45-6, 50, 53-4, 57, 59, 75, 93-4, 96-7, 99, 122, 124, 133, 135, 140, 147, 150, 161, 202, 217

Israeli-Palestinian dispute 137, 197

Italy 62, 72, 76-7, 138-9

J

Japan 16, 78, 106, 117 138, 149, 164-5, 210

Jeddah, Saudi Arabia 35, 45, 81, 188, 217, 219

Jews 14, 38, 53-5, 57, 59, 66, 74-6, 90, 106, 194, 210-11

Jihad, jihadist [see also Islamist jihad] xiii-xvii, 1, 9, 33, 36, 39, 41-2, 44-5, 47, 49-50, 52-3, 57, 66, 68 75, 84, 87, 91, 97, 99, 104-5, 150, 160-2, 166-7, 169, 173-5, 177-80, 182, 188-9, 192-4

Jordan 11, 48, 53, 56, 72, 89, 123, 161, 212

K

Kabal, Afghanistan 118, 142

Kagan, Robert 136, 153

Kaiser, Robert G. 62, 64

Kaplin, Lee 96, 108

Karachi, Pakistan 85

Karbala, Iraq 80

Karpinski, General Janis 170-1

Karzai, President Hamid 118, 142-3

Keiler, Jonathan F. 178-9

Kennan, George 112-3, 129

Kenya 85, 100, 190

Kerry, Senator John 171

Khaled al Faisal ibn Abdul Aziz, Prince 103

Khaled bin Abdul Aziz ibn Saud, King 23, 35, 94, 189, 217

Khaled bin Sultan bin Abdul Aziz al Saud, Prince and General 50, 70, 103-5

Khan, Dr. A.Q. 122

Khomeini, Ayatollah 22, 80, 82, 95, 217

Kissinger, Secretary Henry 210

Koh, Harold Hongju 112, 153

Koran xv-xvii, 4, 9, 29, 31-3, 38-9, 42-3, 49, 52, 63, 65, 67, 75, 77, 188, 209

Korea, North 120-2
Korea, South 138
Kosovo 84, 111, 141
Krauthammer, Charles 206, 213
Kurds 116, 145-6, 165, 177, 180
Kuwait 5-6, 8, 10-1, 13, 18, 71, 82-3, 91, 94, 99, 111, 123, 138, 140, 147, 157-8, 160-2, 166, 176, 189, 212, 215, 217, 219
    Iraq invasion, 1990 82, 99, 111, 189
Kyl, Senator John 88, 108

L

Lebanon 11, 59, 72, 79 83, 147, 198, 206, 219
Lewis, Bernard 50, 64, 101, 109
Libya 53, 84, 122, 140, 147, 196, 198
    Libyan terrorists 83
Lincoln, President Abraham 171
Lindsay, James M. 119, 152
Lindsey, Gene 36
Lippman, Thomas 21-2, 27, 36
Long, David E. 3, 37
Longman, Phillip 61, 64

M

Madrid, Spain 76-7, 102, 193
Majlis 30-2
Malaysia 39
Mann, James 114-5, 119-20, 131, 134, 153
Masland, Tom 153, 185
Mawdudi, Sayyid 41
McKinley, President William 127
McPhee, Michele 109, 167
McVeigh, Timothy 69, 71
Mecca, Saudi Arabia xiii, 3, 5, 7-10, 14, 24-5, 27, 31, 39, 46, 70, 80-1, 93, 98-9, 133, 188-9, 216-7
Medina, Saudi Arabia 3, 5, 7-10, 25, 27, 31, 39, 45-6, 81, 93, 133, 188, 216
Mexico 61
Mintz, John 43, 64, 69, 109
Mir, Mushaf Ali 92

Mohammed xv, xvi, 1, 3, 7, 9, 29, 31-3, 39, 41, 45, 48, 54, 67, 73, 80-1, 88, 209, 215
Morocco 72-3
Moss, Michael 175, 203
Moussaoui, Zacharias 68
Mubarak, President Hosni 57
Munif, Abdul 89, 109
Murawiec, Laurent 78, 92, 109
Musharraf, President Pervez 115, 122
Muslim xiii, xiv, xv, xvii, 1-2, 4, 7-10, 14, 17-8, 24, 28-30, 33, 38-47, 49-50, 52-5, 58-60, 65-68, 71-85, 87, 90-2, 95, 97, 99-102, 104-7, 109-10, 117, 121-2, 124, 130, 132-3, 137, 140-3, 145-8, 151, 167, 169, 173-5, 178, 180, 188-91, 193-9, 203, 206, 208-9, 211-2, 217, 219
Muslim Brotherhood [Brotherhood] 2, 9, 14, 24, 30, 40-50, 66, 78, 81, 87, 90, 95, 106, 188, 191, 193, 209, 211, 217
Muslim World League 46, 92

N

Naimi, Ali al 19
Nasser, Gamal Abdel 44, 188
Nayef bin Abdul Aziz ibn Saud, Prince 23-6, 29, 41, 94, 97
National Front for the Liberation of Iraq 161,
Neo-conservatives 119, 123, 128, 131, 153
Netherlands 72, 76, 118
Nixon, President Richard M. 169
    Twin Pillar Persian Gulf Policy 22
Nordland, Rod 151, 162, 174, 185
North Atlantic Treaty Organization [NATO] 27, 53, 55, 78-9, 107, 116, 118, 121, 134, 149, 198, 201-2

O

O'Hanlon, Michael 182, 185
Oil xiv, xv, xviii, 2-4, 9-22, 24, 26-9, 36, 43, 46, 50-6, 58, 62-3, 78-82, 85, 89-91, 93-5, 98, 101, 105-6, 112, 131, 133, 135-6, 140, 156-8, 160, 166, 173, 183, 188, 194-6, 198, 216, 218, 220

Oman 72, 123, 138

Organization of Petroleum Exporting Countries [OPEC] 13, 17-9, 216

Osama bin Laden [see also Bin Laden] xiii, xiv, xix, 1, 10, 26, 33, 41-7, 77, 79-80, 82, 84, 87, 91-2, 94-5, 98-100, 106, 115, 117, 128, 149, 151, 177, 188-9, 191-2, 195, 204, 207, 212, 216-7

Ottoman Empire 4, 7-8, 39-40, 54, 72-3, 79, 95, 100, 165, 215

P

Pakistan xix, 1, 28, 42, 72-3, 81, 85, 91, 98-9, 115, 117-8, 121-3, 140, 149, 191, 196, 198, 218

Palestine 94, 124, 137, 140, 147, 202, 206, 215

Palestine Liberation Organization [PLO] 88, 137, 155

Paris, France 16, 36, 74, 77, 108, 110

Pentagon xviii, 68, 82, 85, 87, 112, 155, 157, 164-5, 170-1, 173-5, 190, 204, 221

Perle, Richard 119

Persian Gulf xviii, 1-3, 11-2, 14-8, 22, 28, 40, 54, 56, 65, 69, 79, 81, 85, 101, 116, 123, 156, 158, 165, 198, 218

Philby, Harry St. John 11-2

Philippines 14, 39, 69, 131, 206

Pinches, Charles 211, 214

Pipes, Daniel 102, 109

Podhoretz, Norman 102, 128-31, 153

Posner, Gerald 91-2, 109

Powell, Secretary Colin 117-8, 159

Powell Doctrine 159

Putin, Prime Minister Valadimir 115

Q

Qaddafi, President Muammar al 84

Qaeda, al xiii, xv, xvi, xvii, xix, xx, 1, 4, 10, 24, 26-7, 34-5, 38, 41-2, 46-8, 50, 52-3, 63, 67-70, 73, 75-9, 81-2, 84-88, 90-2, 94, 100, 103, 105, 109, 113-7, 122-5, 132-5, 137, 140, 142-4, 147-51, 160, 162, 166-7, 169,

174, 177, 183-4,187, 189-201, 203, 207, 210, 219, 221

Qatar 123, 138

Qusti, Raid 34-5, 37

Qutb, Mohammed 45

Qutb, Sayyid 30, 41, 43-7, 49-50, 87, 90, 106, 211

R

Rahman, Sheik Omar Abdul 48

Reagan, President Ronald 17, 83-4

Ricchiardi, Sherry 169, 185

Rice, Secretary Condoleezza 102, 119, 202

Riyadh, Saudi Arabia 36, 85

Rivilin, Paul 64, 156

Roosevelt, President Franklin D. 128, 137

Roosevelt-Abdul Azziz ibn Saud Meeting, 1945 xix, 12, 19, 21, 93, 94, 95, 114

Roosevelt, President Theodore 205

Rumaylah Oil Fields (Iraq) 158

Rumsfeld, Secretary Donald 113, 119, 132, 137, 158, 160, 161, 164, 165, 171, 172

Russia 17, 106, 115, 119, 123, 136, 139, 149-50, 196, 201

Rwanda 111

S

Sadat, President Anwar 98

Sadr, Muqtada al 168

Sanger, David E. 122, 151

Saladin 39, 54, 215

Salafi or Salafism [see also Wahhabism] xiv, xv, xvii, 1, 2, 4, 7-10, 14, 28, 32, 33, 35, 41, 43, 47-52, 58, 63, 65-6, 69-70, 73, 75-7, 79, 82, 86, 88, 90-1, 95, 100-2, 105-7, 132, 140, 177, 188-9, 193, 196, 198, 208-9, 215

Saud, Muhammad bin 7

Saudi-American relations 19-20, 98, 103

Saudi Arabia xiv, xv, xix, 1-25, 27-41, 43, 45-52, 55-6, 58-63, 65-6, 68-71, 73-4, 76-82, 85-101, 103-9, 112, 122-4, 128, 132-3, 138-

40, 147, 150-1, 161, 187-90, 193, 196-8, 205, 209, 212, 215-9, 221

   Basic Law 30, 31-2, 217

   Consultative Council 30-1, 217-9

   Kingdom 1-5, 7, 9-10, 13, 17, 21, 23, 26-8, 31-4, 37, 52, 63, 72-3, 89-94, 96, 101, 103-5, 124, 128, 182, 187-9, 216

   Majlis 30-2

   Ulama 25, 32-3, 188-9

Schlesinger, Secretary James 171

Schroeder, Chancellor Gerhard 136, 150

Schumer, Senator Charles 88-9, 109

Schwartz, Stephen 75, 109

Schwarzkopf, General Norman 70

Scowcroft, General Brent 140, 153

September 11, 2001 [9/11] xiii, xiv, xviii, xix, xx, 1-2, 9-10, 15, 17, 19-20, 25, 28, 46, 48, 51-2, 57, 62, 67-8, 71, 73-4, 76, 82, 84-8, 90-1, 93-4, 97, 99, 103-4, 106-7, 109, 113-8, 123, 132, 134, 136-7, 139, 143, 149, 151, 164, 169, 187, 190, 192, 194-8, 200-1, 203, 205, 207-8, 210, 212, 219

Shaalan, Hazem 176

Shadid, Anthony 146, 153

Shah of Iran, 17, 22, 26, 80, 95, 98, 188, 217

Shakespeare, William 64

Sharansky, Natan 199, 213

Shiite 9, 17, 21-2, 29, 47, 52, 55, 80-3, 85, 93, 95, 98-9, 116, 133-4, 144-6, 153, 158-9, 162, 165-8, 176, 179-82, 191, 209, 215, 217

   Minority in Saudi Arabia 1, 22, 29, 81, 93

   Majority in Iraq, Iran 80, 134, 144, 162, 163, 168, 180

Shultz, Secretary George P. 131, 141

Sistani, Grand Ayatollah Ali al 52, 146, 168, 179, 180, 183

Somalia 79, 84, 100, 175, 190, 203

Soviet Union 14, 38, 42, 55-6, 70, 81-2, 84, 91, 98-100, 106, 111-2, 114-5, 125, 128, 149, 189, 193, 195, 203, 217

Soviet Union invasion, 1979 80, 99

Spain 13, 24, 39, 54, 76-7, 87, 108, 138-9, 193

Standard Oil of California [SOCAL] 11, 216

Stille, Alexander 164, 185

Stothard, Peter 150, 154

Struck, Doug 146, 153

Sudairi, Hassa bint Ahmad 23

   Sudairi Seven 23-4, 94

Sudan 48, 85, 190

Sufi 9

Sullivan, Andrew 172, 185

Sultan bin Abdul Aziz ibn Saud, Prince 64

Sultan bin Faisal bin Turki, Prince 91, 92

Sunni xvii, 1, 25-6, 33, 40-1, 47, 50, 52-3, 59, 82, 87, 95, 100-1, 118, 133, 143-5,159, 161-2, 164-7, 169, 174, 176-7, 180, 182, 189, 209

Sunni Triangle (Iraq) 25, 143, 159, 162, 166-7, 174, 177

Sweden 72, 77

Syria 9, 24, 45, 49, 53, 55, 72, 95, 133, 136, 147, 161, 177, 193, 198, 206, 212

T

Taheri, Amir 145, 154, 191, 213

Tajikistan 115-6

Takfir wal Hijra 41-2, 47, 177

Taliban xiv, xix, 8, 27, 29, 52, 65, 84, 92, 95, 98, 115-8, 120, 122, 124, 134, 142-3, 149, 180, 191, 195, 218

Tanzania 85, 100, 190,

Taspinar, Omer 76, 110

Taymiyah, Ibn 41, 208

Tehran, Iran 82-3, 116, 147

Tikrit, Iraq 168

Treaty of Versailles 115

Truman, President Harry 21, 124, 137

   Truman Doctrine or Containment Policy 111-2, 123, 125, 127

   Marshall Plan 106

   Point Four Program 21

Tunisia 73

Turkey 29, 53-4, 72-4, 78-9, 101, 118, 133, 138, 142, 162
Turkmenistan 115

U

Ukraine 138, 146, 206
Ulama 25, 32-3, 188-9
Umm Qasr, Iraq 158, 165
Unikewicz, Amy 182, 185
United Arab Emirates 12, 122
United Arab Republic 138
United Kingdom [UK] 72-3, 96
United Nations [UN] 54, 64, 106, 114, 116, 118, 121, 126, 131-2, 135-6, 138-9, 141-3, 147, 149-50, 175, 179, 198, 200-2, 207, 217-9
  General Assembly 131-2
  Resolution 1441 138-9
  Security Council 114, 121, 125, 132, 138-9, 149-50, 201, 217-9
United States [US] xiii, xvii, xviii, xix, xx, 1-2, 7, 10-2, 14-21, 23, 25-9, 43-8, 50, 53, 55-9, 61-3, 66-8, 70-2, 74-5, 77-9, 82-7, 90-100, 102, 106-41, 145-6, 148-52, 155, 159, 162-3, 165, 168-9, 171-2, 175-6, 178, 187, 189-207, 209-12, 218, 221
USS Cole 67, 86, 190
Uzbekistan 115-6

V

Van Gogh, Theo 77
Vienna, Austria 49, 83, 87, 215
Vietnam 79, 85, 119, 166, 169, 175, 184, 203-4
Vistica, Gregory L. 69, 109

W

Walker, Martin 185
Williams, Daniel 213
Wilson, President Woodrow 128
Woodward, Bob 154, 186
Woolsey, R. James 85
World Assembly of Muslim Youth 92
World Trade Center xx, 67, 82, 85, 87, 112, 190
World Trade Organization 105
Wyatt, Caroline 11
  Defense Planning Guidance Proposal of 1992 114, 126
Woodward, Bob 116, 134, 138-9, 154, 157, 159, 186
Woolsey, R. James 85
World Assembly of Muslim Youth 92
World Trade Center xviii, 48, 67, 82, 85, 87, 112, 190
  Bombing, 1993 48, 85, 190
  Twin Towers, 9/11, 2001 xviii, 67, 82, 87, 112, 190
World Trade Organization [WTO] 105
Wyatt, Caroline 77, 110

Y

Yergin, Daniel 112, 154
Yemen 79, 86-7, 100, 123,190

Z

Zahedi, Ardeshir 98
Zakaria, Fareed 164, 186
Zakheim, Dov 119
Zarqawi, Abu Musab al 47, 177
Zawahiri, Ayman al 42, 47-8, 191
Zoellick, Robert 119
Zubaydah, Abu 91-2

978-0-595-35776-5
0-595-35776-8

Printed in the United States
36004LVS00004B/88-105